The Psychology of Digital Media at Work

In many professions daily work life has become unthinkable without the use of a computer with access to the Internet. As technological innovations progress rapidly and new applications of interactional media are invented, organizational behavior continues to change.

The central theme of this book is how digital media affect organizational behavior and employee well-being. A variety of topics are considered:

*   Applications of digital media in both personnel psychology and organizational psychology
*   Tools to improve selection and assessment
*   Issues arising in the context of training, learning and career development
*   The use of online games for education and recreation
*   The impact of mobile devices on organizational life
*   The implications of new forms of collaboration by means of virtual teams

The research documented in this volume consists of high-quality, quantitative studies illustrated by lively practical examples. The combination of science and practice ensures that new insights supported by empirical studies are translated into practical implications. The book will be essential reading for researchers and students in organizational psychology and related disciplines.

Daantje Derks is an Assistant Professor at the Department of Work and Organizational Psychology at Erasmus University Rotterdam, the Netherlands. Her current research interests focus on the impact of computer-mediated communication on daily work life.

Arnold B. Bakker is a Full Professor at the Department of Work and Organizational Psychology at Erasmus University Rotterdam, the Netherlands. His research interests include positive organizational behavior (e.g. performance, flow and engagement at work), burnout, crossover of work-related emotions and serious games on organizational phenomena. Further information can be found at: www.arnoldbakker.com.

Current Issues in Work and Organizational Psychology
Series Editor: Arnold B. Bakker

Current Issues in Work and Organizational Psychology is a series of edited books that reflect the state-of-the-art areas of current and emerging interest in the psychological study of employees, workplaces and organizations.

Each volume is tightly focused on a particular topic and consists of seven to ten chapters contributed by international experts. The editors of individual volumes are leading figures in their areas and provide an introductory overview.

Example topics include:

A Day in the Life of a Happy Worker
Edited by Arnold B. Bakker and Kevin Daniels

New Frontiers in Work and Family Research
Edited by Joseph G. Grzywacz and Evangelia Demerouti

The Psychology of Digital Media at Work

Edited by
Daantje Derks and Arnold B. Bakker

Routledge
Taylor & Francis Group

LONDON AND NEW YORK

First published 2013
by Psychology Press
27 Church Road, Hove, East Sussex, BN3 2FA

Simultaneously published in the USA and Canada
by Psychology Press
711 Third Avenue, New York, NY 10017

Psychology Press is an imprint of the Taylor & Francis Group, an informa business

British Library Cataloguing in Publication Data
A catalogue record for this book is available from the British Library

Library of Congress Cataloging in Publication Data
The psychology of digital media at work / edited by Daantje Derks, Arnold Bakker.
p. cm.
Includes bibliographical references and index.
1. Internet–Social aspects. 2. Organizational behavior. I. Derks, Daantje. II. Bakker, Arnold B.
HM851.P795 2012
302.23'1–dc23

ISBN: 978-1-84872-074-9 (hbk)
ISBN: 978-0-84872-124-1 (pbk)
ISBN: 978-0-203-07414-5 (ebk)

Typeset in Times
by FiSH Books Ltd, Enfield

MIX
Paper from
responsible sources
FSC
www.fsc.org   FSC® C004839

Printed and bound in Great Britain by
TJ International Ltd, Padstow, Cornwall

Contents

1 Introduction

Daantje Derks and Arnold B. Bakker

Many employees feel really handicapped in their work when the Internet is down for a couple of hours. We only seem to realize just how dependent we have become on the Internet on days that the system fails. Especially affected are knowledge-based workers who start a regular day with switching on their computers and mobile devices (e.g. PDA, smartphone, notebook, tablet PC). That work starts when employees enter the office definitely belongs to the past. Work and family life have become highly integrated, facilitated by the technology of digital media.

Digital media affect many tasks in organizational life. The communication with both clients and colleagues is dominated by email communication either handled from a personal computer or on the move by using mobile devices. Virtual teams support international collaborations with the direct consequence that expert input in projects has become time and place independent. Globalization has encouraged this development, in that new media have made access to talent and knowledge more attainable and financially affordable. Furthermore, the application of digital media has had a major impact on organizational training and development programs. Online learning and development programs facilitate lifelong learning in the workplace, which may imply that former transfer problems from the training to the work environment are reduced. Serious games are developed to simulate real work situations to give practice a new dimension without the costs associated with practicing in real life.

In addition, online social network sites made it possible to stay in touch with business associates (LinkedIn) and/or friends and family (e.g. Facebook, MySpace) in a low-effort way. Online gaming during leisure time can facilitate psychological detachment, a precondition for a healthy recovery process resulting in happy and healthy employees. And finally, when an employee decides it is time to make a next move on the labor market, there is a good chance that a webcam test will be a significant part of the selection procedure. In other words, the impact of digital media on organizational life is evident and goes beyond simply facilitating our work. The new innovations in technology have made radical changes to the way we work.

History of digital media in a nutshell

The history of digital media in an organizational context can be divided in two broad categories. The first category entails the development and usage of digital devices aimed at facilitating the interaction between people regardless of time and physical location, formally known as computer-mediated communication.

The second category consists of digital tools within the work context with a goal other than communication. This broad category entails gaming applications for simulation/training purposes and recovery, webcam tests in personnel selection, and e-learning within an organizational context. In the current volume, both categories are represented by a section handling topics relevant for the particular category.

Computer-mediated communication

Text-based email communication has dominated scientific literature for many years (e.g. Byron, 2008; Dawley & Anthony, 2003; Derks & Bakker, 2010; Friedman & Curral, 2003; Kruger, Epley, Parker & Ng, 2005). The reason behind this is that email up till now is still the most used form of computer-mediated communication. Research has examined how the social meaning of interaction is affected by adding the digital component to the conversation, especially in situations where both parties replace face-to-face communication with email communication (Walther & Parks, 2002). Retrospectively, it is hard to imagine that when email was first introduced, people thought it would be confined to the exchange of short task-oriented messages. The lack of nonverbal cues in a text-based medium seems to imply that in the interpretation of email messages we have to rely completely on verbal information (e.g. Burgoon & Saine, 1978; Shaw, 1981; Walther, 1995). However, Derks, Fischer, and Bos (2008) concluded in their review of the field that individuals find new and innovative ways to cope with the restrictions of text-based computer-mediated communication such as the use of emoticons to compensate for the lack of visual cues; or, by acknowledging the restrictions of certain types of media and taking this into account by choosing an outlet for a message.

The introduction of the smartphone gave email a new, mobile dimension. Smartphones could affect social dynamics in the workplace by enabling new forms of interaction and collaboration (Lyytinen & Yoo, 2002a; Pica & Kakihara, 2003). The a-synchronicity of the communication that was so characteristic of email communication has changed into more synchronous communication since many recipients have the habit of answering messages the minute they arrive (Markus, 1994). In return, the organization's expectations regarding reaction times and availability have changed (Davis, 2002; Green, 2001). Furthermore, mobile collaboration provides new challenges like building trustworthy relationships without regular face-to-face interaction.

Managers have started to realize that digital devices may also facilitate interaction between employees, especially those working in different locations. Some of the challenges accompanied by mobile collaboration are also applicable to the virtual collaboration of geographically dispersed teams. Additionally, communicating over different time zones might produce new challenges in interacting. Virtual teams are characterized by members that are geographically dispersed and those members coordinate their work predominantly by electronic information and communication technologies (Hertel, Geister & Konradt, 2005). A virtual team is different from a regular team in that the former predominantly interacts by new media; face-to-face contact, other than that facilitated by videoconferencing (e.g. Skype) is not self-evident. Lipnack and Stamps (1997) state that the members of a virtual *team* interact with each other in order to accomplish common goals.

Many studies have focused on the comparison between traditional teams and virtual teams (e.g. Archer, 1990; Bordia, 1997; Chidambaram & Bostrom, 1993; DeMeyer, 1991; Galegher & Kraut, 1994). However, since virtual teams can also communicate face-to-face and traditional teams can also make use of digital media it might not be useful to draw a clear line between those two types of teams (Hertel *et al.*, 2005). Instead, some authors suggest it might be more useful to consider the relative 'virtuality' of a team and its consequences for management (Axtell, Fleck & Turner, 2004; Bell & Kozlowski, 2002; Griffith & Neale, 2001; Hertel *et al.*, 2005; Kirkman, Rosen, Tesluk & Gibson, 2004). A virtual team is in this view characterized as a team with a high degree of virtuality. The majority of the studies examining the performance of virtual teams has not detected a difference between traditional and virtual teams (for an overview, see Powell, Piccoli, and Ives, 2004).

Besides communicating by email, which is still the preferred medium for task-related communication, it also possible to stay in touch with team members or colleagues by means of social media. Recently, the popular press reported that social networking sites exceed email in the amount of time that people spent on them during a normal day. This is remarkable, since the history of social network sites is relatively short. Online social networks have gained popularity very quickly. Sites can be oriented towards work-related contexts (e.g. LinkedIn.com), shared interests (e.g. MySpace.com), or friends (e.g. Facebook.com) (Ellison, Steinfield & Lampe, 2007). Hampton and Wellman (2003) suggest that social network sites enhance place-based community and facilitate extending your social capital – the accumulation of resources through relationships with other people (Coleman, 1988). A great advantage of the online aspect of these networks is that it creates the ability to maintain valuable connections as one goes through significant life changes. This 'maintained social capital' permits us to stay in touch with a social network after physically disconnecting from it (Ellison *et al.*, 2007).

Applications of digital media other than communication tools

Computer-based alternatives to live training have become more common in recent years (Alexander, Brunyé, Sidman & Weil, 2005). Therefore, in this section of the book, we consider online training from three different, though related, perspectives.

E-learning in the workplace, serious gaming, and gaming during free time share the general factor that we focus on the effects of engaging in these activities on work-related experiences and behaviors. The effects are considered both in terms of improved learning and in terms of transfer to the workplace. Besides these learning centered applications of digital media, the webcam test is included in this part of the book which is an assessment tool. However, even though the goal of the webcam test is different, it is also important that the situations presented in the test resemble the working conditions as best as possible.

E-learning in a general sense is defined as 'a wide set of applications and processes, such as web-based learning, computer-based learning, virtual class-rooms, and digital collaboration' (Kaplan-Leierson, 2002, para. 85). Often cited advantages of e-learning are that it allows organizations to deliver training consistently to all employees; update training content when necessary; and to provide training to employees on demand, anytime, and anywhere (Burgess & Russell, 2003). Furthermore, DeRouin, Fritzsche, and Salas (2005) argue in their review that saving costs is also an appealing factor for organizations to offer e-learning programs to their employees. However, the ultimate purpose of e-learning is not to reduce training expenses, but to improve the way the organization does business (Bersin, 2002). It should be noted though that figures on return of investment are very scarce in all kind of training programs in which e-learning is no exception (DeRouin *et al.*, 2005).

Comparable to the discussion on the virtuality of virtual teams, e-learning does not automatically imply that the entire training is digital and that there is no face-to-face contact at all. Next to e-learning there is also a mixed form called 'blended learning.' In blended learning, traditional classroom sessions are combined with e-learning and self-study (Kovaleski, 2004). Through blended learning, organizations can both profit from the cost savings associated with e-learning and the personal touch associated with classroom instruction (Goodridge, 2001; Masie, 2002).

However, the main question remains how effective these e-learning programs are. DeRouin and colleagues (2005) state that it is difficult to conclude that e-learning is as effective, or perhaps even more effective, at the learning level than traditional classroom-based training. Besides the potential learning effects of e-learning, the transfer of the skills learned in training to the job is just as important (Strother, 2002). In a large-scale survey conducted by Skillsoft (2004), 87% of the e-learners reported using skills and knowledge they had gained from e-learning back on the job. The skills and business areas most improved by e-learning were IT skills, communication with coworkers and customers, business outcomes (e.g. sales), work processes (e.g. project management), and personal skills (e.g. assertiveness, leadership qualities). The results of this survey suggest that employee behavior can be effectively changed as a result of e-learning (Skillsoft, 2004), although it should be noted that the improvements were self-reported.

The effectiveness of online training by e-learning and gaming is not well understood. Overall, the higher the transfer to the operational environment, the more successful the training is considered to be (Alexander *et al.*, 2005).

Alexander *et al.* state that four factors are driving transfer: fidelity, immersion, presence, and user acceptance.

Fidelity refers to the extent to which the virtual environment emulates the real world (e.g. Lane & Alluisi, 1992; Rehman, Mitman & Reynolds, 1995). Especially physical, functional, and psychological fidelity are considered important in relation to transfer (Alexander *et al.*, 2005). Physical fidelity refers to the extent to which the physical simulation looks, sounds, and feels like the operational environment in terms of visual displays, controls, and audio (Baum, Riedel, Hays & Mirabella, 1982). Functional fidelity is defined as the degree to which the simulation acts like the operational equipment in reacting to the tasks executed by the trainee (Allen, Hays & Buffordi, 1986). Finally, psychological fidelity is the degree to which the simulation replicates the psychological factors (i.e. fear, stress) experienced in the real world (Kaiser & Schroeder, 2003). Jentsch and Bowers (1998) emphasize that to determine the relation between fidelity and training performance designers must prioritize the components that need to be realistic and those that do not, based on the requirements of the training. For example, many games offer the unrealistic ability to immediately transport one between locations. While this functionality might improve game play, it differs drastically from the constraints that trainees face in the real world (Alexander *et al.*, 2005).

Immersion refers to the degree to which an individual feels absorbed by a particular experience (Witmer & Singer, 1998). Immersion may contribute to the amount of information acquired, the skills that are developed, and the subsequent transfer of knowledge to real life situations. Situated immersion, also known as presence, points at the subjective experience of actually existing within the computer-mediated environment even when one is physically situated in another environment (Slater & Steed, 2000; Witmer & Singer, 1998). Presence, by definition, increases engagement with training content. Additionally, when trainees are highly engaged with the game or training, it is more likely that they spent more time on it. Time on task is a strong predictor of the acquisition of knowledge and skills (Lombard & Ditton, 1997).

Finally, user acceptance or buy-in is also a factor that may influence the degree of transfer. Buy-in is about the degree to which an individual recognizes that an experience or event is useful for training. The higher the level of buy-in, the more effort a user will invest and the more likely it is that transfer to the real world will take place (Alexander *et al.*, 2005). For example, when the uniforms of the firefighters in the game are not realistic and the vehicles used do not correspond to those used by the practitioners, the user acceptance of the game and consequently the transfer to the work context will decrease (Stapleton, 2004).

Structure of the book

This book includes a range of selected topics that the factors digital media and work have in common. Together, the chapters provide a broad overview of the impact of digital communication media on individuals, teams, and organizations.

The first part of the book has a focus on the interaction and collaboration component of computer-mediated communication. The second part focuses on the impact of gaming and online tests for training, development, and personnel selection.

Online communication and collaboration

In Chapter 2, Rennecker and Derks consider the paradoxical effects of the quick access to information and people facilitated by computer-mediated communication (CMC). They argue that CMC in general and email in particular, has the effect of improving organizational productivity by reducing information delays, while simultaneously hindering individual productivity with excessive communication demands and interruptions. They introduce a typology of email-related 'overload' that more accurately reflects the diversity of workplace experiences reported in the literature. The chapter concludes by considering the implications of extensive communication media use for workers' experience of 'overload.'

In Chapter 3, Stopfer and Gosling illustrate that Online Social Networks (OSNs) impact on professional contexts far beyond screening job applicants. They review the literature and show that OSNs are also relevant for business purposes such as establishing business contacts, improving business purposes, and maintaining business competitiveness. They consider both the perspective of the individual who holds an OSN profile, and the perspective of the organization in using OSNs for marketing purposes.

In Chapter 4, Jarvenpaa and Hedlund address the issue of knowledge-based collaboration in mobile information technology environments. Mobile technology has changed the way individuals engage in their work, but what are the consequences of these changes for the employee? They question whether individuals who collaborate on the move generate novel and useful ideas that are helpful in solving a collaborative goal or problem. They determine that today's reality of mobile collaborations is more focused on social collaboration than on knowledge building, which offers new challenges and opportunities for the future.

In Chapter 5, Krumm and Hertel discuss whether the potential benefits of virtual teams can outweigh the various challenges that come along with working in different locations and/or at different times both for organizations and individual workers. They propose a conceptual model of the knowledge, skills, abilities, and other characteristics (KSAOs) in virtual teams. The chapter closes with practical recommendations to coach virtual team leaders in developing their team members.

Gaming and online tests

In Chapter 6, Xanthopoulou and Papagiannidis explain how engaging in online computer games during free time relates to how individuals function at their work. They integrate psychological spillover models and game literature in order to explain how behaviors exerted in the game may spill over directly or indirectly to the work domain and as a consequence have a beneficial impact on employee performance. Their model illustrates that active learning, leadership, and collaborative behaviors that are commonly manifested in online games may be transferred – directly or indirectly (via game performance and/or self-efficacy) – to work, and in turn enhance job performance.

In Chapter 7, Korteling, Helsdingen, and Theunissen discuss the possibilities and limitations of serious gaming for professional learning and training objectives. They argue that serious games have the potential to train many relevant job-related competencies in a realistic, attractive, and challenging manner. They build a case that gaming is, besides fun, a serious way to train and develop oneself at the workplace. They argue that serious games cannot fully replace traditional training methods, but that they can substantially enrich existing training curricula, and have the potential to inspire and challenge learners

In Chapter 8, van der Klink, Drachsler, and Sloep evaluate the impact of e-learning in the workplace. They give an extensive overview of workplace learning. They indicate that there is a shift from a formalized training to an everyday learning perspective. Learning by doing, by trial and error, is an example of everyday workplace learning. They conclude the chapter by concluding that technology-enhanced workplace learning is increasingly recognized as meaningful and promising.

In the final chapter, Chapter 9, Oostrom, Born, and Van der Molen focus on a webcam test used in personnel selection practices, which makes use of the opportunities provided by digital media. The webcam test is a multimedia situational test with a constructed response format. Oostrom and her colleagues argue that multimedia tests are able to explain additional variance in performance over and above traditional tests.

Why these topics?

The topics covered by this volume are selected for multiple reasons. The main reason for choosing these topics is that they are based on recent observations and developments in organizational life. A strong association with the daily practice of employee functioning within an organizational context using digital media was a first precondition to be included. Second, all topics considered are based on current innovations and applications in both science and practice. Since we aimed to compose a book that is useful for educational purposes and at the same time interesting for practitioners and scientific researchers, we selected topics that have a strong theoretical background in recent research. We think that practitioners can deduct guidelines to optimize the use of digital media in their organizations. Furthermore, we hope that we made practitioners aware of both benefits and pitfalls of extensive media use for employee well-being and job performance. Finally, we aimed to provide new insights in order to encourage scientific research in the field of digital media at work. The scientific work in this area is still scarce and to learn more about the impact of digital media on individual employees and the organization at large, the field is in need of new, innovative research. We hope that the chapters in this book will inspire scholars and researchers to develop new research ideas.

We realize that in making decisions about what to include in this volume, other interesting topics are overlooked. For example the massive popularity of Twitter, the art of microblogging – exchanging and connecting very short messages, is not taken into account in this edition. The reason behind this is that there are still very few empirical studies with solid research designs that handle the impact of Twitter on society and organizational life. Furthermore, the new business opportunities facilitated by Twitter are still in its infancy. Probably in a future edition of this book there will be enough material available to write a chapter on Twitter.

We dedicated one chapter to online social network sites (OSNS). However, the consequences of, for example, having a Facebook profile in the selection process is still under researched and therefore excluded. Online impression formation using OSNS is based on minimal cues and might therefore not be accurate. Observations in practice show that where applicants hope to make a first impression at a job interview, usually the first impression has already been formed by the information that is online available about the applicants. The privacy issues related to this topic are also interesting to consider.

Finally, another important topic that is probably extensive enough to fill a volume of its own, is the 'new way of working.' The new way of working is a recent interpretation of home-based teleworking. However, in its current interpretation, the new way of working perspective is characterized by collective arrangements regarding the flexibility and mobility of employees facilitated by new media. Organizations have discovered that this downsizes their overheads and it saves employees time in commuting. However, the consequences for work engagement and work-family balance are unclear. Some studies show that it is beneficial for keeping a healthy balance between work and family domains (Duxbury, Higgins & Neufeld, 1998; Raghuram & Weisenfeld, 2004), where others argue that the blurring of boundaries is detrimental for maintaining an acceptable work-family balance (Igbaria & Guimaraes, 1999; Standen, Daniels & Lamond, 1999).

Future research

All chapters have included suggestions for future research. We have argued in this chapter that well-designed empirical studies are still scarce in most of the topics included in this volume. Therefore, there is ample room for new research ideas linking digital media to an organizational context. In fact, digital media can also be very useful in collecting data for example. Online questionnaires are easily widespread by the use of social media and it has become much easier to conduct diary studies since it is possible to fill them out anytime, anywhere by means of smartphones or tablets. We suggest that innovation is not restricted to the content of new research ideas, but also by using and inventing new paradigms and data collection tools.

References

Alexander, A. L., Brunyé, T., Sidman, J., Weil, S. A. (2005) *From gaming to training: A review of studies on fidelity, immersion, presence and buy-in and their effects on transfer in PC-based simulations and games.* Woburn, MA: DARWARS Training Impact Group.

Allen, J. A., Hays, R. T. & Buffordi, L. C. (1986) Maintenance, training, simulator fidelity, and individual differences in transfer of training. *Human Factors*, 28, 497–509.

Archer, N. P. (1990) A comparison of computer conferences with face-to-face meetings for small group business decisions. *Behaviour & Information Technology*, 9, 307–317.

Axtell, C. M., Fleck, S. J. & Turner, N. (2004) Virtual teams: Collaborating across distance, in C. L. Cooper & I. T. Robertson (eds), *International Review of Industrial and Organizational Psychology*, 19. Chichester: Wiley.

Baum, D. R., Riedel, S., Hays, R. T. & Mirabella, A. (1982) *Training effectiveness as a function of training device fidelity: Current ARI research* (Technical Report, 593). Alexandria, VA: US Army Research Institute for the Behavioral and Social Sciences. (Defense Technical Information Center No. ADA133104).

Bell, B. S. & Kozlowski, S. W. J. (2002) A typology of virtual teams: Implications for effective leadership. *Group and Organization Management*, 27, 14–49.

Bersin, J. (2002) Measure the metrics: How to link e-learning to business strategy. *E-learning*, 3, 26–28.

Bordia, P. (1997) Face-to-face versus computer-mediated communication: A synthesis of the experimental literature. *The Journal of Business Communication*, 34, 99–120.

Burgess, J. R. D. & Russell, J. E. A. (2003) The effectiveness of distance learning initiatives in organizations. *Journal of Vocational Behavior*, 63, 289–303.

Burgoon, J. K. & Saine, T. (1978) *The unspoken dialogue: An introduction to nonverbal communication.* Boston: Houghton Mifflin.

Byron, K. (2008) Carrying too heavy a load? The communication and miscommunication of emotion by e-mail. *Academy of Management Review*, 23, 309–327.

Chidambaram, L. & Bostrom, R. (1993) Evolution of group performance over time: A repeated measures study of GDSS effects. *Journal of Organizational Computing*, 3, 443–469.

Coleman, J. S. (1988) Social capital in the creation of human capital. *American Journal of Sociology*, 94, S95–S120.

Davis, G. (2002) Anytime/anyplace computing and the future of knowledge work. *Communications of the ACM*, 45, 67–73.

Dawley, D. D. & Anthony, W. P. (2003) User perceptions of e-mail at work. *Journal of Business and Technical Communication*, 17, 170–200.

DeMeyer, A. (1991) Tech talk: How managers are stimulating global R&D communication. *Sloan Management Review*, 32, 49–59.

DeRouin, R. E., Fritzsche, B. A. & Salas, E. (2005) E-learning in organizations. *Journal of Management*, 31, 920–940.

Derks, D. & Bakker, A. B. (2010) The impact of e-mail communication of organizational life. *Cyberpsychology: Journal of Psychosocial Research on Cyberspace, 4,* article 1. Retrieved August 4, 2011 from http://cyberpsychology.eu/view.php?cisloclanku= 2010052401&article=1.

Derks, D., Fischer, A. H. & Bos, A. E. R. (2008) The role of emotion in computer-mediated communication: A review. *Computer in Human Behavior*, 24, 766–785.

Duxbury, L. E., Higgins, C. & Neufeld, D. (1998) Telework and the balance between work and family: Is telework part of the problem or part of the solution? in M. Igbaria & M. Tan (eds), *The Virtual Workplace*. Hershey, PA: Idea Group, pp. 218–255.

Ellison, N. B., Steinfeld, C. & Lampe, C. (2007) The benefits of Facebook 'friends': Social capital and college students' use of online social network sites. *Journal of Computer-Mediated Communication*, 12, 1143–1168.

Friedman, R. A. & Currall, C. (2003) Conflict escalation: Dispute exacerbating elements of e-mail communication. *Human Relations*, 56, 1325–1347.

Galegher, J. & Kraut, R. E. (1994) Computer-mediated communication for intellectual teamwork: An experiment in group writing. *Information Systems Research*, 5, 110–138.

Goodridge, E. (2001) E-learning blends in with classrooms. *Information Week*, 834.

Green, N. (2001) Who is watching whom? Monitoring and accountability in mobile relations. In B. Brown, N. Green & R. Harper (eds), *Wireless world: Social and interactional aspects of the mobile age*. London: Springer, pp. 32–44.

Griffith, T. L. & Neale, M. A. (2001) Information processing in traditional, hybrid, and virtual teams: From nascent knowledge to transactive memory. *Research in Organizational Behavior*, 23. Amsterdam: Jai-Elsevier Science, pp. 379–421.

Hampton, K. & Wellman, B. (2003) Neighboring in Netville: How the Internet support community and social capital in a wired suburb. *City & Community*, 2, 277–311.

Hertel, G., Geister, S. & Konradt, U. (2005) Managing virtual teams: A review of current empirical research. *Human Resource Management Review*, 15, 69–95.

Igbaria, M. & Guimaraes, T. (1999) Exploring differences in employee turnover intentions and its determinants among telecommuters and non-telecommuters. *Journal of Management Information Systems*, 16, 147–164.

Jentsch, F. & Bowers, C. A. (1998) Evidence for the validity of PC-based simulations in studying aircrew coordination. *International Journal of Aviation Psychology*, 8, 243–260.

Kaiser, M. K. & Schroeder, J. A. (2003) Flights of fancy: The art and science of flight simulation, in P. S. Tang & M. A. Vidulich (eds), *Principles and practice of aviation psychology*. Mahwah, NJ: Erlbaum, pp. 435–471.

Kaplan-Leierson, E. (2002) *E-learning glossary*. Retrieved July 27, 2011 from http://www.learningcircuits.org/glossary.html.

Kirkman, B. L., Rosen, B., Tesluk, P. E. & Gibson, C. B. (2004) The impact of team empowerment on virtual team performance: The moderating role of face-to-face interaction. *Academy of Management Journal*, 47, 175–192.

Kovaleski, D. (2004) Blended learning in focus. *Corporate Meetings & Incentives*, 23, 35–36.

Kruger, J., Epley, N., Parker, J. & Ng, Z. W. (2005) Egocentrism over e-mail: Can we communicate as well as we think? *Journal of Personality and Social Psychology*, 89, 925–936.

Lane, N. E. & Alluisi, E. A. (1992) *Fidelity and validity in distributed interactive simulation: Questions and answers* (Report No. IDA-D-1066). Alexandria, VA: Institute for Defense Analysis.

Lipnack, J. & Stamps, J. (1997) *Virtual teams*. New York: John Wiley.

Lombard, M. & Ditton, T. (1997) At the heart of it all: The concept of presence. *Journal of Computer-Mediated communication*, 3. Retrieved July 27, 2011 from http://jcmc.indiana.edu/vol3/issue2/lombard.html.

Lyytinen, K. & Yoo, Y. (2002a) Issues and challenges in ubiquitous computing. *Communications of the ACM*, 45, 63–65.

Markus, M. L. (1994) Finding a happy medium: Explaining the negative effect of electronic communication on social life at work. *ACM Transactions on Information Systems*, 12, 119–149.

Masie, E. (2002) Blended learning: The magic is in the mix, in A. Rosett (ed.), *The ASTD e-learning handbook*. New York: McGraw-Hill.

Pica, D. & Kakihara, M. (2003) The duality of mobility: Designing fluid organizations through stable interaction. Paper presented at the 11th European Conference on Information Systems, Naples, Italy.

Powell, A., Piccoli, G. & Ives, B. (2004) Virtual teams: A review of current literature and directions for future research. *The DATABASE for Advances in Information Systems*, 35, 6–36.

Raghuram, S. & Wiesenfeld, B. (2004) Work-nonwork conflict and job stress among virtual workers. *Human Resource Management*, 43, 259–277.

Rehman, A. J., Mitman, R. & Reynolds, M. (1995) *A handbook of flight simulation fidelity requirements for human factors research* (Technical Report No. DOT/FAA/CT-TN95/46). Wright-Patterson, AFB. OH: Crew Systems Ergonomics Information Analysis Center.

Shaw, M. E. (1981) *Group dynamics: The psychology of small group behavior.* New York: McGraw-Hill.

Skillsoft (2004) *EMEA e-learning benchmark survey: The user's perspective.* Middlesex, UK: Author.

Slater, M. & Steed, A. (2000) A virtual presence counter. *Presence: Teleoperators and Virtual Environments*, 9, 413–434.

Standen, P., Daniels, K. & Lamond, D. (1999) The home as a workplace: Work-family interaction and psychological well being in telework. *Journal of Occupational Health Psychology*, 4, 368–381.

Stapleton, A. (2004) *Serious games: Serious opportunities.* Paper presented at the Australian Game Developers' Conference, Academic Sumit, Melbourne, VIC.

Strother, J. B. (2002) An assessment of the effectiveness of e-learning in corporate training progams. *International Review of Research in Open and Distance Learning* [online], 3.

Walther, J. B. (1995) Relational aspects of computer-mediated communication: Experimental observations over time. *Organizational Science*, 6, 186–203.

Walther, J. B. & Parks, M. R. (2002) Cues filtered out, cues filtered in: Computer-mediated communication and relationships. In M. L. Knapp & J. A. Daly (eds), *Handbook of interpersonal communication*, 3rd edn. Thousand Oaks, CA: Sage, pp. 529–563.

Witmer, B. & Singer, M. (1998) Measuring presence in virtual environments: A presence questionnaire. *Presence: Teleoperators and Virtual Environments*, 7, 225–240.

Part 1

Online communication and collaboration

2 Email overload

Fine-tuning the research lens

Julie Rennecker and Daantje Derks

Email has changed the way we work. A significant proportion of the communication in organizational life, with clients and colleagues, far away or in close proximity, takes place online (Renaud, Ramsay & Hair, 2006). The reputation of email is that it is less time consuming, more reliable and more efficient than face-to-face meetings or phone calls (e.g. Berghel, 1997). People can be reached easily and quickly (Manger, Wicklund & Elkeland, 2003), and communicating asynchronously facilitates collaboration with individuals irrespective of geographical location (Renaud *et al.*, 2006).

One of the great accomplishments of email documented in early studies of workplace computer-mediated communication was that it enabled the receipt of more information from more – and more diverse – sources (Sproull & Kiesler, 1991) than traditional, manager-filtered information channels, e.g. department meetings and memos. Workers given access to email for the first time reported feeling 'more connected' and 'more informed' (Sproull & Kiesler, 1991).

Other studies, however, foreshadowed the cries of 'overload' that were to come. Hiltz and Turoff (1985) foresaw that when email, then available primarily to academics and government employees, became widely available across industry, workers would struggle with managing the inflow of messages. Subsequent studies of the 'overload' workers experience related to email use have continued to emphasize the amount of information being received and processed via email as well as strategies to improve throughput (Edmunds & Morris, 2000; Eppler & Mengis, 2004; Farhoomand & Drury, 2002; Hemp, 2009). A handful of studies, however, have found that workers' perceived overload stems from aspects of their email use other than, or in addition to, the number and length of messages received. Other factors contributing to perceived overload have included pressures to respond quickly (Derks & Bakker, 2010; Thomas *et al.*, 2006); unanticipated tasks generated by received messages (Thomas *et al.*, 2006; Zeldes, Sward & Louchheim, 2007); interruptions and task-switching associated with responding to emails (Dabbish & Kraut, 2006; Russell, Purvis & Banks, 2005); numerous and diverse role demands (Derks & Bakker, 2010); and lack of control over incoming messages (Allen & Shoard, 2005; Bawden & Robinson, 2009; Zeldes *et al.*, 2007). These suggest the need for a more multi-dimensional conceptualization of workers' overload experiences than that implied by the label 'information overload.'

In the following pages, we explore these additional dimensions. After a review of the existing literature, we introduce a typology of 'email overload' that distinguishes between *information* overload, *work* overload, and *social* overload that, we argue, better captures the diversity of experiences reported in the literature. We then discuss the implications of the typology for doing studies that will produce finer-grained analyses, leading, in turn, to more fruitful recommendations for knowledge workers and their managers. Finally, we close by considering the ongoing proliferation of communication media and the implications of this proliferation both for research and for workers' lived experiences of 'overload.'

Email and information overload

The terms 'email overload' and 'information overload' are often used interchangeably, but studies of 'information overload' predate widespread computer-mediated communication (Chervany & Dickson, 1974; Galbraith, 1974; O'Reilly, 1980; Schroder, Driver & Streufert, 1967; Milgram, 1970). These studies repeatedly argued and demonstrated that humans have a limited capacity to receive, interpret, assimilate, and apply information. While the limit(s) varies somewhat between individuals, within individuals over time, and in response to contextual influences, limits do nonetheless exist, and when they are exceeded, cognitive performance – i.e. decision-making, prioritization, organizing skills – declines.

As email adoption became widespread, information overload researchers turned their attention to the information-processing implications of email use. Study after study highlighted a recurring paradox – email communication facilitated information distribution and reduced information delays, improving *organizational* productivity, while simultaneously overwhelming workers' information processing capabilities, often resulting in decreased *individual* effectiveness and increased stress (Allen & Wilson, 2003; Dabbish & Kraut, 2006; Edmunds & Morris, 2000; Eppler *et al.*, 2004). Studies across disciplines considering diverse information types and sources (Jacoby, 1984; Keller & Staelin, 1987; Schick, Gordon & Haka, 1990; Swain & Haka, 2001) have found that information overload results in inefficiency, demotivation, stress, confusion, and decreased decision quality (Eppler & Mengis, 2004; O'Reilly, 1980).

Hiltz and Turoff (1985), however, argued that perceived overload related to email use was for most users a transient state in a user's learning curve that passed when use of the interface became routine and when users developed effective strategies for filtering and prioritizing messages. In short, they argued that email overload need not be an inevitable result of email use.

At the time of their writing, that may have been the case. Since then, however, a number of factors have contributed to an explosion in email volume (Zeldes et al., 2007). Organizations have become more geographically and temporally distributed, requiring increased reliance on email, rather than telephone or other synchronous media, to manage organizational communication. The result is a '24/7' flow of work-related email. In addition, marketers, professional associations, utility companies, social groups, health centers, and others outside the organizational boundary have since adopted email for interaction with their members and clients, further increasing the volume of emails received. Finally, there is evidence that email encourages people to communicate more (Balter, 1998; Sproull & Kiesler, 1991), so that email users can expect to be contacted more frequently, even if communicating with the same people and organizations as before adopting email. In addition, other contextual factors, such as job characteristics (Dabbish & Kraut, 2006) and organizational climate (Allen & Wilson, 2003), may contribute to workers in particular roles or in particular organizations using email even more than their contemporaries in other organizational contexts.

While email users typically both send and receive messages, a systematic bias exists for receiving more messages than one sends. Because email allows one sender to address multiple recipients simultaneously, the average workplace email user receives slightly more than twice the number of message s/he sends (Dabbish & Kraut, 2006; Radicati, 2010). In addition, the tendency to communicate more and the incongruity between the number of messages sent and received may also be explained in part by the difference in marginal costs per message experienced by the sender and the receiver. Renaud and colleagues (2006) have argued that senders enjoy a disproportionate share of the benefits of email communication while recipients shoulder a disproportionate share of the costs. For instance, in addition to the time and energy involved in reading and responding to another's information request, recipients also tend to interrupt their own work to continuously monitor incoming emails to satisfy senders' expectations of a timely reply (Dabbish & Kraut, 2006; Derks & Bakker, 2010; Iqbal & Horvitz, 2007; Russell, Purvis & Banks, 2005).

In addition to the *volume* of electronic communication, both researchers and businesses have more recently taken notice of the productivity and performance costs of CMC-related *interruptions* (Dabbish & Kraut, 2006; Hemp, 2009; Richtel, 2008; Zeldes *et al.*, 2007). A study at Microsoft found that workers took 24 minutes, on average, to return to their work after checking email (Hemp, 2009), a particularly startling finding considering another study by an independent research firm (*Trends*, 2009) reporting that an average knowledge worker checks email 50 times per day and uses instant messaging 77 times during that same time period. While a bit of simple arithmetic reveals the incompatibility of the two studies' findings,[1] suggesting variations in measurement schemes and the type of workers studied, they both highlight the potentially disruptive effects of unmanaged computer-mediated communication (CMC). Other studies by Spira and Feintuch (2005), Gantz, Boyd, and Dowling at IDC (2009), and Zeldes *et al.* (2007) all report similar findings in studies of global knowledge workers spanning industries and job roles. Conservative calculations by Zeldes *et al.* (2007), estimate that the average worker loses 6 hours per week to interruptions and 2 hours per week to processing unnecessary email, for a total productivity loss of 8 hours per week – or 392 hours per year – per employee. For a large multinational firm with 50,000 employees, this translates into a cost of approximately €764,366,394, or one-billion U.S. dollars at current exchange rates.

And time is not all that is lost. Hewlett-Packard found that a worker performing a cognitive task while distracted by electronic communication exhibited twice the degradation in IQ scores during the task as a person smoking marijuana (Hemp, 2009). While not necessarily a perfect measure of available cognitive capacity, the use of IQ scores provides a common measure for comparing performance during distracted and non-distracted states. Psychologists have long referred to this phenomenon – i.e. degradation in focal task performance when trying to perform a second task – as *dual-task interference* (Matthews *et al.*, 2000), though they do not yet agree on the underlying explanation.

That chronic multi-tasking could have an enduring performance impact, however, is a relatively new finding. In studies of multi-tasking students at Stanford, Ophir, Nass & Wagner (2009) found that 'high media multi-tasking' (HMM) students, those who frequently engaged in multi-tasking involving five or more simultaneous information streams, scored poorly on standard judgment, recall, and reaction-time tasks compared to their 'low media multi-tasking' (LMM) peers. It is important to note that the students were *not* engaged in multi-tasking when performing the standard evaluation tasks, indicating that the negative performance impacts of multi-tasking persist, even when the multi-tasking behavior stops. These findings challenge the decades-old conventional wisdom that multi-taskers accomplish more as well as the widely-accepted notion that a new generation of workers who have grown up multi-tasking and using electronic communication tools have, as a result, developed more complex neural pathways allowing them to multi-task effectively (Tapscott, 1997).

Numerous sources including consultants, academic researchers, and time-management specialists have recommended both individual and organizational strategies for managing the communicative load associated with email and mitigating its impacts on personal productivity (Allen, 2001; Hemp, 2009; Hiltz & Turoff, 1985). Because email overload is typically called 'information overload,' the recommended remedies tend to focus on strategies to facilitate information processing. The phenomena described in empirical studies to date, however, suggest that the challenges workers experience do not stem only from the *amount of information* they receive via email but rather that 'overload' is a multi-dimensional experience.

The impacts of email overload on workers' home lives and health have not been as clearly quantified as the impacts on performance but are an increasing focus of study. The introduction of the smartphone, which facilitates email communication outside the office, has contributed to the emergence of a norm of continual communication (e.g. Castells, 1996; Hassan, 2003; Hörning, Ahrens & Gerhard, 1999) regardless of location or time of day. There is evidence that use of smartphones leads to difficulties in managing a healthy work-home balance (Davis, 2002; Grant & Kiesler, 2001; Green, 2002; Higgins & Duxbury, 2005; Jarvenpaa & Lang, 2005) and that negative spillover, or work-home interference (WHI), is related to poor well-being. For example, WHI is associated with negative affect (e.g. Burke, 1993; MacEwen & Barling, 1994), exhaustion, poor physical health, reduced relationship satisfaction (Bakker, Demerouti & Burke,

2009), and psychosomatic symptoms (e.g. Frone, Russell & Cooper, 1991; Frone, Russell & Barnes, 1996; Kinnunen & Mauno, 1998). Clearly, email overload and information overload are not interchangeable concepts.

Fine-tuning our lens

In reviewing the information overload literature associated with email use, we found that in spite of general agreement on the formal definition of 'information overload,' in practice, the phenomena observed reflect more than a mismatch between workers' cognitive capacity and the information processing demands introduced by email use. Several research teams have highlighted additional dimensions to be considered, but without challenging the 'information overload' label. Even prior to the widespread use of email, Schick, Gordon & Haka (1990) proposed the definition of information overload be refined to emphasize the temporal aspects of an information processing situation, in addition to an individual's cognitive capacities, in order to address conflicting findings in the literature: 'information processing demands on an individual's time to perform [them]...exceed the supply or capacity of time available for such processing' (p.199). Other researchers have highlighted emotional and social factors influencing workers' perceived level of 'overload.' Thomas *et al.*, (2006), avoiding the term 'information overload' altogether, identified characteristics of email interaction stemming from the social processes within which the exchanges occurred that impacted on whether and to what degree workers experienced 'email overload.' Finally, a study by Gantz *et al.* (2009), identified 'information diversity' as a prime contributor to knowledge workers' experience of information overload. All of these studies indicate that additional factors, namely time, tasks, relationships, and lack of control, figure significantly in workers' felt experience of overload.

Based on a close examination of the phenomena described in the studies we reviewed, we propose a three-part typology of email overload experiences, distinguishing among the causes of email overload – *information* overload, *work* overload, and *social* overload – any one of which can contribute, individually or in combination, to a worker's *perceived* overload, or 'email-related stress' (Dabbish & Kraut, 2006). In this typology, the term *information overload* is restricted to situations fitting the classic definition, i.e. the condition where the *cognitive* demands associated with an information-processing task exceed an individual's information-processing capacity, typically resulting in lower-quality decisions (O'Reilly, 1980). In contrast, *work overload* results when the physical and temporal processing demands associated with a particular volume of messages exceed the *physical capabilities* of a normal person to complete the processing in the available time. This includes the short-term tasks required to respond to the messages, such as locating information, compiling existing data, or coordinating schedules (Thomas *et al.*, 2006; Zeldes *et al.*, 2007). Finally, *social overload* occurs when the number and variety of social exposures and the associated social information received exceeds an individual's *interaction capacity*, that is, a person's ability to process the information and respond appropriately (McCarthy & Saegert, 1978).

Though analytically distinct, we appreciate that these three sources of over-load, in practice, can and do occur simultaneously and most likely have an additive, if not a synergistic, impact on real and perceived overload. Nonetheless, maintaining the analytic distinctions will allow for a more accurate understanding of observed and reported phenomena as well as for more situation-specific remedies. For instance, a technology that filters and prioritizes messages or a no-personal-email policy will not necessarily lighten the load of a manager receiving 150–300 work-related messages per day.

Information overload is well-researched and supported by a long history of psychological (Cutrell, Czerwinski & Horvitz, 2001; Librowski, 1975) and, more recently, neuroscience (Carpenter, Just & Reichle, 2000) studies that have outlined the limitations of human information processing. *Work overload* and *social overload*, on the other hand, are less well explicated, and the relationships among these three analytically-distinct sources of email overload have not yet, to our knowledge, been explored. In the following section, we first expand upon the definition of each overload type, and then consider the application of the typology to the analysis of email-induced overload in the workplace.

Information overload

When popular media invoke the term 'information overload' with respect to email use, the author is typically referring to the rapid growth in email volume that has occurred since the mid-1990s (Gantz *et al.*, 2009; Zeldes *et al.*, 2007). In this chapter, however, we are distinguishing between the cognitive demands of perceiving, interpreting, and applying the information contained in those messages, the traditional focus for academic writings on *information overload*, and the time required to physically process a volume of messages, or *work over-load*, which we discuss in the subsequent section.

Though researchers have, over time, proposed a number of nuanced refinements, most accept the classic cognition-based definition of *information overload* as their starting point. That is, information overload results when the information-processing requirements (IPR) of a task or situation exceed an individual's information-processing capacity (IPC) (Edmunds & Morris, 2000; Eppler & Mengis, 2004; Galbraith, 1974; Keller & Staelin, 1987; Muller, 1984; O'Reilly, 1980; Schneider, 1987; Sparrow, 1999; Tushman & Nadler, 1978). We propose retaining this definition, with its emphasis on cognition, arguing that it has both practical and theoretical value and is supported by psychological (Cutrell, Czerwinski & Horvitz, 2001; Matthews, Davies, *et al.*, 2000: Miller, 1956; Rubinstein, Meyer & Evans, 2001), work group (Dennis, 1996; Grise & Gallupe, 1999/2000; Heninger, Dennis & Hilmer, 2006; Schultze & Vandenbosch, 1998) and neuroscience research (Carpenter, Just & Reichle, 2000). For purposes of this typology, we would not modify the classic definition but would qualify it by limiting the focus to information received via email.

Miller (1956) may have been the first to articulate and to quantify the limits of humans' ability to perceive and make judgments about received information.

Though his 'magical number seven, plus or minus 2' is widely cited in both academic and popular publications discussing the information-processing limits of humans, his work focused primarily on perception and recall of discrete bits of novel information, which does not accurately represent either the complexity nor the mix of familiar and novel information characterizing knowledge workers' email interactions. While debates continue regarding the underlying neural architecture, theorists agree – and empirical studies confirm – the existence of information processing limits across diverse information types. In contrast to the *fixed* resource model implicit in Miller's '7 +/– 2' rule and much of the business and management literature, however, the psychology literature has favored more *variable* resource models (Matthews *et al.*, 2000), recognizing that an individual's information-processing capacity will vary over time, fluctuating with mental and physical energy levels (ibid.) as well as other idiosyncratic conditions. Additional studies have explored how the context of consumption (Engle, Kane & Tuholski, 1999), recipient knowledge (or long-term memory, see Ericsson & Delaney, 1999), and attention levels (Norman & Bobrow, 1975) further impact on information comprehension, retention, and recall.

Another important stream of research for understanding the conditions under which information overload is most likely to occur involves the role of long-term memory in information processing. Ericsson and Delaney (1999) have argued that as knowledge workers develop expertise in a domain, they refine their selection, storage, and retrieval mechanisms, enabling them to more easily attend to, remember, and recall important information while being less distracted by irrelevant information (see also Engle *et al.*, 1999). Thus, we would expect novices to be more quickly overloaded than experts, and for all workers to be more quickly overloaded by content addressing novel domains than by information on familiar topics. While this perspective resonates intuitively with most knowledge workers, information novelty/familiarity is rarely mentioned in the business psychology literature on overload.

In recent years it has become popular to assert that a younger generation of workers who have grown up using a suite of multimedia tools have developed more complex neural pathways, purportedly freeing them from the cognitive limits on which much information overload research is based (Tapscott, 1997, 2008). As mentioned earlier, more recent studies now refute that claim (Bergen, Grimes & Potter, 2005; Hembrooke & Gay, 2005; Ophir *et al.*, 2009), showing that people who chronically attend to multiple simultaneous information streams perform more poorly on standard experimental tasks for judgment and decision-making than people who typically attend to no more than two simultaneous information channels. In addition, Ophir *et al.* found that the high media multi-taskers (HMM) felt more confident about their performance than their low media multi-tasker (LMM) counterparts, similar to O'Reilly's (1980) findings that decision makers who received more information inputs made poorer decisions but felt more confident about those decisions than those with access to less information. Other laboratory studies of 'task-switching' and 'interruptions,' both closely related to multi-tasking, have obtained similar results (Carpenter *et al.*, 2000; Matthews *et al.*, 2000 (see Chapter 5); Rubinstein, Meyer & Evans, 2001).

Taken together, these findings suggest that 'objective' information overload (Eppler & Mengis, 2004), the point at which information perception, interpretation, and judgment quality decline, is further exacerbated by common email consumption practices – e.g. interruptions, task-switching, and multi-tasking – that erode workers' capacity for assimilating and applying the information associated with any particular task. In addition, the multi-tasking behaviors that give workers an increased sense of control over email volume (Allen & Shoard, 2005: Mazmanian *et al.*, 2005) are also likely to boost the workers' confidence regarding their information-processing competence, suggesting that 'subjective' information overload (Haksever & Fisher, 1996), the point when an individual *perceives* him or herself to be overloaded, may occur substantially later than an objective performance decline.

When workers use the term 'overload,' however, they may be referring to a sense of being overwhelmed from trying to deal with the sheer volume of messages received, the topic of the next section.

Work overload

Many academic studies fail to differentiate between the information-processing load associated with particular decisions or actions, or *information load*, as discussed in the previous section, and a worker's total email *workload* (Thomas *et al.*, 2006). We define *work overload*, with respect to workplace email, as receiving, and being expected to respond to (Zeldes *et al.*, 2007), a volume of messages that exceed a worker's physical capability to do so in the allotted time, even when the messages are processed efficiently by a competent worker.

Researchers began grappling with issues of information quantity and processing time limitations long before email became commonplace. Keller and Staelin (1987), for example, introduced the distinctions of 'quantity' and 'quality' into the information overload dialog in the marketing community, and Schick *et al* (1990) argued for a 'temporal approach' to information overload that would take into consideration the time required to process the necessary information. Both of these studies, however, were still primarily concerned with how the number of information inputs bearing on a particular decision task impacted an individual's cognitive performance, i.e. *information* overload. What we propose here, however, is that the total quantity of email messages sent and received for all tasks – or the *communication workload* – warrants attention in its own right if we are to fully understand and explore ways to relieve workers' real and perceived overload (Zeldes *et al.*, 2007).

To illustrate the work overload concept, we use data from a 2008 survey of 2,300 Intel employees (Hemp, 2009) to estimate the amount of time required by each worker on a daily basis to deal with the volume of received email, assuming a competent, motivated employee and the unrealistic conditions that all messages would be processed on the day received and without interruption. The Intel workers received, on average, 350 messages per week (70 messages per work day), while executives received 300 messages *per day* (Hemp, 2009). Email volume data from multiple sources (Dabbish & Kraut, 2006; Fisher, Brush, *et al.*, 2006; Gantz, *et al.*, 2009; Radicati, 2010; Zeldes *et al.*, 2007) suggests that the Intel numbers offer a reasonable approximation of the email workload of a typical knowledge worker in a medium-to-large organization whose work requires ongoing communication and coordination with others. Our calculations are summarized in Table 2.1.

Table 2.1 Estimated time required to process email volumes reported in Intel study, 2008

	Message types	Estimated time (on average) to process each message type	Daily hours devoted to email
Staff member 70 messages/day	1/3 unnecessary[1] = 23 messages	30 seconds/ message	11.5 minutes
	1/3 necessary[2] = 24 messages	2 minutes/ message	48.0 minutes
	1/3 important[3] = 23 messages	5 minutes/ message	115.0 minutes
			174.5 min = 2.9 hrs
Executive 300 messages/day	1/3 unnecessary = 100 messages	30 seconds/ message	50 minutes
	1/3 necessary = 100 messages	1 minutes/ message	100 minutes
	1/3 important = 100 messages	5 minutes/ message	500 minutes
			650 minutes = 10.8 hrs

1　Based on Intel survey findings. Assumed processing consists of scanning sender, subject line, and content, then deleting without responding.
2　Assumed processing consists of reading and sending a brief reply with known or readily-available information.
3　Assumed processing consists of reading, thinking, researching needed information and/or coordinating with others prior to responding, and a response that requires attention to word choice, recipient list, and clarity.
4　Note, however, that Intel employees only reported spending approximately two hours per day completing email.

We categorized one third of messages as 'unnecessary' based on the Intel study, but the estimated proportions of messages categorized as 'necessary' and 'important' and the time allotted to process messages of each type are gross-level approximations based on our respective field observations, used here for illustration purposes. We anticipate that field studies of actual workers' email management practices would result in a more complex message typology and greater variation in response times due to factors not considered here. For instance, IT professionals responding to an online industry study identified eight message types accounting for a significant proportion of their email traffic (Vile & Collins, 2004).

Studies of smartphone users report that workers are processing email during meetings and at home (Derks & Bakker, 2010; Middleton, 2007) in order to manage the volume (Govindaraju & Sward, 2005) and exert some control (Allen & Shoard, 2005; Mazmanian, Orlikowski & Yates, 2005) over when and how their email workload is handled. Unfortunately, these tactics can backfire due to the negative impacts on workers' information-processing capacities, as described earlier.

A second aspect of email-related work overload is the additional work generated by received messages. Analyzing message threads in a sample of 1,727 emails, Thomas, King, et al (2006) found that 70% of the received messages took one minute or less to read and required little or no response. The remaining messages were also brief, requiring little time to read, but often included requests for urgent action. The workers reported that their experience of overload did not result from the volume of messages they received or the amount of information in those messages so much as the unanticipated, and often urgent, activity triggered by implicit and explicit requests in the messages. In addition, Thomas *et al.*'s analysis revealed that the senders of the urgent requests often followed their initial request with additional messages modifying the original request, even as the requested work was being carried out. In these messages, they asked for more or different information, changed the task deadline or who was to receive the work product, and/or the format of the work product (e.g. email message, report, PowerPoint presentation), increasing both the message and task loads.

Thomas *et al.*'s findings hint at a third dimension of *work overload* and a recurring finding in other studies – lack of control over the incoming message stream heightens feelings of overload (Zeldes *et al.*, 2007). The proliferation of smartphones has increased workers' vulnerability to these requests outside normal working hours. The opportunity to be accessible anywhere, anytime, seems to have become an obligation to be accessible everywhere, all the time (Bawden & Robinson, 2009; Brown, 2001; Cooper, 2001; Katz & Aarhus, 2002; Mazmanian, Orlikowski & Yates, 2005), further eroding workers' sense of control over their own time and work, thus increasing feelings of 'overload.'

In the preceding discussions of both information and work overload, we have emphasized the time, task, and cognitive demands of email messages. In the next section we turn our attention to an under-examined aspect of email overload, the number and diversity of interpersonal encounters – and the associated role demands – enabled by email communication.

Social overload

Social overload, a term borrowed from sociology and urban studies (McCarthy & Saegert, 1978), occurs when 'the number of social exposures exceed a person's interaction capacity' or 'the amount of social information received exceeds an individual's ability to process incoming social stimuli' (p.253). This differs from the concepts of role demands, role overload, and role conflict (Coverman, 1989) studied by psychologists for decades because it makes explicit the demands of interpersonal interaction – or choosing not to interact – and encompasses the cost of encounters beyond one's formal role obligations as employee and family member.

People have always performed multiple roles and interacted with diverse groups, so role diversity, role-switching, and social adaptations are not new phenomena. What is new is the 'density' of social interaction enabled by computer-mediated communication (Hiltz & Turoff, 1985). In extensive studies of interpersonal interaction, Goffman (1966) noted how people used physical barriers – e.g. walls, doors, distance – to segregate, contain, and serialize interactions and their accompanying role demands. The limitations of the then-available communication technologies, e.g. single-line, location-based telephones with no 'call waiting,' also limited the total number of roles and encounters experienced on any given day.

In the world of computer-mediated communication, however, the number of encounters and the associated interaction demands are no longer constrained by physical barriers or technology limitations. Teleworking may enable us to get away with working in our pajamas, but the expectations persist that we speak in a particular language with appropriate syntax and tone, that we exhibit a relationship-appropriate level of authority or deference, and that we respond at a rate reflecting our role in and regard for each relationship. In any given hour of the workday, one may receive messages from one's boss, spouse, important/unimportant client, child's soccer coach, preferred/negligible vendor, child, dentist, religious organization, professional organization, and former classmate, to name just a few, each with a unique request and a particular time horizon for responding. Not only does the recipient have to cognitively-process the content of the message and reply appropriately, but each interaction must be prioritized within the broader ecology of one's relational life.

Social overload has not yet been discussed in studies of workplace communication, but it is emerging as a growing concern in the public media (Campbell, 2008; Spivak, 2004). In a lengthy but articulate weblog posting, Spivak details the numerous ways his participation in professional and social networking sites has increased the volume and diversity of his electronic encounters. Many of these encounters occurred in the form of email messages from mere acquaintances, calling upon him to perform professional favors for someone he did not know at all, extending his social exposure well beyond his immediate circles of coworkers, family, and friends.

Additionally, social networking sites have intruded on organizational life (see also Stopfer & Gosling, this volume). Employees are spending an increasing amount of time during office hours updating their Facebook and LinkedIn profiles and interacting with people accessible through those channels. Though Facebook emphasizes users' private lives, and LinkedIn users' professional relationships, in practice the boundaries between these domains are becoming less distinct, further increasing the social load workers encounter during work hours.

Studies of physical or geographical density predating widespread electronic communication (McCarthy & Saegert, 1978) found that people living in more densely-populated areas unconsciously contract the physical range of their social circle, effectively limiting the number of relationships and day-to-day encounters. In contrast, Spivak's blog indicates that an increase in the density of his computer-mediated world serves to further expand the circle of his encounters, exceeding his personal social limits. We argue that at least some portion of the workers experiencing 'overload' are similarly overwhelmed by a number and diversity of social encounters (and associated role demands) that exceeds their personal interaction capacities.

Table 2.2 summarizes and illustrates the three components of the typology. In the next section we consider the implications of applying the typology to future studies of email-related overload.

Table 2.2 A typology of email overload

Types of email overload	Definition	Sample behavioral/performance indicators
Information overload	The condition of decreased cognitive performance that results when the processing demands of information received via email with respect to a particular task or situation (e.g., comparing, synthesizing, deciding) exceed an individual's information-processing capacity	• Difficulty making signal-noise distinctions resulting in oversight of key facts • Inappropriately weighting the associated facts and considerations • Inability to make decisions resulting from inability to sort and prioritize information
Work overload	Receiving, and being expected to respond to, a volume of messages that exceed the time available to do so, even when the messages are processed efficiently by a competent worker	• Inability to respond to received messages in a timely manner despite committed effort to do so • A growing backlog of unanswered messages • Overlooking important messages due to the volume of messages received • Sense of being overwhelmed or hopelessness about ever 'catching up'
Social overload	A sense of being overwhelmed stemming from the number and diversity of email interactions (and associated role demands) that exceed an individual's personal interaction capacity	• Reports of feeling 'fragmented' related to one's email interactions • Sending messages that are uncharacteristically inappropriate in tone or content • Difficulty prioritizing messages requiring a response • Distorted perceptions of the emotional demands associated with particular messages

Applying the typology: implications for research

Current studies often make declarative statements about which factors *do* and *do not* contribute to 'information overload' without recognizing that the communicative practices in the work environment(s) being studied may differ significantly from those in another study where different conclusions were drawn. Using the typology as a data collection framework will allow researchers to produce more precise descriptions of workers' experiences and to make cross-study comparisons, allowing both for more specific and more accurate generalizations.

In proposing this typology, we are also implicitly arguing for more empirical field studies. Laboratory studies could be useful for testing each element of the typology and for developing scales and indices to quantify observations, and observation studies could be validated with larger survey studies, but to fully understand the conditions in the workplace that should be guiding managers and technology designers, we recommend field studies with access to participants' actual email interactions and working conditions.

The assessment of information overload could borrow techniques used in studies of group decision support systems (GDSS) (Heninger, Dennis & Hilmer, 2006; Williams, Dennis, Stam & Aronson, 2007). These include measures of the amount of information related to a particular task or decision, the number of different sources supplying that information, the time period over which the information arrives, and the time available for making the decision.

We also suggest collecting quantitative data on three common practices that erode worker cognition: interruptions, task-switching, and multi-tasking. In practice, interruptions and task-switching are closely related, but to improve consistency across studies, we suggest defining *interruptions* as work disruptions initiated by someone other than the focal worker. For instance, a received phone call, a visual or auditory message alert, or a person arriving at one's desk would all constitute interruptions. Interruption data should include the frequency and duration of interruptions. *Task-switching*, on the other hand, would be initiated by the worker him/herself, such as when a person stops working on a report to check for or respond to incoming email messages or works intermittently on multiple tasks in response to emerging information and requests received via email. Finally, *multi-tasking* is the simultaneous engagement in more than one activity, such as listening to a conference call and writing emails at the same time. Multi-tasking data should include the number and type of activities being engaged in simultaneously – e.g. email, instant messaging, telephone conference, face-to-face meeting, child care – and the amount of time spent in multi-tasking mode.

The dependent variables important for assessing *information* overload include indicators of cognitive performance, such as making accurate signal-noise distinctions and situation assessments in addition to decision quality and efficiency. Self-report measures of the perceived level of overload as well as of cognitive performance, such as the ability to organize information received via email and the perceived ease or difficulty of making decisions with this same information, should also be collected. While it will most likely be impossible in a field situation to obtain a cognition baseline and demonstrate statistically-significant erosion of cognitive performance corresponding with a particular information load, having data on both the cognitive demands of the incoming email stream and on workers' performance indicators will, when analyzed within the context of the full typology, allow for finer-grained analyses of the cause(s) and consequences of each case of overload and, therefore, more effective remedies.

Evaluating whether, or to what degree, workers' perceived email overload is a consequence of *work overload,* the second element in our typology, will require collecting data on the received messages – e.g. number, length, type, and importance – the amount of time required to process each message type, and the time required to complete any tasks necessary to respond to the received messages. In practice, many messages will deal with ongoing projects that unfold over weeks and months, but these are not the 'tasks' we are suggesting to be captured. Instead, we mean activities such as looking up information, calling a coworker, or extracting data from an existing report that are necessary to compose a reply.

Corresponding dependent variables would include the average time per day spent processing email communication, both within and outside regular work hours, the average lapsed time between message receipt and message response for each message type,[2] and the proportion of each day's messages that go unread. These measures will vary among individuals and across organizations depending on a variety of factors, including the geographical dispersion of the organization and the role of email in the organization's ecology of communication media,[3] so there are no absolute thresholds for these measures to differentiate between 'normal' and 'overload' conditions. Instead, these measures will need to be analyzed in conjunction with workers' perceptions regarding the appropriateness of the volume of received email and of their own effectiveness in managing it. The strategies employed to manage the volume of messages should also be documented, to allow researchers to better compare studies across contexts.

In a study where *work* overload seems to be a significant factor, researchers should also be asking *why* this is happening: Are large volumes of unnecessary messages being sent, as suggested by the Intel study (Hemp, 2009)? Or is the volume of messages, perhaps with lengthy 'cc:' recipient lists, the result of an organizational climate of mistrust, prompting workers to over-communicate and over-document out of fear of being unfairly blamed for errors, project delays, or poor decisions (Allen & Wilson, 2003)? Or are workers simply engaged in too many simultaneous projects or organizational initiatives, resulting in an unmanageable communicative volume? Each of these causes of email-related work overload would call for a different remedy.

Finally, evaluating the contribution of email-related *social overload,* the third element in the typology, to workers' overload experience calls for descriptive statistics (e.g. min, max, mean, median, and mode) of a worker's interaction partners over the course of a work day (or week) and the number of different social contexts represented by these contacts. Though we are aware of no formal investigations of social overload in computer-mediated communication, the urban studies literature suggests that receiving 50 messages from ten different people, all within the organization and participating on a common project, would create less social load than 50 messages from 25 people representing ten unique social contexts. To test this presumption as well as to illuminate any contribution of social overload to a worker's perceived overload, researchers would also need to gather additional subjective data, such as ratings of perceived 'stress' or feeling 'focused' versus 'fragmented' at intervals throughout the study period (e.g. hourly, daily). These ratings would then need to be mapped against the social density of the interval – i.e. the number of unique message senders and the number of discrete social contexts represented by that interval's message senders – to identify any correlations between the subjective measures and the message characteristics.

More objective measures of social overload include the time required to compose response messages and the appropriateness and tone of the language used. As individuals become socially overloaded, they may become less adept at making role transitions. Consequently, it may require a worker longer to compose a relationally-appropriate response or s/he may respond quickly but without making the appropriate shifts in vocabulary and tone.

Investigation of social overload would also include an evaluation of the nature and extent of work-home interference (WHI) taking place. A comprehensive evaluation would include both the encroachment of work on family life *and* time spent at work distracted by family-related emails. Both of these situations can be equally stressful because they increase a worker's interaction density and require him or her to simultaneously enact competing roles. An exploration of WHI should also identify the coping strategies employed by workers to either minimize WHI or to mitigate its emotional impacts. Derks, ten Brummelhuis, Zecic and Bakker (2012) found that, contrary to the perceived mastery and control reported by Allen and Shoard (2005), smartphone users did *not* manage to increase the recovery strategies that lead to psychological detachment, relaxation, mastery and feelings of autonomy compared to a control group of non-smartphone users that did.

Finally, any field investigation of email overload should also include an exploration of the workers' proficiency with features of the email system such as filters that facilitate screening, organization, and prioritization of incoming messages. Any team-level practice conventions, such as beginning the subject line of emails with the project name or formatting the content for easy consumption, should also be noted (Orlikowski & Yates, 1994). Filtering features and formatting conventions can give workers a greater sense of control over their consumption of messages even if they have no control over the messages being sent.

Though studies of information overload have repeatedly demonstrated an 'inverted-U' relationship between the amount of information to be processed and an individual's cognitive performance, no such established relationships are known for work overload or social overload. We have suggested performance, perception, and behavioral measures to be mapped against theoretically-informed characteristics of workers' incoming email messages, and we anticipate that, if not an 'inverted-U,' researchers will see a 'breaking point' in the curve where a threshold is reached, whether in information, work, or social load, and increases in that independent variable beyond the threshold are expected to result in performance declines and increased stress.

We have also conjectured that these analytically-distinct types of overload are, in practice, quite interrelated, but at this point, we do not know the dynamics of those interrelationships. For instance, do the types of overload always co-vary, or is it possible to suffer from work overload without experiencing either information overload or social overload? And in cases where workers report feeling overloaded, and the metrics for their email communication indicate more than one form of overload, are the effects of each component of overload additive or synergistic? Finally, how do workers' perceptions of the source(s) of their overload correspond with their email metrics? Answers to these types of questions will be required before remedies can be prescribed with precision. Meanwhile, both industry and individuals move ahead, looking for and testing a variety of remedies in search of relief. In the next section, we summarize those most consistently suggested in the literature.

Transcending overload: strategies to try and to test

Information systems scholars (Hiltz & Turoff, 1985) and organizational practitioners (Allen, 2001; Hemp, 2009) have suggested a number of strategies for dealing with email overload, from systemic-level interventions in technology design, and organizational policy to individual practice changes. Though each strategy addresses at least one source of email overload, no single strategy addresses all the sources and so will not alleviate all cases of overload. In addition, one or more of the strategies may not be financially, technically, or politically feasible in all organizational contexts. Nonetheless, each offers a point of departure for developing more refined and targeted strategies aimed at particular causes of email overload.

Systemic strategies

Interventions at the system level have the opportunity for the most widespread benefit and send a symbolic message that an organization is invested in mitigating the negative effects of email overload. For many years, recommendations focused primarily on creating or modifying technology features, such as filtering and message threading, to facilitate message prioritization and processing (Hiltz & Turoff, 1985; Hemp, 2009). Other technology advances, such as the smartphone, initially expected to increase employee flexibility by making email accessible on-the-go have, in many cases, simply resulted in longer working hours (e.g. Middleton, 2007). Formation of the Information Overload Research Group (http://iorgforum.org/), a consortium created by high-tech companies that now includes academics, consultants, and executives, seems to be indicating an emerging recognition that social solutions, such as organizational policies and practices, will also be required.

Technology strategies

Intelligent technology tools now exist to offload some of the work of managing one's inbox by prioritizing messages based on a worker's history with various senders; sorting email into threads by project; and filtering out messages sent to a group if another recipient has already responded to the initial request. Others automate the translation of email messages into calendar appointments or tasks. These tools typically need to be implemented at the system level, particularly in larger organizations where security protocols keep individual users from down-loading, installing, or modifying programs.

Organizational policies

One of the reasons commonly given for 'email addiction' behaviors (Middleton, 2007) – i.e. checking email in the bathroom and on weekends and vacations (Hemp, 2009) – is the perception that such behavior is expected and that failure to do so will result in negative perceptions. For managers with busy meeting schedules during the day, it might be useful to check and respond to emails during evening and weekend hours, but this practice may inadvertently create a belief that work outside office hours is expected. Organizational policies restricting hours for email communication not only give individuals 'permission' to not check their email but make it inappropriate to do so. Intel, Microsoft, and Hewlett-Packard are now experimenting with policies, such as 'no email Thursdays' and 'no email after 6:00 p.m.' (Hemp, 2009). These sorts of policies can offer psychological safety by removing the personal risks of 'missing out' on something important, 'failing to respond,' or being the only one 'out of the loop.' To the degree that these types of policies also decrease interruptions and allow for periods of focused concentration, we would also expect them to yield productiv-ity gains in addition to decreasing stress and improving employee job satisfaction (Perlow, 1997). Again, we would encourage verification in field settings.

Individual strategies

In the absence of supportive organizational policies, individuals can feel as if they have no control over their email communication except to become a more strate-gic communicator and a faster typist. Even in the most unforgiving environments, however, individuals can take steps to help themselves. First, learning to use one's email application efficiently can be a big help. For instance, many email applications have 'filtering' capabilities, a feature that sorts incoming messages, based on the sender ID or subject line – into project and topic-specific folders before the user sees them. This allows the user to process all the messages related to a particular project in one batch, taking advantage of the mind's ability to process and recall large amounts of information if properly 'chunked' (Miller, 1956) or 'clustered' (Schuff, Turetken & Darcy, 2006). Even in the absence of such filtering capability or knowledge of how to use it, a user can read and respond to all the messages related to a particular project or task before moving to the next topic. Both approaches minimize the cognitive process losses associated with task-switching and improve information assimilation, decreasing worker stress by increasing perceived control and improving efficiency.

Users can also *dis*able email 'features,' such as auditory and visual message alerts, to decrease the disruptive nature of email messages. Then discipline is required to only check messages at pre-determined times, such as every hour; every two hours; or morning, lunch, and 4:00 p.m.

Finally, users often overlook the opportunity of defining a personal 'policy' for dealing with social and family-related emails as a way to increase personal control over one's email communication. We suggest composing the equivalent of an 'auto-response' style message that can be sent to all *non*-work-related emails: 'I have received your message and will respond...' The user completes the statement with a personally appropriate time interval.

Group practices

Work groups can also create their own policies for project-related emails to decrease email volume and improve reading efficiency. Examples of such group-level practice policies include always including the project name in the message 'Subject' line, only sending necessary emails, and properly using the CC and BCC options. Many collaborative groups have fallen into the habit of copying all the group members on every group-related email message. Consequently, many received emails are copies of messages not directly addressed to the recipient but only sent to inform him or her. In many instances, it is not expected or necessary for the recipient to act on these messages, but it still takes time and cognitive resources to process them, resources that could be better applied elsewhere.

Finally, project teams and work groups can agree upon guidelines for when to use email and when to opt for other media, such as the telephone, audio-conferencing, or a group document repository. Email is often a default choice rather than a conscious one.

A look to the future

While advances in information and communication technology can be exciting, many bode poorly for email overload. For instance, social networking tools, such as Facebook and Twitter, could be argued to decrease social overload by making it possible to keep in touch with many friends and family members simultaneously – i.e. a single posting of a child's photographs are available for viewing by everyone in one's network. At the same time, however, these applications decrease the cost and increase the reach of one-to-many communication. So with a couple of mouse clicks, a user can send an invitation or an alert to hundreds of people without knowing their email addresses or other contact information. Recently we have seen how these features can be used constructively in the self-organization of political activities, but for most day-to-day interactions, they can be an additional source of unnecessary – and distracting – emails.

Continued advances in smartphone technology that allow it to increasingly replace the computer promise to increase worker flexibility but also reinforce the ties to work that transcend time and place (Arnold, 2003). In addition, there is new evidence that smartphone users become less capable of engaging in 'recovery' strategies, coping methods that allow psychological detachment, relaxation, and feelings of mastery and autonomy, than non-smartphone users, and so find it more difficult to disengage from work psychologically (Derks, ten Brummelhuis, Zecic & Bakker, 2012). In combination with predictions of continued growth in email volume (Radicati, 2010) and increased adoption of smartphones, the Derks *et al.* study suggests that email-related stress will also increase due, in part, to impaired coping.

Finally, trends in the physical configuration of organizations, such as teleworking where employees work remotely, often from a home office, can also be expected to further increase reliance on email communication. 'Hoteling,' another trend common in the U.S.'s high-tech industry, replaces assigned desks and offices with reservable work spaces for the days when traveling or teleworking employees are in the office. Intended to decrease overheads while providing location and scheduling flexibility for workers, the unpredictability of coworkers' locations makes email one of the most reliable communication channels.

To regain some of the benefits of physical proximity, Cisco Systems, IBM, and Sun Microsystems (now Oracle) are all experimenting with proprietary versions of 'virtual immersive environments,' similar to video games in that workers are represented by 'avatars,' to support 'virtual collocation.' In these electronic office spaces, geographically-dispersed workers can work 'side-by-side.' These tools are still used primarily in each company's research department and for occasional 'worldwide' meetings, so the implications of their wide-scale adoption for email communication remain to be seen.

As mentioned earlier, however, there is a growing backlash against email overload in the industry community and some mobilization to decrease unnecessary message distribution and to develop tools and policies for managing the load that remains. We anticipate that our typology will be useful in both designing and evaluating the interventions that emerge.

Conclusion

Email has come to be seen as 'a pre-requisite for doing business in the modern commercial world' (Vile & Collins, 2004), and it offers a number of advantages over its predecessors (Hiltz & Turoff, 1985; Sproull & Kiesler, 1991; Thomas *et al.*, 2006). Management of the endless flow of incoming messages, however, is becoming increasingly critical for both organizational productivity and knowledge worker health and satisfaction.

In this chapter, we have suggested that the term 'information overload' is insufficient for representing workers' day-to-day email experiences and have presented a typology consisting of three distinct bases for workers' feelings of email-related 'overload': *information overload, work overload,* and *social overload. Information overload* occurs when the amount of information to be consumed and assimilated, particularly with respect to a particular task or decision, exceeds the individual's information processing capacity. *Work overload* occurs when the volume of messages received and the time required to respond appropriately exceeds the hours available in the workday. This may be due to receipt of a large number of unnecessary messages, a low-trust culture that prompts users to 'cc:' many recipients, a worker being engaged in too many simultaneous projects, or insufficient group or organizational norms to promote judicious use of email. Finally, *social overload* occurs when a worker receives email messages from too many different people evoking too many distinct roles and social contexts, exceeding the recipient's interaction capacity.

We argued that these distinctions are necessary both to facilitate comparisons across studies and to inform researchers' recommendations. We suggested possible lines of inquiry and metrics to be collected for each element in the typology so that researchers can provide data-based recommendations for relieving email overload and decreasing worker stress, which we expect to simultaneously improve worker performance and satisfaction.

Finally, we considered the implications of contemporary trends in technology use for user experiences of overload. Without intentional practice changes at the individual, group, and organizational levels, we expect workers' feelings of overload to intensify. Common responses to extended periods of stress include depression, apathy, and withdrawal. For both workers' and organizations' sakes, we encourage researchers, managers, and workers to be proactive in seeking ways to stem the flow.

Notes

1   Checking email 50 times per day $\times$ 24 minutes before returning to work after checking email = 1,200 minutes or 20 hours!
2   The message *types* are best defined from the recipients' perspective so the type categories will be emergent and based on the data available.
3   In some organizations, workers rely primarily on instant messaging (IM) for task-related communication, using email primarily for broadcast messages without time-sensitive content or to document decisions already made via IM. In these organizations, it would be more appropriate to focus on workers' use of IM rather than, or in addition to, email.

References

Allen, D. (2001) *Getting things done: The art of stress-free productivity.* New York: Penguin Books.

Allen, D. K. & Shoard, M. (2005) Spreading the load: mobile information and communication technologies and their effect on information overload. *Information Research*, 10, paper 227. Retrieved January 15, 2011 from http://InformationR.net/ir/10-2/paper227.html.

Allen, D. & Wilson, T. D. (2003) Information overload: context and causes. *The New Review of Information Behaviour Research*, 4, 31–44.

Arnold, M. (2003) On the phenomenology of technology: the 'Janus-faces' of mobile phones. *Information and Organization*, 13, 231–256.

Baethge, A. & Rigotti, T. (2010) *Interruptions and multitasking. A comprehensive overview of theories and empirical research with special regard to age differences*, 1st edn. Dortmund: Federal Institute for Occupational Safety and Health, Germany. Retrieved January 20, 2010 from http://www.baua.de/de/Publikationen/ Fachbeitraege/F2220.pdf?__blob=publicationFile&v=4

Bakker. A. B., Demerouti, E. & Burke, R. (2009) Workaholism and relationship quality: A spillover–crossover perspective. *Journal of Occupational Health Psychology*, 14, 23–33.

Balter, O. (1998) *Electronic mail in a working context*. Unpublished dissertation, Kungl Tekniska Hogskolan, Stockholm, Sweden.

Bawden, D. & Robinson, L. (2009) The dark side of information: Overload, anxiety, and other paradoxes and pathologies. *Journal of Information Science*, 35, 180–191.

Bergen, L., Grimes, T. & Potter, D. (2005) How attention partitions itself during simultaneous message presentations. *Human Communication Research*, 31, 311–336.

Berghel, H. (1997) E-mail – The good, the bad and the ugly. *Communcations of the ACM*, 40, 11–15.

Brown, B. (2001) Studying the use of mobile technology. In B. Brown, R. Harper & N. Green (eds), *Wireless world: Social and interactional aspects of the mobile age*. New York: Springer, pp. 3–14.

Burke, R. J. (1993) Work-family stress, conflict, coping, and burnout in police officers. *Stress Medicine*, 9, 171–180.

Campbell, Janice 'Social Overload?!' Weblog posted July 23, 2008, retrieved January 21, 2011 from http://blogs.sun.com/janicec/entry/information_overload

Carpenter, P. A., Just, M. A. & Reichle, E. D. (2000) Working memory and executive function: Evidence from neuroimaging. *Current Opinion in Neurobiology*, 10, 195–199.

Castells, M. (1996) *The Rise of Networked Society*. Oxford: Oxford University Press.

Chan, S. Y. (2001) The use of graphs as decision aids in relation to information overload and managerial decision quality. *Journal of Information Science*, 6, 417–426.

Chervany, N. & Dickson, G. (1974) An experimental evaluation of information overload in a production environment. *Management Science*, 10, 1335–1344.

Cooper, G. (2001) The mutable mobile: social theory in the wireless world, in B. Brown, R. Harper & N. Green (eds), *Wireless world: Social and interactional aspects of the mobile age*. New York: Springer, pp. 19–31.

Coverman, S. (1989) Role overload, role conflict, and stress: Addressing consequences of multiple role Demands. *Social Forces*, 64, 965–982.

Cutrell, E., Czerwinski, M. & Horvitz, E. (2001) Notification, disruption, and memory: Effects of messaging Interruptions on memory and performance. Paper presented at the Human-Computer Interaction – Interact '01, Tokyo.

Dabbish, L. & Kraut, R. (2006) Email overload at work: An analysis of factors associated with Email Strain. *Proceedings of the 2006 Conference on Computer-Supported Cooperative Work*.

Davis, G. (2002) Anytime/anyplace computing and the future of knowledge work. *Communications of the ACM*, 45, 67–73.

Dennis, A. R. (1996) Information processing in group decision-making: You can lead a group to information, but you can't make it think. *MIS Quarterly*, 20, 433–458.

Derks, D. & Bakker, A. B. (2010) The impact of e-mail communication on organizational life. *Cyberpsychology: Journal of Psychosocial Research on Cyberspace*, 4.

Retrieved from http://cyberpsychology.eu/view.php?cisloclanku=2010052401& article=1.

Derks, D., ten Brummelhuis, L. L., Zecic, D. & Bakker, A. B. (2012) Switching on and off…Does smartphone use obstruct the possibility to engage in recovery activities? *European Journal of Work and Organizational Psychology.*

Duxbury, L., Higgins, C. & Lee, C. (1994) Work-family conflict: A comparison by gender, family type, and perceived control. *Journal of Family Issues*, 15, 449–466.

Edmunds, A. & Morris, A. (2000) The problem of information overload in business organizations: A review on the literature. *International Journal of Information Management*, 20, 17–28.

Eppler, M. J. & Mengis, J. (2004) The concept of information overload: A review of literature from organization science, accounting, marketing, MIS, and related disciplines. *The Information Society*, 20, 325–344.

Ericsson, K. A. & Delaney, P. F. (1999) Long-term working memory as an alternative to capacity models of working memory in everyday skilled performance, in A. Miyake and P. Shah (eds), *Models of Working Memory: Mechanisms of Active Maintenance and Executive Control.* Cambridge, UK: Cambridge University Press, pp. 257–297.

Farhoomand, A. F. & Drury, D. H. (2002) Managerial information overload. *Communications of the ACM*, 45, 127–131.

Fisher, D., Brush, A. J., Gleave, E., Smith, M. A. (2006) Revisiting Whittaker & Sidner's 'Email overload' ten years later. Proceedings of Conference on Computer-Supported Cooperative Work (CSCW), Banff, Alberta, Canada, pp. 309–312.

Frone, M. R., Russell, M. & Barnes, G. M. (1996) Work-family conflict, gender, and health-related outcomes: A study of employed parents in two community samples. *Journal of Occupational Health Psychology*, 1, 57–69.

Frone, M. R., Russell, M. & Cooper, M. L. (1991) Relationship of work and family stressors to psychological distress: The independent moderating influence of social support, mastery, active coping and self-focused attention. *Journal of Social Behavior and Personality*, 6, 227–250.

Galbraith, J. R. (1974) Organization design: An information processing view. *Interfaces*, 3, 28–36.

Gantz. J., Boyd, A. & Dowling, S. (2009) Cutting the clutter: Tacking information overload at the source. IDC White Paper, sponsored by Xerox Corporation.

Goffman, E. (1966) *Behavior in public places: Notes on the social organization of gatherings.* New York: Free Press.

Govindaraju, M. & Sward, D. (2005) Effects of wireless mobile technology on employee work behavior and productivity: An Intel case study, in C. Sorensen, Y. Yoo, K. Lyytinen, and J. DeGross (eds), *Designing ubiquitous information environments: Socio-technical issues and challenges.* New York: Springer, pp. 349–351.

Grant, D. & Kiesler, S. (2001) Blurring the boundaries: Cell phones, mobility and the line between work and personal life. In B. Brown, R. Harper & N. Green (eds), *Wireless world: Social and interactional aspects of the mobile age.* New York: Springer, pp. 121–131.

Green, N. (2002) On the move: Technology, mobility, and the mediation of social time and space. *The Information Society*, 18, 281–292.

Grise, M. L. & B. Gallupe. (1999/2000) Information overload: Addressing the productivity paradox in face-to-face electronic meetings. *Journal of Management Information Systems*, 16, 157–185.

Haksever, A. M. and Fisher, N. (1996) A method of measuring information overload in construction project management. Proceedings CIB W89 Beijing International Conference, 310–323.

Hassan, R. (2003) Network Time and the New Knowledge Epoch. *Time & Society*, 12, 225–241.

Hembrooke, H. & Gay, G. (2003) The lecture and the laptop: Multitasking in wireless learning environments. *Journal of Computing in Higher Education*, 15, 46–65.

Hemp, P. (2009) Death by information overload. *Harvard Business Review*, September, 83–89.

Heninger, W. G., Dennis, A. R. & Hilmer, K. M. (2006) Individual cognition and dual task interference in group support systems. *Information Systems Research*, 17, 415–424.

Higgins, C. & Duxbury, L. (2005) Saying 'No' in a culture of hours, money and non-support. *Ivey Business Journal,* July/August, 1–5.

Hiltz, S. R. & Turoff, M. (1985) Structuring computer-mediated communication systems to avoid information overload. *Communications of the ACM*, 28, 680–689.

Hörning, K. H., Ahrens, D. & Gerhard, A. (1999) Do technologies have time? New practices of time and the transformation of communication technologies. *Time & Society*, 8, 293–308.

Iqbal, S. T. & Horvitz, E. (2007) Disruption and recovery of computing tasks: Field study, analysis, and directions. *Proceedings of CHI2007, April 28–May 3, 2007*, San Jose, CA.

Jacoby, J. (1984) Perspectives on information overload. *Journal of Consumer Research*, 10, 432–436.

Jarvenpaa, S. & Lang, K. (2005) Managing the paradoxes of mobile technology. *Information Systems Management Journal*, 22, 7–23.

Katz, J. E. & Aarhus, M. A. (2002) Making meaning of mobiles: A theory of apparatgeist. In J. E. Katz & M. A. Aarhus (eds), *Perpetual contact: Mobile communication, private talk, public performance.* Cambridge: Cambridge University Press, pp. 301–318.

Keller, K. L. & Staelin, R. (1987) Effects of quality and quantity of information on decision effectiveness. *Journal of Consumer Research*, 14, 200–213.

Kinnunen, U. & Mauno, S. (1998) Antecedents and outcomes of work-family conflict among employed women and men in Finland. *Human Relations*, 51, 157–177.

Kock, N., Del Aguila-Obra, A. R. & Padilla-Melendez, A. (2009) The information overload paradox: A Structural equation modeling analysis of data from New Zealand, Spain, and the USA. *Journal of Global Information Management*, 17, 1–19.

Librowski, Z. (1975) Sensory and information inputs overload: Behavioral effects. *Comprehensive Psychiatry*, 16, 199–221.

MacEwen, K. E. & Barling, J. (1994) Daily consequences of work interference with family and family interference with work. *Work & Stress*, 8, 244–254.

Manger, T., Wicklund, R. A. & Eikeland, O. (2003) Speed, communication and solving social problems. *Communications*, 28, 323–337.

Matthews, G., Davies, D. R., Westerman, S. J. & Stammers, R. B. (2000) *Human performance: Cognition, stress, and individual differences*. Philadelphia and East Sussex, UK: Psychology Press.

Mazmanian, M. A., Orlikowski, W. J. & Yates, J. (2005) Crackberries: The social implications of ubiquitous wireless e-mail devices. In C. Sorensen *et al.* (eds), *Desiging ubiquitous information environments: Socio-technical issues and challenges*. New York: Springer, pp. 337–344.

McCarthy, D. & Saegert, S. (1978) Residential density, social overload, and social withdrawal. *Human Ecology*, 6, 253–272.

Meier, R. L. (1963) Communications overload: Proposals from the study of a university library. *Administrative Science Quarterly*, 7, 521–544.

Middleton, C. (2007) Illusions of balance and control in an always-on environment: A case study of Blackberry users. *Continuum: Journal of Media & Cultural Studies*, 21, 165–178.

Milgram, S. (1970) The experience of living in the cities. *Science*, 13, 1461–1468.

Miller, G. (1956) The magical number seven, plus or minus two: Some limits on our capacity for processing information. *Psychological Review*, 63, 81–97.

Muller, T. E. (1984) Buyer response to variations in product information and load. *Psychological Review*, 63, 81–97.

Norman, D. A. & Bobrow, D. G. (1975) On data-limited and resource-limited processes. *Cognitive Psychology*, 7, 44–64

Ophir, E., Nass, C. & Wagner, A.D. (2009) Cognitive control in media multi-taskers. *Proceedings of the National Academy of Sciences*, 106, 15583–15587.

O'Reilly, C. (1980) Individuals and information overload in organizations: Is more necessarily better? *Academy of Management Journal*, 23, 684–696.

Orlikowski, W. J. & Yates, J. (1994) Genre repertoire: Examining the structuring of communicative practices in organizations. *Administrative Science Quarterly*, 39, 541–574.

Perlow, L. (1997) *Finding time: How corporations, individuals, and families can benefit from new work practices.* Ithaca, NY: Cornell Press.

Radicati, S. (2010) Email Statistics Report, 2010. Palo Alto, CA: The Radicati Group. Retrieved February 22, 2011 from http://www.radicati.com/wp/wp-content/uploads/2010/04/Email-Statistics-Report-2010-2014-Executive-Summary2.pdf

Renaud, K., Ramsay, J. & Hair, M. (2006) You've got mail…Shall I deal with it now? Electronic mail from a recipient's perspective. *Journal of Human-Computer Interaction*, 21, 313–332.

Richtel, M. (2008) Lost in e-mail, tech firms face self-made beast. *The New York Times*, June 14, 2008. Retrieved January 15, 2011 from http://www.nytimes.com/2008/06/14/technology/14email.html.

Rubinstein, J. S., Meyer, D. E. & Evans, J. E. (2001) Executive control of cognitive processes in task switching. *Journal of Experimental Psychology – Human Perception and Performance*, 27, 763–797.

Russell, W., Purvis, L. M. & Banks, A. (2005) Describing the strategies used for dealing with email interruptions according to different situational parameters. *Computers in Human Behavior*, 23, 1820–1837.

Schick, A. G., Gorden, L. A. & Haka, S. (1990) Information overload: A temporal approach. *Accounting, Organizations, and Society*, 15, 199–220.

Schneider, S. C. (1987) Information overload: Causes and consequences. *Human Systems Management*, 7, 143–153.

Schroder, H. M., Driver, M. J. & Streufert, S. (1967) *Human Information Processing – Individuals and Groups Functioning in Complex Social Situations.* New York: Holt, Rinehart & Winston.

Schuff, D., Turetken, O. & Darcy, J. (2006) Managing e-mail overload: Clustering to increase attention supply. *Decision Support Systems*, 42, 1350–1365.

Schultze, U. & Vandenbosch, B. (1998) Information overload in a groupware environment: Now you see it, now you don't. *Journal of Organizational Computing and Electronic Commerce*, 8, 127–148.

Science & Technology News (2006) US office workers get interrupted 11 times an hour, Dec 14, 2006. Retrieved January 16, 2011 from http://www.impactlab.net/2006/12/14/

us-office-workers-get-interrupted-11-times-an-hour/.

Sonnentag, S. & Kruel, U. (2006) Psychological detachment from work during off-job time: The role of job stressors, job involvement, and recovery-related self-efficacy. *European Journal of Work and Organizational Psychology*, 15, 197–217.

Sparrow, P. R. (1999) Strategy and cognition: Understanding the role of management knowledge structures, organizational memory, and information overload. *Creativity and Innovation Management*, 8, 140–149.

Spira, J. and Feintuch, J. (2005) The cost of not paying attention: How interruptions impact knowledge worker productivity. Basex Industry Intelligence. Retrieved 01 Mar 2012 from http://www.basex.com/web/tbghome.nsf/23e5e39594c064ee852564ae004fa010/ea4eae828bd411be8525742f0006cde3/$file/costofnotpayingattention.basexreport.pdf

Spivak, N. (2004) The emerging problem of 'social overload'. Weblog post Jan 25, 2004. Retrieved January 24, 2011 from http://novaspivack.typepad.com/nova_spivacks_weblog/2004/01/the_emerging_pr.html.

Sproull, L. & Kiesler, S. (1991) *Connections: New ways of working in the networked organization*. Cambridge, MA: MIT Press.

Swain, M. R. & Haka, S .F. (2000) Effects of information load on capital budgeting decisions. *Behavioral Research in Accounting*, 12, 171–199.

Tapscott, D. (1998) *Growing Up Digital: The Rise of the Net Generation*. New York: McGraw-Hill.

Tapscott, D. (2008) *Grown-up Digitial: How the Net Generation is Changing the World.* New York: McGraw-Hill.

Tarafdar, M., Tu, Q., Ragu-Nathan, T. S. & Ragu-Nathan, B. S. (2011) Crossing to the dark side: Examining creators, outcomes, and inhibitors of technostress. *Communications of the ACM*, 54, 113–120.

Thomas, G. F., King, C. L., Baroni, B., Cook, L., Keitelman, M., Miller, S. & Wardle, A. (2006) Reconceptualizing e-mail overload, *Journal of Business and Technical Communication*, 20, 252–287.

TRENDS E-Magazine (2009) Managing information overload. October, 32–34.

Tushman, M. L. & Nadler, D. A. (1978) Information processing as an integrating concept in organizational design. *Academy of Management Review*, 3, 613–625.

Tuttle, B. & Burton, F. G. (1999) The effects of a modest incentive on information overload in an investment analysis task. *Accounting, Organizations, and Society*, 24, 673–687.

Vile, D. & Collins, J. (2004) Email: business or pleasure? – Mission criticality meets personal interest. Quocirca, Ltd., Independent research division. Retrieved January 10, 2011. Now accessible by direct inquiry to www.quocirca.com.

Vollmann, T. E. (1991) Cutting the Gordian knot of misguided performance measurement. *Industrial Management & Data Systems*, 1, 24–26.

Williams, M. L., Dennis, A. R. , Stam, A. & Aronson, J. E. (2007) The impact of DSS use and information load on errors and decision quality. *European Journal of Operations Research*, 176, 468–481.

Zeldes, N., Sward, D. & Louchheim, S. (2007) Infomania: Why we can't afford to ignore it any longer. *First Monday*, 12, August 6, 2007. Retrieved March 6, 2012 from http://firstmonday.org/htbin/cgiwrap/bin/ojs/indes.php/fm/rt/printerFriendly/1973/1848

3 Online social networks in the work context

Juliane M. Stopfer and Samuel D. Gosling

The following two news stories offer vivid illustrations of how Online Social Networks (OSNs) can have a significant impact in professional contexts:

> Van Allen runs a company that recruits job candidates for hospitals and clinics across the country. With physicians in short supply, he was happy to come across the résumé of a well-qualified young female psychiatrist. As part of his due diligence check, Allen looked her up in Facebook, a popular social networking Web site, and found things that made him think twice. 'Pictures of her taking off her shirt at parties,' he said. 'Not just on one occasion, but on another occasion, then another occasion.' Concerned about those pictures, he called the candidate and asked for an explanation. She didn't get the job.
>
> (Wei Du, 14.08.2007)

> After graduating from Notre Dame in 2005, the 25-year-old landed a position in the ad-sales department of an upscale magazine. Her future employers checked out her Facebook profile and saw pictures of her scuba diving, traveling through Italy and helping introduce computers to a small African village. On the flip side, there were photos of her at a tailgate party with a beer in hand and a guy playfully planting a kiss on her cheek. But those pictures didn't bother the employer, who offered her the job anyway. 'They were looking for someone who would mesh with their community,' she says. 'My profile showed I'm a well-rounded person.'
>
> (Simmons, 04.01.2008)

The impact of these news stories goes well beyond screening job applicants (Brady & Libit, 2006; Kluemper & Rosen, 2009; Lorenz, 2009). OSNs are also relevant for business purposes such as establishing business contacts, improving business processes, and maintaining business competitiveness (Fortino & Nayak, 2010). In this chapter, we aim to review the OSN literature placing an emphasis on how OSNs interface with occupational contexts. We start by describing what OSNs are and how they work, explaining key features of Facebook and LinkedIn, the two OSNs with the greatest relevance to professional contexts. Next we review the numerous ways in which OSNs interface with work contexts followed by a discussion of how OSNs are used by organizations for marketing purposes. We conclude the chapter by identifying some important directions for new research in this domain.

OSNs are Web-based services that enable users to articulate and make visible their social networks (Boyd & Ellison, 2007). Since their emergence in 1997, these Internet platforms have experienced a phenomenal growth: There are 1.5 billion people worldwide using OSNs (Kreutz, 2009) like MySpace, Facebook, and LinkedIn. As of November 2010, the world's largest OSN, Facebook, had more than 582 million unique users (socialbakers, 06.12.2010). Individuals in virtually all societies and cultural settings now routinely use Web 2.0 tools, often for considerable amounts of time (Fortino & Nayak, 2010). Recent estimates suggest that people spend three times more time on Facebook than they do on Google (Ostrow, 17.09.2009). OSNs are used as a primary medium for communication and networking (Boyd & Ellison, 2007; Valkenburg & Peter, 2009). On Facebook, for example, users spend on average 7 hours per month (nielsenwire, 2010) with women spending 30% more time on OSNs than men (Radwanick, 2010).

The routine use of OSNs has spread into other social domains as well. For example, OSNs have been used for aiding criminal investigations and college disciplinary hearings (Kornblum & Marklein, 2006) and to monitor the college party scene (Brady & Libit, 2006). Recently, OSNs have become significant vehicles for major marketing (Leitner & Grechenig, 2008), political, and social-awareness campaigns (Gievert, 2009).

What are OSNs and how do they work?

OSNs can be defined as interactive Web technologies that allow their users to present themselves with a public or semi-public profile and to establish visible connections to other users of the same network (see Boyd & Ellison, 2007; Lenhart & Madden, 2007). A distinction can be made between internal OSNs and public OSNs (sometimes also termed general vs. enterprise OSNs; Wang & Kobsa, 2009). Internal OSNs, such as *SocialBlue* (formerly known as *Beehive*) at IBM, *WaterCooler* at HP, and *D Street* at Deloitte, are run by organizations for their own internal use. Public OSNs, in contrast, are predominantly run by commercial providers, with the software and data residing in the providers' own servers. In the following section, we describe the key features of the two most important public OSNs, Facebook and LinkedIn, in more detail (see Rooksby *et al.*, 2009 for a review of the major public OSNs around the world). We focus on these two OSNs because they currently have the greatest penetration into work contexts and, therefore, have the greatest potential to influence professional businesses. Then we give a short overview of internal OSNs.

Facebook – an OSN for personal use

Facebook, launched in 2004 in the United States, was created for people who want to connect to and communicate with their real-life friends. Anyone holding a valid email address can create a personal profile on Facebook. The profile page gives other people an idea about who the user is by displaying information about the user he or she has chosen to share; information typically provided includes such items as a profile picture, fore- and surname, sex, date of birth, interests, education and work background, and contact information (e.g. IM screen name, phone number, address, website). Users establish visible links to other Facebook members by sending them friend requests, which can be accepted or declined. By connecting to someone else, users can keep track of that person's activity on the site. Each individual's network of friends is visually displayed on his or her profile. The average Facebook user has 130 friends (Facebook, 2011).

In addition to the personal profile, users have a 'Home page,' which is the first to appear whenever a user logs in. The Home page includes a news feed that keeps users updated about what their friends are up to (Facebook, 2011). Facebook offers a variety of ways to interact with other users, such as chatting, sending personal messages (similar to email), poking (a content-free way to say 'just thinking of you'; Joinson, 2008), wall posting (writing comments on another user's profile that are visible for other Facebook members), and providing status updates (Facebook, 2011).

Facebook's focus is on sharing media and photos, videos, and music with friends. Members can start interests groups, announce and join events, or play games. Facebook also provides access to many third-party applications (e.g. *Jobmagic*, a social media recruiting platform). In total, people can interact with over 900 million objects on Facebook (Facebook, 2011). Content from other sites (e.g. Twitter) can be integrated into Facebook as well (Skeels & Grudin, 2009). Facebook also has a development platform that enables companies and engineers to integrate with the Facebook website and to gain access to Facebook users (Facebook, 2011).

OSN profiles are typically established by individuals but business owners, artists, and public figures can also create Facebook profiles, termed *Pages*. Instead of becoming friends with the owners of these accounts, users *like* these Pages by clicking a *Like* button. In the remainder of the chapter we will mainly focus on OSN profiles used by individuals to demonstrate the various uses of OSNs in the workplace. However, we do mention organizational OSN Pages where relevant (e.g. in the section on Marketing).

LinkedIn – an OSN for professional use

LinkedIn, created in 2003, is an OSN designed specifically for the purpose of professional networking, such as finding a job, discovering sales leads, and connecting with potential business partners. According to Roos (no date), LinkedIn is the No. 1 online destination for professional networking. LinkedIn audiences are people who want to stay in touch or get back in touch with former colleagues and classmates, active job seekers and job posters, and full-time recruiters and headhunters. As of January 2011, LinkedIn had over 90 million users (LinkedIn, 2011).

In contrast to Facebook, a LinkedIn profile is much more focused on the individual (Gralla & Widman, 2008). It reads like a professional résumé with a focus on education and employment history. Users can, for example, specify their school's name and degree earned as well as job title, employer, industry, and a short description of what the job entailed. Compared to Facebook where many users frequently change their status settings and engage in day-to-day social activities, LinkedIn profiles tend to be associated with less activity and fewer profile changes (Skeels & Grudin, 2009).

Users can invite other LinkedIn users to become member of their network (which is similar to the *friends* concept on Facebook). People who are part of an individual's network are called the user's connections. These direct connections (the average LinkedIn user collects two or three dozen connections; Roos, no date) can easily be contacted via email. Contacting direct connection's connections (two degrees away) and their connections (three degrees away) requires special LinkedIn tools called introductions, InMail or OpenMail. To use InMail or OpenMail LinkedIn users must upgrade their memberships to a premium membership (Personal Plus, Business, or Pro), paying monthly or annual subscription fees.

Services like posting job openings or reference searches also cost money.

SocialBlue, WaterCooler, and D Street – examples of internal OSNs

Businesses are creating their own internal OSNs which can be tailored to the respective workplace and can keep information behind the firewalls (Giles, 2010). We focus on the description of IBM's *SocialBlue*, HP's *WaterCooler*, and Deloitte's *D Street*, because there is very little information available about other internal OSNs (Rooksby *et al.*, 2009; but see Richter, Kneifel & Ott, 2009 for details on Accenture's *People Pages*).

SocialBlue (launched in May 2007), *WaterCooler*, and *D Street* (both launched in June 2007) have taken inspiration from public OSNs such as Facebook (Rooksby *et al.*, 2009). Their features include profiles and connections to other users as well as the ability to post status messages, pictures, lists, and comments (*SocialBlue*), blogging, tagging, filtering, and building virtual teams (*WaterCooler*), and suggesting things to do when visiting local areas (*D Street*; Rooksby *et al.*, 2009). These internal OSNs are not the central focus of this chapter so interested readers are directed to DiMicco, Millen, Geyer, Dugan, Brownholtz, and Muller (2008), Brzozowski (2009), and Romeo (2008) for more detailed overviews of the internal OSNs *SocialBlue*, *WaterCooler*, and *D Street*.

Another example of an enterprise OSN is Yammer, launched in September 2008. Yammer is used by about 80,000 companies (Cutler, 20.07.2010) for sharing internal information between employees within an organization or between organizational members and pre-designated groups by posting status updates similar to Facebook or Twitter (Cox, 14.03.2011). We anticipate that Yammer will soon become a focus of empirical research on OSNs in work contexts. However, due to the lack of existing studies of Yammer we do not review it here.

Having described the key features of the most influential OSNs, we next turn to the various ways in which OSNs are used the work context.

OSN use within the workplace

Do employees actually use OSNs at work? According to a survey of 1,654 corporate IT and IS managers and computer end users across all sizes of organization in North America, the United Kingdom, and Europe, the use of OSNs like Facebook and LinkedIn is widespread at work for both work and personal purposes (FaceTime, 2010). Facebook appears to be the leading site for personal social networking at work, with 93% of end users accessing the site for personal reasons, with 48% using LinkedIn (FaceTime, 2010). For professional purposes, however, Facebook was used by 36% and LinkedIn by 86% of respondents. Of those who admitted using LinkedIn for work purposes, 38% were from the computing and technology sector and 10% from the financial services. Facebook, however, was reported to be utilized for work purposes equally across a variety of industries (FaceTime, 2010). The internal OSN *WaterCooler* was more used by people who work in engineering or marketing than by those in sales, finance, or operations (Brzozowski, 2009).

OSNs were accessed at least once per day by 61% of respondents, with 15% admitting to using OSNs 'constantly throughout the day' (FaceTime, 2010). Another study reported corporate users spending an average of 18 minutes on a typical workday using OSNs, or about 4% of their workday (Osterman Research, 2010).

One study of workplace use of Facebook and LinkedIn conducted a survey and focused interviews among Microsoft employees, finding that 52% of survey participants used LinkedIn and 49% used Facebook (Skeels & Grudin, 2009). However, daily use of Facebook was reported by only 17% and daily use of LinkedIn by only 4%. Facebook use was exceptionally high among the youngest respondents (72% of the under 25-year-old employees), dropping steadily with age (46% of the over 46-year-old employees), whereas LinkedIn use was highest among employees between 26 to 45 years (61–64%).

What do people use OSNs for at work? According to the FaceTime survey, the most common work-related purposes for using OSNs are professional networking with colleagues (79%), learning about colleagues (66%), research (61%), sales prospecting (37%), marketing communications with costumers (37%), setting up meetings (25%), and sharing work-related project information (18%; FaceTime, 2010).

There were slight differences in how Microsoft employees used Facebook and LinkedIn. The employees used Facebook to reconnect with colleagues from previous jobs and old friends, maintain awareness of the personal and professional lives of their connections and to keep in touch with their contacts, build social capital, and gather professional information. The employees used LinkedIn for a number of reasons, including recruiting, learning more about people one has met or one soon will meet, and getting quick answers to professional questions from LinkedIn groups (Skeels & Grudin, 2009). IBM employees reported using the internal OSN *SocialBlue* for three main reasons: connecting with coworkers at a personal level, career advancement in the company, and campaigning for their projects (DiMicco *et al.*, 2008).

In the next section we draw on the useful framework proposed by Rooksby *et al.* (2009) to organize the different functions of workplace communication: (1) social searching and social browsing, (2) people finding and information finding, (3) group formation, and (4) social capital. We also discuss the issues of procrastination and time wasting as well as privacy and content controls.

Social searching and social browsing

In the context of OSNs, social searching refers to the search for specific people with whom the user shares an offline connection to learn more about them via their OSN profile. Social browsing is the search for random people or groups online with whom users would want to connect offline (Lampe, Ellison & Steinfield, 2006). Employers and employees can use OSNs to engage in both social searching and social browsing. We next focus on these two domains of OSN usage.

Social searching: seeking additional information about job applicants

Workers perform social searching when trying to gather information about a known person from his or her OSN profile (e.g. employees seeking information about coworkers or advisors; organizations supervising employees). In a broader sense, social searching also includes checking out the OSN profiles of specific people with whom the user has not yet established an offline connection, such as job applicants or prospective advisors. Forty-five percent of employers reported using OSN profiles to evaluate job candidates' suitability for open positions (Grasz, 24.08.2009). Three-quarters of organizations even have formal policies that require their recruiters and human resources professionals to research candidates online (cross-tab, 2010). Despite this widespread institutionalized use of OSNs for screening, only 7% of U.S. consumers surveyed believe that online data affected their job search (cross-tab, 2010). Yet, one recent study showed experimentally that applicants whose OSN profiles emphasized family orientation or professional orientation were seen as more suitable for the job and were more likely to be interviewed than applicants whose OSN profiles stressed drinking alcohol. Also, the chances of being offered significantly higher starting salaries increased for the family orientation and professional orientation conditions as compared to the alcohol condition (Bohnert & Ross, 2010). However, the question of the extent to which people, who are positively judged on the basis of their OSN profile, actually perform better in their jobs, has yet to be addressed. One step into this direction was an experimental study, which showed that people can reliably and accurately distinguish high from low performers based on viewing their OSN profiles, especially if the raters were more intelligent and emotionally stable (Kluemper & Rosen, 2009).

How can Facebook be utilized to seek additional information about job applicants? A Facebook profile, which is created for personal use, can contain a lot of private information about its owner and might therefore provide a broad picture of the applicant's personality. According to Back *et al.* (2010) people form accurate impressions of profile owners' personalities solely from viewing their Facebook profiles.[1] Importantly, personality impressions based on users' Facebook profiles were not influenced by profile owners trying to portray themselves in a positive light (Back *et al.*, 2010). This finding supports the idea that Facebook constitutes an extended real life context where users express their actual personalities and act authentically (Gosling, Augustine, Vazire, Holtzman & Gaddis, in press). Thus, collecting information about a potential employee from his or her Facebook profile might help to make decisions in the recruiting process.

An applicant's LinkedIn profile, on the other hand, might not provide additional information to what a recruiter already knows from the applicant's résumé. Most of the available data focuses on education- and career-related information, with little or no information about hobbies, political orientation, religious affiliations, favorite movies or music (Skeels & Grudin, 2009). Furthermore, it is not clear to what extent users might engage in impression management when presenting themselves on LinkedIn. Research is needed to determine the accuracy of impressions based on LinkedIn profiles.

For internal OSNs such as 'the Facebook-like *SocialBlue*' (Skeels & Grudin, 2009), similar mechanisms as those described for Facebook can be expected. However, the role of impression management in internal OSNs has yet to be specified, because users typically connect to coworkers, not friends and family as they would do on Facebook.

Social browsing: seeking candidates for jobs or projects

People perform social browsing if there is a need to find experts to help solving certain problems (Rooksby *et al.*, 2009) or to identify appropriate candidates for a certain job. For this purpose, OSNs typically offer search options that require entering a key word of interest. People can also engage in social browsing by clicking on tagged items on a user's profile. In the nonprofessional context, Facebook is used more often for social searching than for social browsing (Joinson *et al.*, 2008; Lampe *et al.*, 2006). However, Facebook offers a variety of applications for browsing lists of job seekers such as BullToss, Zoho Recruit, or Job Tracker.

LinkedIn supplies recruiters and headhunters with enhanced search tools and management software to find qualified passive candidates (individuals who already have a job and are not actively looking for a new one; HR.com, 23.04.2007). Professionals can do references search to see what the applicant's former colleagues say about him or her (receiving recommendations and credentials). Salespeople can search within a target industry for people who might be interested in their products. Entrepreneurs can use LinkedIn to search out potential business partners, clients, and vendors.

According to DiMicco *et al.* (2008), IBM employees regularly use the internal OSN *SocialBlue* for social browsing. People aimed to discover and connect with coworkers they did not know in addition to building stronger bonds with their weak ties. However, we do not know of any empirical research examining the use of Facebook, LinkedIn, or internal OSNs for social browsing in the work context.

People finding and information finding

An issue especially related to social browsing (where users aim to find unacquainted people who match certain criteria) is finding people vs. finding information in order to solve a problem. In some cases, such as trying to solve a technical issue, it might be most helpful to quickly locate an expert in the field who can be asked for a solution instead of finding the solution itself. OSNs might be one way to locate knowledgeable people, as we demonstrate in the following two sections.

People finding and information finding: asking questions using OSN status messages

Internal information technologies of large organizations are often used to find people who would know the answer to a question rather than finding the answer itself (Nardi, Whittaker & Schwarz, 2000). One fast and easy way to ask questions of one's OSN connections is through status updates. A recent survey shows that 89% of Facebook users use this function, with users sharing 5 billion pieces of information each week through status updates (FaceTime, 2010). A survey of Microsoft employees explored the usage of status messages on Facebook and Twitter to ask questions to their online connections in order to satisfy their information needs (Morris, Teevan & Panovich, 2010). OSNs were especially used to ask opinion questions (e.g. asking for a rating of a specific item), recommendation questions (e.g. open-ended requests for suggestions), and factual knowledge questions (Morris *et al.*, 2010). The most popular question topics were technology, entertainment, home and family, and professional (e.g. jobs, education, events; Morris *et al.*, 2010).

So far there has not been an empirical investigation to determine the success of using Facebook, LinkedIn, or internal OSNs to locate experts in the professional context. It might, for example, be equally or even more effective to find experts by using Internet search engines like Google. Recently more and more institutions have started to engage in crowdsourcing, which is the act of taking a function once performed by employees and outsourcing it to an undefined (and generally large) network of people in the form of an open call (Howe, 02.06.2006).[2] One famous example is Amazon Mechanical Turk, a Web-based marketplace that helps companies find people to perform tasks (termed HITs, human intelligence tasks) such as identifying items in a photograph, transcribing podcasts, or completing a survey (Buhrmester, Kwang & Gosling, 2011; Howe, 2006). However, one vital advantage of using OSNs instead of other Internet sources to locate experts might be the stronger trust in the responses provided by known people (Morris *et al.*, 2010). Employees in the Morris *et al.* (2010) study believed that OSNs were better than search engines for subjective questions (i.e. seeking opinions or recommendations). To what extent asking one's OSN connections is advantageous for other types of questions, too, should be subject to further research. It would also be interesting to explore the extent of trust in answers provided by a user's connection's connection (e.g. a potential expert might be a friend's friend on Facebook) or even a stranger. People can accurately perceive a user's personality (including conscientiousness) solely from his or her OSN profile (Back *et al.*, 2010), so we would expect that users also can accurately decide whether answers provided by unknown OSN users are trustworthy or not. Facebook status messages are viewed only by a user's connections but the Facebook application, Facebook Questions, allows users to pose questions to the entire Facebook community in order to get a broad set of answers and learn information from people knowledgeable on a range of topics. After asking a question, users also have the option of adding a photo or a poll (Ross, 28.07.2010). This new Facebook function allows promising lines of research concerning the use of OSNs to find people who might know the answer to a question.

People finding and information finding: seeking a job via OSNs

A job seeker might take advantage of his or her network of online connections in an OSN. For example, upon being notified about a job seeker's current situation, members of his or her network can spread the word to prospective employers, share their personal insight and experience, and make suggestions (Ideboen, 2010).

On Facebook, there are several applications for job searches such as Facebook Marketplace or Jobster Career Network (Gralla & Widman, 2008). LinkedIn is known to provide instruments a job seeker can utilize to become employed according to his or her skills, ambition, and qualifications (Ideboen, 2010). Methods for searching out contacts on LinkedIn are uploading email contacts, colleague search, classmate search, name search, and advanced search (allows searching for LinkedIn members using several different criteria such as keywords, name, title, company, location, and industry). According to a survey conducted by Verrilli, 2010, 'connecting to other LinkedIn members' was found to be the most effective LinkedIn tool for finding a job.

Further than from case scenarios, we do not know about studies that compare traditional job searches such as those conducted via job centers or Internet search engines with job searches using OSNs like Facebook, LinkedIn, or internal OSNs. However, we expect job searches via OSNs might have some significant advantages. For example, connections to other members of the network are visually displayed on the OSN profile, so that job seekers become aware of their existing direct and indirect (connections' connections) social relationships. This information might foster the effective utilization of one's social network for job search purposes. Another advantage of the visual display of a user's connections might be that potential employers get an impression of a job seeker's social relationships, for example to high status members. This might promote the trust in a person's performance, because connections to others always require a confirmation by the other user and therefore cannot be faked.

Group formation

As described earlier, OSNs can be used to build groups, either by displaying already existing teams online or by forming a new group of unacquainted people (Rooksby *et al.*, 2009). These groups can be defined by location, special interests, or any other topic. In some cases it might be useful to form groups quickly and to focus on an immediate issue (e.g. organizing a business trip), in other situations (e.g. exchange experiences with a new software tool) group formation might be valuable over the long term (Rooksby *et al.*, 2009). OSNs can support group formation online by social searching and social browsing, as described above.

Group formation: building and joining interest groups in OSNs

A survey by FaceTime (2010) revealed that 51% of respondents who use Facebook for professional purposes use the group function (FaceTime, 2010). For example, by January 2011, the Facebook group *HEWLETT PACKARD* had 1,554 members (Facebook, 2011). One potential advantage of an OSN group might be the visual display of the group members in terms of their OSN profiles so that they are no longer anonymous entities. This function might increase accountability and trust in the work relations among group members. Also, group activities in OSNs are typically stored over a certain period of time. This makes it easy to refer to past comments, but also to store, supervise, and evaluate all communication processes. However, research is needed to clarify the potential advantages of building groups in OSNs such as higher productivity and member satisfaction.

According to DiMicco and Millen (2007), IBM employees who used Facebook to 'relive the college days' (belong to a large number of school networks, have few connections in their professional networks) were the ones with the highest number of Facebook groups. They were especially likely to join political groups, social clubs, friend (and insider joke) groups, religious organizations, and sexual orientation groups, whereas only a small number of them were part of job-related groups (often associated to internships or a local corporate group). These findings suggest an emphasis of free time-oriented uses of Facebook groups for those 'relive the college days' Facebook users. Respondents who used Facebook to 'dress to impress' (i.e. those who have a relatively high number of corporate members in their networks), however, had slightly more job-related Facebook groups than did those with fewer corporate members in their networks (DiMicco & Millen, 2007).

LinkedIn is an OSN designed for professional purposes so it tends to have more work-oriented groups. By January 2011, there were 816,832 groups on LinkedIn (LinkedIn, 2011). For example, 47,240 users joined the LinkedIn group

HP Connections. The largest group on LinkedIn is *Linked:HR (#1 Human Resources Group)* with 358,583 members (LinkedIn, 2011). In addition to such usage data, research is needed to specify the processes by which groups form and how they are used in Facebook, LinkedIn, and internal OSNs.

Social capital

Social relationships are crucial to virtually all work contexts and OSNs are used to actively build and maintain such relationships (Steinfield, DiMicco, Ellison & Lampe, 2009). The resources that derive from the relationships among people in varying social contexts are termed social capital (Coleman, 1988). Lin (1999) defines social capital as an 'investment in social relations by individuals through which they gain access to embedded resources to enhance expected returns of instrumental or expressive actions' (p. 39). Reciprocity implies that individuals both obtain benefits from the network and give benefits back to it.

Putnam (2000) differentiates between bridging social capital and bonding social capital. Bridging social capital means connecting to 'weak ties' such as acquaintances and friends of friends (Putnam, 2000). These connections are more likely to provide new information and diverse perspectives. According to Ellison and colleagues (Ellison, Steinfield & Lampe, 2007; Steinfield, Ellison & Lampe, 2008) there is a strong connection between the use of Facebook and higher levels of bridging social capital among undergraduates. Employees from IBM and Microsoft also reported using OSNs to support weak ties (DiMicco *et al.*, 2008; Skeels & Grudin, 2009).

Bonding social capital refers to the kinds of support from close acquaintances such as intimate friends and family (Putnam, 2000). These strong relationships are more likely to provide emotional support and concrete benefits such as financial loans. There is also a relation between OSN use and bonding social capital (Ellison *et al.*, 2007). In particular, intense Facebook use, high self-esteem, and satisfaction with university life were associated with higher self-reported bonding social capital.

The constructs of bonding and bridging are equally relevant within an organizational setting (Steinfield *et al.*, 2009). Bonding social capital in an organization implies that there is trust and a sense of obligation that encourages reciprocity, while bridging social capital is associated with the kinds of weak ties that facilitate access to non-redundant information.

The social capital within an organization enables individuals to locate useful information and also to draw on resources and make contributions to the network (Sherif, Hoffman & Thomas, 2006).

Social capital: professional networking in OSNs

OSNs may help people creating and maintaining social capital because users can interact with a large network of social connections (Steinfield *et al.*, 2009). Professional networking refers to communication between workers with similar areas of interest, background, and profession who are linked to share and contribute important personal professional information for career advancement and human resource management (Fortino & Nayak, 2010). Fortino and Nayak have argued that Facebook does not fit the professional networking needs. However, others have shown that Facebook is viewed as a place for both non-professional and professional networking (DiMicco & Millen, 2007).

Several authors agree that LinkedIn clearly meets the professional networking needs (e.g. Fortino & Nayak, 2010; Verrilli, 2010). According to DiMicco *et al.* (2008) IBM employees who use the internal OSN *SocialBlue* reported using it to connect to others through writing comments to achieve the goals of career advancement and promotion of projects. However, social capital is hard to quantify in terms of productivity because the value of any time spent socializing on OSNs is difficult to measure. There are no quantifications for improving trust, reciprocity, and understanding between coworkers through using OSNs.

Procrastination and time wasting

According to Donoghue and Rabin (2000) people procrastinate when they delay doing unpleasant tasks that they wish they could do sooner. OSNs might be used as a means of procrastination because they offer hundreds of features a user can interact with instead of finishing a working task. Twenty-eight percent of respondents of the FaceTime (2010) survey indicated using Facebook at work to play games such as Farmville, Mafia Wars, or Scrabble.

Socializing on OSNs might also be seen as a source of time wasting. It is not clear if any social activity on OSNs is worthwhile (Rooksby *et al.*, 2009) because there is no strict boundary between strengthening social ties and wasting time. For example, might writing a funny comment on a coworker's Facebook status update lead to a stronger collegial relation, which in turn leads to more efficient collaboration on work-related issues in the long run? Or was the time used to formulate the funny statement just wasted? In the FaceTime survey, 27% of respondents who use Facebook for work purposes reported purchasing and giving gifts to other users and 20% reported that they uploaded, tagged, and shared photos (FaceTime, 2010). It is hard to determine the extent to which these online activities actually are work-related (e.g. aimed at building and maintaining social capital).

It is possible that the breaks provided by OSNs serve to rejuvenate employees. For instance, a short and unobtrusive period of using Twitter or Facebook at work or general 'workplace Internet leisure browsing' may help employees get refreshed and help them keep focus and thus increase their productivities (see Wang & Kobsa, 2010).

Privacy and content controls

Privacy in OSNs has been the topic of numerous studies (e.g. Acquisti & Gross, 2006; Joinson, 2008; Kolek & Saunders, 2008; Lewis, Kaufman & Christakis,

2008). One finding to emerge is that people say they value their privacy, but in practice they often act otherwise (Acquisti & Gross, 2006). People might not sufficiently think through the consequences of what they post on their OSN profiles, which is why organizations often worry about employees posting inappropriate content (Kuhn, 2008).

OSNs provide their users with control over their profile entries such that users can choose which information they want to make public and keep private. On Facebook, for example, users can delete comments on their profile posted by other users. Further, the visibility of each profile entry can be customized, so that certain profile information can only be seen by some users but not by others. Such profile adjustments might help to avoid possible tensions when using OSNs in the work context, such as tensions from crossing hierarchy, status, and power boundaries and the tension over disclosing confidential information on OSNs (Skeels & Grudin, 2009). However, based on interview data, Rooksby *et al.* (2009) argue that it can be hard to separate social and work-oriented interactions. For example, on Facebook, people report having a mix of work and social connections. Some users put great care into making only appropriate connections and making sure nothing is available that might be embarrassing. The negotiation of the users' identity across contexts involves a decision about who should have access to what kinds of information (Donahue, Robins, Roberts & John, 1993). However, in order to use OSNs effectively, a user's profile content needs to be visible to an audience larger than one's direct connections so that users can get in touch with new people online (DiMicco *et al.*, 2008).

DiMicco *et al.* (2008) observed the absence of privacy concerns within the internal OSN *SocialBlue*. Interviewees reported being willing to share more information on the internal OSN than on public OSNs and being less concerned about ramifications of sharing personally identifying information and opinions about IBM.

OSNs in marketing

After talking about individuals' OSN uses, we now present one example of an organizational use of OSNs: Marketing. OSNs have begun to attract the attention of marketing scholars (e.g. Dholakia, Bagozzi & Pearo, 2004; Kozinets, 2002; Trusov, Bodapati & Bucklin, 2010). OSNs are appealing from a marketing perspective because they provide a medium for propagating recommendations through people with similar interests (Leskovec, Adamic & Huberman, 2007).

On Facebook, for example, organizations can use various options for marketing purposes, such as applications (*Apps*), advertisements (*Ads*), OpenGraph (which connects Facebook to an organization's Web page, including *Like* buttons and other social plugins), groups, and Pages (Roth & Wiese, no date). As noted in Section 2 above, companies can create a Page on Facebook to present pictures, news, or statistics of the organization. Facebook users who have connected to the Page via the *Like* button receive status updates of the company (Roth & Wiese, no date). Thus, organizations can easily communicate commercial messages to hundreds of thousands of potential clients via Facebook Pages (for example, as of January 2011, 198,314 people like HP on Facebook). Organizations can also broadcast advertisements with Facebook Ads, which include a picture or video and the advertisement text. Facebook Engagement Ads additionally allow users to interact with the advertisement, for example by joining an event, taking a survey, or liking a Page (Roth & Wiese, no date). In addition to increasing interaction with customers, companies' OSN Pages provide continuous consumer feedback, which can act as a valuable source of information to adapt and improve products (Pantano, Tavernise & Viassone, 2010).

In a case study of a bakery in Houston, Dholakia and Durham (2010) set up a company's Facebook Page and surveyed the effect on customer behavior. According to self-reports, after becoming Facebook fans of the bakery, customers visited the store more frequently and generated more positive word of mouth than nonfans. They also reported greater emotional attachment to the bakery (Dholakia & Durham, 2010). These outcomes might result from the foot-in-the-door effect, a tactic for enhancing compliance (Freedman & Fraser, 1966). If someone was made to agree to a small request (e.g. liking a Facebook Page), he or she may later be more willing to agree to a large favor (e.g. visiting a store, spread positive word of mouth).

Similar to Facebook, companies can reach their customers on LinkedIn, for example by taking out advertisements or creating company Pages. There are more than 1 million companies with LinkedIn company Pages. These company Pages can be followed by LinkedIn users (for example, as of January 2011, HP has 188,011 followers on LinkedIn; LinkedIn, 2011).

However, as is the case for personal OSN profiles, organizations must devote time and effort to establish and maintain the relevance of their Pages. There might be only a small number of customers who actually connect to the organization's OSN Page; hence OSNs should be used by companies as just one niche tool among others (Dholakia & Durham, 2010). On the other hand, using OSNs for marketing might be especially effective because analyzing social networks allows the company to acquire new customers who otherwise would not have been identified based on traditional attributes (Hill, Provost & Volonsky, 2006). Thus, social media tools like OSNs can provide organizations with 'eyes' and 'ears' like never before (Hewlett-Packard Development Company, L.P., no date).

Conclusions and future directions

OSNs are now tightly integrated into people's everyday social interactions. In professional contexts too, OSNs are beginning to play an increasingly prominent role. In this chapter we provided an overview of relevant findings for understanding how OSNs can impact work contexts. A summary of this overview is provided in Table 3.1.

The research to date has provided some fascinating glimpses into the use of OSNs in work contexts but has only begun to scratch the surface of this domain. As a consequence, our review raises rather more questions than it provides

Table 3.1 Examples for OSN use in the workplace, organized according to the functions of workplace communication (Rooksby *et al.*, 2009), and proposed usefulness of Facebook, LinkedIn, and internal OSNs

Workplace communication function	Examples for OSN use in the workplace	Used by…	Usefulness of		
			Facebook	LinkedIn	internal OSNs
Social searching	Seeking additional information about job applicants	Organization	+	–	+/–
Social browsing	Seeking candidates for jobs or projects	Organization	+/–	+	+
People finding & information finding	Asking questions using OSN status messages	Employee	+	+	+
	Seeking a job via OSNs	Employee	+	+	+/–
Group formation	Building and joining interest groups in OSNs	Organization/ employee	+	+	+
Social capital	Professional networking in OSNs	Employee	+	+	+

Note: + OSN seems to be useful for the respective workplace communication function, – OSN does not seem to be useful, +/– it is unclear whether the OSN is useful.

answers. For example, it does suggest that OSN profiles are used to evaluate job applicants, or to get quick answers from one's online connections, or to engage in marketing, but it also raises the question of how to determine success in the usage of OSNs for locating experts, seeking jobs, forming groups, building social capital.

Thus, the field is still wide open in terms of questions to be addressed. Here we highlight just two issues that seem to us to be in particularly urgent need of research attention: Age differences and non-users. Age differences in the usage of OSNs might be important in two ways. First, there are age differences in the willingness to use OSNs. Researchers have shown that older people express more privacy concerns with regard to OSNs (e.g. Acquisti & Gross, 2006; Lehtinen, Näsänen & Sarvas, 2009). Also, younger users have a larger network of online connections (Pfeil, Arjan & Zaphiris, 2009). Thus, the important question is raised whether older adults might be at a disadvantage when going on the job market and in other work contexts from their less intense use of OSNs. Second, according to equal employment opportunity law in the U.S., applicants do not have to indicate age and sex in the application letter. However, in OSN profiles, users typically reveal their real name, date of birth, and gender. As a result, the ethics and legality behind screening job applicants using OSNs has become an important issue (Zeidner, 2007).

A similar problem results from investigating only people who use OSNs but not collecting data on those who are not OSN members. It strikes us as particularly important to explore whether non-users are affected by disadvantages (e.g. not receiving important information, exclusion from group activities) resulting from not using Facebook, LinkedIn, or internal OSNs (Taylor, 23.09.2009). On the other hand, non-users could reap advantages in the work context conferred by the greater control they retain over their personal information and the opacity of their social networks.

Given that OSNs are so young, it is not surprising that research examining their impact in work contexts is rather sparse. In addition to the numerous specific findings from the studies done to date, the research literature as a whole points to the fact that OSNs do have an impact on work contexts and issues from work contexts are having an impact on OSNs (e.g. in terms of OSN design, applications, and practices). As OSNs evolve and work practices adapt to OSNs, the links between the two are set to become even more tightly entwined. Increasingly then, a full understanding of OSNs and work practices, will require an understanding of how the two domains are connected.

Notes

1   Recently, Facebook established a new profile design. The new Facebook profile includes a feature where it is possible to restrict unknown viewers to seeing a quick overview of basic information such as where the user is from, went to school, and works as well as a row of recently tagged photos of the user (Wiseman, 05.12.2010). The study reported here as well as all research referred to in this chapter involves Facebook's former design.
2   For example, the translation of the aforementioned OSN Yammer into various languages was crowdsourced to the Yammer users (Gobry, 08.12.2010).

References

Acquisti, A. & Gross, R. (2006) Imagined communities: Awareness, information sharing, and privacy on the Facebook. *Proceedings of the 6th Workshop on Privacy Enhancing Technologies*. Cambridge, UK.

Back, M. D., Stopfer, J. M., Vazire, S., Gaddis, S., Schmukle, S. C., Egloff, B. & Gosling, S. D. (2010) Facebook profiles reflect actual personality, not self-idealization. *Psychological Science*, 21, 372–374.

Binder, J., Howes, A. & Sutcliffe, A. (2009) The problem of conflicting social spheres: Effects of network structure on experienced tension in social network sites. *Proceedings of the 27th International conference on Human factors in computing system*. Boston, MA.

Bohnert, D. & Ross, W. H. (2010) The influence of social networking web sites on the evaluation of job candidates. *Cyberpsychology, Behavior, and Social Networking*, 13, 341–347.

Boyd, D. M. & Ellison, N. B. (2007) Social network sites: Definition, history, and scholarship. *Journal of Computer-Mediated Communication*, 13, 210–230.

Brady, E. & Libit, D. (09.03.2006) Alarms sound over Facebook time; Students see website as a friendly community; Schools fear postings make athletes vulnerable. *USA Today*, p. 1C.

Brzozowski, M. J. (2009) WaterCooler: Exploring an organization through enterprise social media. Group '09: *Proceedings of the 2009 International ACM Conference.* Sanibel Isl., FL: USA.

Buhrmester, M. D., Kwang, T. & Gosling, S. D. (2011) Amazon's Mechanical Turk: A new source of cheap, yet high-quality, data? *Perspectives on Psychological Science*, 6, 3–5.

Coleman, J. S. (1988) Social capital and the creation of human capital. *The American Journal of Sociology*, 94 (Supplement), S95–S120.

Cox, L. (14.03.2011) *Yammer gets workers hooked first, then woos bosses.* Retrieved April 11, 2011 from http://www.technologyreview.com/business/35078/?a=f.

cross-tab (2010) *Online reputation in a connected world.* Retrieved January 20, 2011 from http://www.marketingtecnologico.com/ad2006/adminsc1/app/marketingtecnologico/up loads/Estudos/dpd_online%20reputation%20research_overview.pdf.

Cutler, K.-M. (20.07.2010) *Yammer, the Twitter for businesses, crosses 1 million users.* Retrieved April 11, 2011 from http://venturebeat.com/2010/07/20/yammer-1-million-users/.

Dholakia, U. M., Bagozzi, R. P. & Klein Pearo, L. (2004) A social influence model of consumer participation in network- and small-group-based virtual communities. *International Journal of Research in Marketing*, 21, 241–263.

Dholakia, U. M. & Durham, E. (2010, March) One café chain's Facebook experiment. *Harvard Business Review*, 88, 26–26.

DiMicco, J. M. & Millen, D. R. (2007) Identity management: Multiple presentations of self on Facebook. Group '07: *Proceedings of the 2007 International ACM Conference on Supporting Group Work '07.* Sanibel Isl., FL: USA.

DiMicco, J., Millen, D. R., Geyer, W., Dugan, C., Brownholtz, B. & Muller, M. (2008) Motivations for social networking at work. CSCW '08: *Proceedings of the 2008 International ACM Conference on Computer supported cooperative work.* San Diego, CA: USA.

Donahue, E. M., Robins, R.W., Roberts, B. W. & John, O. P. (1993) The divided self: Concurrent and longitudinal effects of psychological adjustment and social roles on self-concept differentiation. *Journal of Personality and Social Psychology*, 64, 834–846.

Ellison, N., Steinfield, C. & Lampe, C. (2007) The benefits of Facebook 'friends': Social capital and college students' use of online social network sites. *Journal of Computer-Mediated Communication*, 12, 1143–1168.

Facebook (2011) *Press room.* Retrieved January 20, 2011 from http://www.facebook.com/press/info.php?statistics.

FaceTime (2010) *The Collaborative Internet: Usage Trends, End User Attitudes and IT Impact.*

FaceTime Communications, Inc., 5th Annual Survey, March 2010. Retrieved January 20, 2011 from http://www.slideshare.net/cinthiashields/facetime-survey-report-fifth-annual-survey

Fortino, A. & Nayak, A. (2010) An architecture for applying social networking to business. *Applications and Technology Conference (LISAT), 2010,* Long Island Systems.

Freedman, J. L. & Fraser, S. C. (1966) Compliance without pressure: The foot-in-the-door technique. *Journal of Personality and Social Psychology*, 4, 195–202.

Gievert, S. (2009) Wahlkampf auf studiVZ: Gruscheln mit Guido (Election campaign on studiVZ: Gruscheln with Guido). Retrieved April 27, 2009 from http://www.studivz.net/l/politikfibel.

Giles, M. (30.01.2010) A world of connections: A special report on social networking. *The Economist.* Retrieved March 2, 2010 from http://www.economist.com/specialreports/displayStory.cfm?story_id=15351002.

Gobry, P.-E. (08.12.2010) *Yammer comes in several languages, opens the rest to crowdsourcing.* Retrieved April 11, 2011 from http://www.businessinsider.com/yammer-comes-in-several-languages-opens-the-rest-to-crowdsourcing-2010-12.

Gosling, S. D., Augustine, A. A., Vazire, S., Holtzman, N. & Gaddis, S. (in press) Manifestations of personality in online social networks: Self-reported Facebook-related behaviors and observable profile information. *Cyberpsychology, Behavior, and Social Networking.*

Gralla, P. & Widman, J. (2008) *Facebook vs. LinkedIn: Which is better for business?* Retrieved January 20, 2011 from http://www.computerworld.com/s/article/9065398/Facebook_vs._LinkedIn_Which_is_better_for_business_.

Grasz, J. (24.08.2009) *45% Employers use Facebook-Twitter to screen job candidates.* Retrieved January 20, 2011 from http://oregonbusinessreport.com/2009/08/45-employers-use-facebook-twitter-to-screen-job-candidates/.

Hewlett-Packard Development Company, L.P. (no date) Why you can't ignore social media. Retrieved January 21, 2011 from http://h10134.www1.hp.com/insights/perspectives/innovation/why-you-can-ignore-social-media/.

Hill, S., Provost, F. & Volinsky, C. (2006) Network-based marketing: Identifying likely adopters via consumer networks. *Statistical Science*, 21, 256–276.

Howe, J. (02.06.2006) *Crowdsourcing: A definition.* Retrieved January 26, 2011 from http://crowdsourcing.typepad.com/cs/2006/06/crowdsourcing_a.html.

Howe, J. (2006) The rise of crowdsourcing. *Wired magazine, 14.06.* Retrieved January 20 2011 from http://www.disco.ethz.ch/lectures/fs10/seminar/paper/michael-8.pdf.

HR.com (23.04.2007) *LinkedIn corporate solutions offers new tools for corporate staffing departments.* Retrieved January 20, 2011 from http://www.hr.com/en/communities/linkedin-corporate-solutions-offers-new-tools-for-_f0wh29b0.html

Ideboen, A. (30.04.2010) *Can LinkedIn really help you get a job?* Retrieved January 20, 2011 from http://www.suite101.com/content/can-linkedin-really-help-you-get-a-job-a232170.

Joinson, A. N. (2008) Looking at, looking up or keeping up with people? Motives and uses of Facebook. *CHI '08: Proceeding of the twenty-sixth annual SIGCHI conference on Human factors in computing systems.* New York, NY: USA, pp. 1027–1036.

Kluemper, D. H. & Rosen, P. A. (2009) Future employment selection methods: Evaluating social networking web sites. *Journal of Managerial Psychology*, 24, 567–580.

Kolek, E. A. & Saunders, D. (2008) Online disclosure: An empirical examination of undergraduate Facebook profiles. *NASPA Journal*, 45, 1–25.

Kornblum, J. & Marklein, M. B. (09.03.2006) What you say online could haunt you: Schools, employers scrutinize social websites such as MySpace and Facebook. *USA Today,* 1A.

Kozinets, R. V. (2002) The field behind the screen: Using netnography for marketing research in online communities. *Journal of Marketing Research*, 39, 61–72.

Kreutz, C. (19.06.2009) *The next billion – the rise of social network sites in developing countries*. Retrieved January 20, 2011 from http://www.web2fordev.net/component/content/article/1-latest-news/69-social-networks.

Kuhn, S. (2008) SelectMinds: Social networking in organisations. Paper presented at the Workshop on Social Networking in Organizations, CSCW 2008, San Diego, CA.

Lampe, C., Ellison, N. & Steinfield, C. (2006) A Face(book) in the crowd: Social searching vs. social browsing. Paper presented at the ACM Special Interest Group on Computer-Supported Cooperative Work, Banff, Canada.

Lehtinen, V., Näsänen, J. & Sarvas, R. (2009) 'A little silly and empty-headed': Older adults' understandings of social networking sites. *HCI 2009, People and Computers XXIII, Celebrating people and technology*, pp. 45–54.

Leitner, P. & Grechenig, T. (2008) Social networking sphere: A snapshot of trends, functionalities and revenue models. *IADIS International Conference on Web Based Communities 2008*, Vienna.

Lenhart, A. & Madden, M. (2007, January) *Social networking websites and teens: An overview*. Retrieved December 7, 2007 from http://www.pewinternet.org/pdfs/PIP_SNS_ Data_Memo_Jan_2007.pdf.

Leskovec, J., Adamic, L. A. & Huberman, A. (2007) *The dynamics of viral marketing*. ACM Transactions on the Web, 1.

Lewis, K., Kaufman, J. & Christakis, N. (2008) The taste for privacy: An analysis of college student privacy settings in an online social network. *Journal of Computer-Mediated Communication*, 14, 79–100.

Lin, N. (1999) Building a network theory of social capital. *Connections*, 22, 28–51.

LinkedIn (2011) *About us*. Retrieved January 20, 2011 from http://press.linkedin.com/about.

Lorenz, M. (20.08.2009) *Nearly half of employers use social networking sites to screen job candidates*. Retrieved January 20, 2011 from http://thehiringsite.careerbuilder.com/2009/08/20/nearly-half-of-employers-use-social-networking-sites-to-screen-job-candidates/.

Morris, M. R., Teevan, J. & Panovich, K. (2010) What do people ask their social networks, and why? A survey study of status message q&a behavior. *CHI 2010, April 10–15, 2010*, Atlanta, GA: USA.

Nardi, B., Whittaker, S. & Schwarz, H. (2000) It's not what you know, it's who you know: Work in the information age. *First Monday, 5*.

nielsenwire (16.02.2010) Facebook users average 7 hrs a month in January as digital universe expands. Retrieved January 20, 2011 from http://blog.nielsen.com/nielsenwire/online_mobile/facebook-users-average-7-hrs-a-month-in-january-as-digital-universe-expands/.

O'Donoghue, T. & Rabin, M. (2001) Choice and procrastination. *Quarterly Journal of Economics*, 116, 121–160.

Osterman Research (2010) *Why you need to focus on social networking in your company*. Osterman Research White Paper, July, 2010. Retrieved January 20, 2011 from http://www.slideshare.net/Actiance/face-time-osterman-why-you-need-to-focus-on-social-networking-in-your-companypdf-4947176.

Ostrow, A. (17.09.2009) *People spend 3x more time on Facebook than Google*. Retrieved January 20, 2011 from http://mashable.com/2009/09/17/facebook-google-time-spent/.

Pantano, E., Tavernise, A. & Viassone, M. (2010) Consumer perception of computer-mediated communication in a social network. *4th International Conference on New Trends in Information Science and Service Science,* Gyeongju, Korea.

Pfeil, U., Arjan, R. & Zaphiris, P. (2009) Age differences in online social networking: A study of user profiles and the social capital divide among teenagers and older users in MySpace. *Computers in Human Behavior,* 25, 643–654.

Putnam, R. D. (2000) *Bowling along: The collapse and revival of American community.* Simon & Schuster, New York.

Radwanick, S. (28.07.2010) *Social networking sites reach a higher percentage of women than men worldwide.* Retrieved January 20, 2011 from http://www.comscore.com/ Press_Events/Press_Releases/2010/7/Social_Networking_Sites_Reach_a_Higher_ Percentage_of_Women_than_Men_Worldwide.

Richter, A., Kneifel, D. & Ott, F. (2009) Fallstudie: Social Networking bei Accenture (Case study: Social networking at Accenture). *Wirtschaftsinformatik & Management,* 1, 78–81.

Romeo, P. (2008) The D Street case study. Paper presented at the Workshop on Social Networking in Organizations, CSCW 2008, San Diego, CA.

Rooksby, J., Baxter, G., Cliff, D., Greenwood, D., Harvey, N., Kahn, A. W., Keen, J. & Sommerville, I. (2009) Social networking and the workplace. *Report of the UK large scale complex IT systems initiative.* Retrieved January 10, 2011 from http://www.lscits.org/pubs/HOReport1b.pdf.

Roos, D. (no date) *How LinkedIn works.* Retrieved January 10, 2011 from http://computer.howstuffworks.com/internet/social-networking/networks/linkedin.htm.

Ross, B. (28.07.2010) *Searching for answers? Ask Facebook questions.* Retrieved January 20, 2011 from http://www.facebook.com/blog.php?post=411795942130.

Roth, P. & Wiese, J. (no date) Facebook Marketing Einführung & Überblick (Facebook marketing intoduction and overview) Retrieved January 20, 2011 from http://facebook-marketing.de/einfuehrung-ueberblick.

Simmons, A. (04.01.2008) *How to click and clean your online profiles.* Retrieved January 10, 2011 from http://www.jobbound.com/news/article/how-to-click-and-clean-your-online-profiles.

Skeels, M. & Grudin, J. (2009) When social networks cross boundaries: A case study of workplace use of Facebook and LinkedIn. *Proceedings of Group 2009,* Sanibel Island, FL: USA, pp. 95–104.

Sherif, K., Hoffman, J. & Thomas, B. (2006) Can technology build organizational social capital? The case of a global IT consulting firm. *Information & Management,* 43, 795–804.

socialbakers (06.12.2010) *Top growing countries on Facebook in November.* Retrieved January 10, 2011 from http://www.socialbakers.com/blog/93-top-growing-countries-on-facebook-in-november/.

Steinfeld, C., DiMicco, J., Ellison, N. & Lampe, C. (2009) Bowling online: Social networking and social capital within the organization. *Proceedings of the Fourth International Conference on Communities and Technologies (C&T 2009),* State College, PA: USA.

Steinfield, C., Ellison, N. & Lampe, C. (2008) Social capital, self-esteem, and use of online social network sites: A longitudinal analysis. *Journal of Applied Developmental Psychology,* 29, 434–445.

Taylor, V. (23.09.2009) *Social not-working: The perils of too much communication.* Retrieved January 20, 2011 from http://www.betternetworker.com/articles/view/ marketing/social-networking/social-not-working-the-perils-of-too-much-communication.

Trusov, M., Bodapati, A. V. & Bucklin, R. E. (2010) Determining influential users in internet social networks. *Journal of Marketing Research*, 47, 643–658.

Valkenburg, P. M. & Peter, J. (2009) Social consequences of the internet for adolescents: A decade of research. *Current Directions in Psychological Science*, 18, 1–5.

Verilli, D. (2010) *Action research: How to find a job using LinkedIn.* Retrieved January 10, 2011 from http://dianeverrilli.com/wp-content/uploads/file/ActionResearchLinkedIn.pdf.

Wang, Y. & Kobsa, A. (2009) Privacy in online social networking at workplace. *IEEE Int'l Conference on Computational Science and Engineering.* Vancouver, Canada, pp. 975–978.

Wei Du (14.08.2007) *Job candidates getting tripped up by Facebook.* Retrieved January 10, 2011 from http://www.msnbc.msn.com/id/20202935/ns/business-personal_finance/.

Wiseman, J. (05.12.2010) *Introducing the new profile.* Retrieved January 20, 2011 from http://blog.facebook.com/blog.php?post=462201327130.

Zeidner, R. (2007) How deep can you probe? *HR Magazine*, 52, 57–62.

4 Mobilizing knowledge collaboration

Today's reality vs. future possibility

Sirkka L. Jarvenpaa and Turid Hedlund

Widespread proliferation of wireless communication networks, portable devices, and mobile applications render mobile information technology (IT) commonplace in our work and social lives. Mobile IT has made it possible for people to connect and coordinate ubiquitously on the move. Mobile IT promises potential for 'individuals, groups, and organizations to co-create services, applications, and content' (Tilson, Lyytinen & Sorensen, 2010). But is mobile IT offering possibilities for knowledge collaboration that relate to the workplace? Are mobile environments serving the purposes of collaborative problem solving and joint knowledge production?

In this chapter we examine possibilities for mobile knowledge collaboration. We begin by reviewing knowledge collaboration in online environments. For example, on Wikipedia.org, individuals can add knowledge and integrate the knowledge of others with whom they have had no prior contact and little direct dialogue. We also review selected mobile IT literature for examples and explanations of mobile collaboration. We find little evidence that knowledge collaboration is taking place in mobile IT environments. To further explore the possibilities for mobile collaboration, we introduce the affordance concept (Gibson, 1979). We theorize about affordances that individuals need to perceive for knowledge collaboration to take place in mobile IT environments. Finally we conclude by studying two examples from the literature that we initially believed exemplified the three sets of affordances that we introduced; affordances of ubiquitous interaction, affordances of knowledge processing and affordances of human motivations. A closer examination proved us otherwise since the examples illustrated rather limited mobile knowledge collaboration. In the case of the jazz festival, uploading and tagging of files was experienced as distracting and interfering with the overall festival experience. We conclude the study by stressing that the framework we presented urges the importance of more research on support processes where the support for interaction ubiquity, motivational aspects and knowledge creation is studied not separately but together.

Defining mobility

Ubiquitous mobile connectivity (more briefly, mobility) allows individuals to access the Internet's World Wide Web and various mobile application services while physically being in motion from place to place. Particularly with smart-phones and tablets, individuals have dramatically increased their use of the Internet while on the move (Ling & Stald, 2010; Morgan Stanley Research, 2010). Today, mobility means much more than a mobile phone, however. Mobile IT refers to managing a portfolio of mobile technologies 'consisting of more than one mobile phone, a dedicated mobile email client, a notebook computer with wireless Internet access, and perhaps peripheral equipment interacting with the devices in Personal Area Networks (PANs), such as Bluetooth headsets, cameras, photo printers and speakers' (Sorensen, 2011a). In particular, mobile messaging in social networking applications has propelled the growth in mobile network traffic (Morgan Stanley Research, 2010).

The use of mobile IT does not necessarily imply mobility. Individuals might access the Internet with their mobile phones or digital tablets from their home or office while remaining stationary, or while focusing on certain applications or tasks monochronically. Mobility assumes movement in (1) spatial, (2) temporal, and (3) contextual dimensions (Kakihara & Sorensen, 2000). Spatial mobility refers to geographical or physical movements of objects (e.g. people, data, or images). Temporal mobility refers to the movement that allows time to be ordered, divided, and reconfigured in different, nonlinear ways. Contextual mobility refers to both the situatedness of interaction and the transcending of traditional physical spatial boundaries, such as home lives and work lives. Mobility is important because the use of technology that transcends space, time, and context can have an impact on behavior and interaction (e.g. individual atten-tion, participation, decision making, relationships). The use of mobile messaging can help transcend temporal boundaries and allow more parallel execution of previously sequentially executed tasks and decision processes (e.g. information gathering, dissemination, discussion, deliberation, and deciding). A nurse using mobile IT at the point of patient can simultaneously (as opposed to sequentially) engage with the patient, and access and process catalogued medical information (Junglas, Abraham & Ives, 2009).

Mobility supports information searching, communication, and transaction capa-bilities for nomads (i.e. people, objects, other resources) as they move in a transparent, integrated, convenient, and adaptive manner (Ali-Hassan, Nevo & Nevo, 2010; Kleinrock, 2001; Lyytinen & Yoo, 2002). An often-mentioned benefit of mobility is that people travelling or commuting (e.g. whilst on board of a train) can use their travelling time productively by using mobile technology (Axtell, Hislop & Whittaker, 2008). Sales personnel and distance workers are able to be in contact with their office by using mobile devices (Daniels, Lamond & Standen, 2001).

Focusing on work environments, Yuan, Archer, Connelly, and Zheng (2010) developed a mobile task model that identified task characteristics of mobile work and mobile support functions that fit with the task characteristics. In Yuan *et al.* (2010), the task characteristics included mobility, location dependence, and time criticality. Mobility was defined as a location variety (the frequency that a person was away from the standard office). Location dependence related to the location-related information that was required to perform the task. Time criticality related to the task's time urgency and rigidity in temporal structuring. The mobile work support functions included location tracking (identify and notify a moving target), notification (brief messages about scheduled or urgent events such as alerts), and online job dispatching (assignment of scarce resources to completing tasks). In an empirical study of 550 mobile workers, Yuan *et al.* (2010) found that perceived usefulness of mobile location notification and real-time mobile job dispatching support functions were positively related to task characteristic of mobility; location tracking and navigation were perceived most useful in tasks involving location dependence; mobile notification and location tracking were perceived most useful in time-critical tasks.

In the prevailing literature, mobile work activities rally around the functions of *connecting* and *coordinating* interactions between the stationary office administration and the mobile work force or within the mobile work force. This is illustrated in examples from mobile police technology (Sorensen, 2011b, pp. 101–110) that support mobile work and the interdependences needed to coordinate actions during a work shift of two police officers. Mobile data services are an integral part of operational management of distributed police forces. The control room and the mobile police units are in constant contact through a car-based computer, car-based and personal radios and car-based and personal mobile phones. The work practices and how they are adapted are deeply intertwined with the adaptive use of mobile IT in the handling of critical incidents and emergencies.

The work of Sorensen (2011a, 2011b) highlights the importance of work context in understanding mobility. Although the mobile task model can provide general guidelines for the development and use of mobile work support systems, the specific use context needs to be incorporated to understand mobility. A location-based mobile crisis management service requires mobility in the form of real-time technological, psychological, and social adaptability to the constraints of the environment as individuals, groups, devices and environment interact with each other for the varied emergency purposes (Majchrzak & More, 2011). A stationary use of a notebook with wireless connections involves a low degree of mobility as only a simple manual reconfiguration to a specific place is needed. *We define mobility as a dynamic process that involves interaction of the individuals, the mobile IT environment, and the social context.*

The dynamic nature of mobility introduces a set of fundamental paradoxes (Jarvenpaa & Lang, 2005) that can be complex even in rather simple tasks. While mobility is depicted as free of access, time, and place restrictions, it also is highly interwoven and entrenched in the mutual interdependencies of the specific context (Arnold, 2003). In addition, technology destroys distance but at the same time destroys closeness; in other words, 'We can move, but we are always there' (Arnold, 2003). Mobile environments can tightly control the actions of individuals while at the same time supporting high levels of discretion and improvisation (Jarvenpaa & Lang, 2005). Sorensen (2011a, 2011a) highlights how social and organizational practices of mobile users simultaneously have a presence of transparency and opacity.

The implication of these paradoxes is that effective personal and organizational use of mobile IT even with tasks of connecting and coordinating requires individuals to engage in complex coping strategies in situ. Lyytinen and Yoo (2002) discuss interactions in nomadic environments and the challenges regarding technical and social mechanisms – particularly social roles – when a group of individuals engages or interacts in mobile environments. An individual can be simultaneously involved in micro, local, and remote interactions; for example, she might access medical records (micro) while talking real time with medical technicians and nurses elsewhere in the building (local), and reading emails left last night by specialists located on another continent (remote) (Luff & Heath, 1997). These interactions can be interleaved by personal instant messages. Managing multiple parallel interactions and the resulting complexity require coping with divided attention, multiple social roles, and a plethora of interface and access issues (Reinsch, Turner & Tinsley, 2008; Dennis, Rennecker & Hansen, 2010). These coping strategies have to accommodate ever more complex demands in mobile knowledge collaboration. Can mobile IT environments support knowledge collaboration? To explore this question, we start by looking at knowledge collaboration in online environments.

Online knowledge collaboration

Great organizational interest in knowledge collaboration has emerged with the advanced, Internet-based interactive infrastructures, including online communities and collectives (Albors, Ramos & Hervas, 2008; McAfee, 2006). The latest social media technologies have led to a rise of online collaboration at a scale and scope not previously witnessed (Kane, 2009). The technologies allow individuals to interact with others and with the content that they share. Such collaboration might range from joining online support groups that offer helpful suggestions, to remixing videos and music, to developing content as well as review, comment and change content provided by other persons in the online Wikipedia encyclopedia. Such forms of collaboration involve a complex set of social and cognitive behaviors, including participation, information acquisition, information sharing, and most importantly knowledge transformation.

Faraj, Jarvenpaa, and Majchrzak (2011) define online collaborative work broadly as the sharing, transfer, accumulation, transformation, and co-creation of knowledge. They argue that in offline, or face-to-face context, knowledge transformation is typically conceptualized as exhibiting convergence after divergence, social identification, repeated interactions, goal sharing, and feelings of interdependence. However, in many *online* contexts, knowledge transformation lacks these characteristics. For example, in many Wikipedia contributions, collaboration can occur among people not known to each other and who share different interests, and there is little direct dialogue or interaction among participants. The interaction is indirect via commenting, corrections, and editing of submissions by many different individuals whose online community memberships may have little or no temporal overlap (Ransbotham & Kane, 2011).

Instead, what is emphasized implicitly or explicitly about knowledge collaboration with advanced digital technologies is its generative capacity (Avital & Te'eni, 2009; Faraj *et al.*, 2011). Avital and Te'eni (2009) introduced the concept of 'generative capacity' to emphasize perpetuating, combinative capability that offers the potential to create something new or novel in a particular context. Generative capacity assumes the presence of heterogeneous resources; an open and participatory culture; permeable boundaries allowing for entry and exit of people; and virtual space where people can engage in various sharing, collaboration, and transformational activities (Van Osch & Avital, 2010). Generative capacity depends on those activities that involve interaction with the inputs and outputs of the creative process; devotion of time and of the members' talents; and the digital platform. Generative capacity is fueled by clear although often multiple goals and rapid feedback that spur further collective action (Kane, Azad, Faraj & Majchrzak, 2011). Rapid feedback might take the form of, for example, easy commenting or voting. Van Osch and Avital (2010) further extended the generative capacity concept to online collectives and defined it as 'the ability to engage in acts of rejuvenating, reconfiguring, reframing, and revolutionizing within a particular goal-driven context.'

Open source software communities often exhibit generative capacity. They involve voluntary work done with the aim of serving the community. Developers contribute their time, effort and programming skills to develop software that is distributed free to potential users. The community structure is strong and the persons involved in open source projects are highly committed to the community and the aim to produce high quality software for free use. There is a great deal of transparency to work and who is doing what and what matters to others, all of which helps building on each other's work as well as jointly solving problems. There is a continuous improvement of software with new releases (Aksulu & Wade, 2010).

Hence, the online Internet-based infrastructure and its potentials for knowledge collaboration is known and well covered in literature. The interesting research question that follows is what happens when the setting is mobile IT. How well is knowledge collaboration supported in mobile IT environments?

Mobile knowledge collaboration

Chatterjee and Sarker (2007) define mobile collaboration as involving 'cooperative work, towards a specific goal, by individuals who are spatially and/or contextually dispersed, and the relevant foci of the individuals change with time during the cooperative act.' They conceptualize knowledge collaboration involving agents solving unanticipated ad hoc problems under time pressure, where different agents have knowledge of different aspects of the problem. As an exemplar of mobile collaboration, Chatterjee and Sarker (2007) discuss a case of mobile road inspectors who identify, report, and repair defects in the road infrastructure. The inspectors are on the move, creating memos in the form of voice recordings, using their GPS receivers to automatically record the position of the defect, sharing the information with other inspectors, and collaborating on solution approaches. Hence, mobile collaboration can involve multiple and multi-level interactions that are interleaved with workflow, co-presence (i.e. temporal convergence of individuals interacting with one another), and shared objects.

While Chatterjee and Sarker (2007) depict mobile collaboration as a collective activity, Sorensen (2011a) and Junglas *et al.* (2009) emphasize individual agency. Mobile collaboration shifts the intelligence and control to the edge – namely, to the individual agents who negotiate access, knowledge, cognitive effort, and social support in a collective setting. According to Sorensen (2011a; 2011b), the paradoxical effects of mobile IT are fundamentally experienced at the individual level (e.g. when organizational control over the uses of mobile devices is seen as too tight or too loose because of how it affects the individual). Individuals on the same mobile team may use widely differing mechanisms to deal with the opportunities and constraints facing the team. This is because of their individual perceptions, preferences, choices, and moods in a particular in-situ context. Some might perceive that providing transparency (e.g. tweets) of their changing locations leads to fewer interruptions and disturbances by other mobile team members. Others might perceive that providing less visibility for others in terms of their locations, actions, movements, and interactions reduces interruptions and distractions. The environmental constraints, such as a slow or unstable connection, might be perceived by one individual, while another is more aware of the sound quality compared to face-to-face encounters. Some individuals might consider the alerts and triggers that technologically track changes in content or actions of others as useful in deciding when to contribute to a collective collaboration; others might perceive that such capabilities constrain and limit their collaboration (Kane *et al.*, 2011). Thus, individuals in the collective settings can act in highly varying ways according to their localized agency. Because they perceive the mobile environment and the social context differently, individuals are likely to use mobile environments in unexpected and diverse ways even when collaborating in the same group or collective. A high degree of individualization takes place in the course of goal-oriented behavior, even when the individual behaviors together constitute mobile knowledge collaboration.

Given the individualized nature of phenomena in action, how can collective goals be maintained so that individual actions render collaborative problem solving or joint knowledge production? In the late 1990s, Luff and Heath (1997) reported both successful and unsuccessful cases of mobile collaboration. Tamaru, Hasuike, and Tozaki (2005) report successful examples of mobile collaborative problem solving with simple mobile phone technology. However, failures are also common in the literature (e.g. Er, 2007; Fomin, 2008). Examining collaborative behaviors of individuals waiting in a snow storm for a bus that never came to take them to work, Fomin (2008) reports that both the need for mobile collaboration and the technology existed, but the collaborative behaviors were not part of the individual's nor the collective's mobile behavior repertoire. Chatterjee, Chakraborty, Sarker, Sarker, and Lau (2009) found that, in the applications of healthcare mobile IT, there was little evidence of collaborative problem solving. Collaborative problem solving requires individuals to engage in effortful cognitive and social processes in unstructured tasks. Exercising such demanding processes is difficult even in face-to-face; let alone in mobile IT environments where individuals are challenged by communication connectivity, small screen sizes, and cumbersome interfaces and input mechanisms. Chatterjee *et al.* (2009) found that mobile information technologies were used for structured tasks and primarily for communication, such as paging a doctor on call. Studying mobile IT environments of the medical staff, Shen, Yoo, and Lyytinen (2006) found that mobile technologies improved communication and coordination among individuals, but at the same time, the technology created its own urgencies that at times disrupted the linear temporal flow of the work execution. Junglas *et al.* (2009) found that in the healthcare context, integrating mobile IT with the nurse's workflow improved nurse's work performance; however, interface issues such as limiting typing skills and 'fumbling with the computer in front of a patient' negatively impacted the professional identity of the nurses. The nurses also struggled with divided attention: bonding with the patient versus interacting with the mobile IT.

In summary, mobile knowledge collaboration is a complex phenomenon in which the pursuit of collective goals of problem solving or joint knowledge production is driven by individual agents in situ. Mobile collaboration requires high levels of adaptive interaction to balance the collective goals of the collaboration with the individualized coping strategies. The mobile IT literature contains several examples of complex coordination in work settings, but knowledge collaboration can mean even more demanding cognitive and social processes. The literature fails to make clear in what situations this localized agency, adaptation, and interaction can make knowledge collaboration possible in mobile IT environments.

Affordances of mobile collaboration environments

To explore possibilities for mobile knowledge collaboration, we relate to Gibson's (1979) 'affordance' concept that can help explain how people perceive objects to afford action in their environments. The concept of affordances provides an ecological account of a goal-directed behavior in situ and how different technologies render different ranges of uses and constraints in different environments. Gibson's work focused on the psychology of perception and how humans, along with animals, birds, etc., orient to objects and see possibilities that these objects offer for action given their needs (Hutchby, 2001). For example, an animal perceives a stone as a shelter, whereas a human perceives the same stone as a rock. Hence, what is perceived are not the properties of objects, but rather affordances, or 'the acts or behaviors that are afforded or permitted by an object, place, or event' (Michaels & Carello, 1981, p. 17 in Markus & Silver, 2008. 'We would say that humans do not perceive chairs, pencils, and doughnuts; they perceive places to sit, objects with which to write, and things to eat' (Michaels & Carello, 1981, p. 42). Importantly, the affordances do not necessarily change when the needs change. So a chair is still a place to sit rather than a decoration in a room even when a person has no need to sit (Hutchby, 2001).

We theorize about affordances of mobile IT to promote mobile knowledge collaboration. The affordances are presented as emergent functional properties that can facilitate mobile collaboration. Affordances, or emergent functional properties, are highly situational orientations and judgments that are not only affected by the task, individual preferences, choices, and moods, but also are constantly shaped by the broader environment in which the action takes place (Zammuto *et al.* 2007).

We begin by reviewing the affordances discussed in the mobile and online IT literatures. The affordances we review fall under three different facets: (1) ubiquitous interaction, (2) knowledge processing and accumulation, and (3) human motivation. Although these affordances are particularly relevant for mobile knowledge collaboration, there may be others as well.

Affordances of ubiquitous interaction

Ubiquity is a core concept discussed in the mobile IT literature (Lyytinen & Yoo, 2002). Ubiquitous interaction involves managing multiple contexts (e.g. micro, local, and remote contexts) and their many ongoing interactions.

Sorensen (2010) identifies four affordances of ubiquitous interaction: connectors, filters, mediators, and coordinators. Connectors are unprioritized encounters, such as requests for interaction, messages, and alerts. Filters, meanwhile, denote prioritized interactions but without memory of past history. For example, a personal network on LinkedIn is an example of a filter. Mediators support ongoing relationships by incorporating memories of past conversations, but they do not filter or prioritize current interactions; and coordinators support filtered interactions of ongoing relationships while remembering the content of conversations, tracking status, and outstanding actions.

Sorensen (2010) underscores how a portfolio of these affordances is needed to support ubiquitous interaction. In a case study of operational policing, all four affordances were present (Sorensen, 2010). A personal radio was mounted on the officer's shoulder, providing an uninterrupted, two-way flow of information between the officer and the control room during an incident (mediator). The police also had mobile data terminals in their cars that streamed relevant dedicated information before they arrived at the place of a crime (filter). In another example of filter, an audio channel broadcast reported on other nearby incidents. The officers applied highly selective filtering when they provided information on a main shared frequency. In terms of connectors, the officers also used mobile phones to contact witnesses and used short message service (SMS) to communicate with colleagues in other police cars (connector). Finally, the officers had access to a data terminal that listed all active incidents and allowed officers to choose and identify the ones for which they were available (coordinator). However, even with all these affordances present, the case conveys primarily complex coordination, rather than collaborative problem solving or joint knowledge production.

Also examining mobile IT environments in emergency response, Landgren and Nulden (2007) report how an ad hoc response team established team members' differing expertise and interacted and negotiated with the team members who came from a wide range of organizations to address the threats presented by an incident. The case study illustrates coordination activities at the level of a dyad, a team, and the broader multi-organizational network. These examples clearly demonstrate that mobile environments are facilitating coordination of work not just in mundane environments (e.g. Ling, 2004), but also in large-scale catastrophes that require fast-paced sense-making across a large group of individuals – including individuals who might not have had any prior contact (Landgren & Nulden, 2007). Perhaps counter-intuitively, Landgren and Bergstrand (2010) argue that short, live-video sequences convey more information to an emergency control center than much longer ones because the latter require a much longer attention span than what is generally available in the midst of an emergency. The authors describe complex sense-making processes that short video sequences facilitate at the control center. The case illustrates well the importance of the first responder's discretion of which events are broadcast and which ones are not, so that the control center can take appropriate action. But here again, the activity between the first responder and the control center represents coordination more so than knowledge collaboration.

Affordances of knowledge processing

Faraj *et al.* (2011) argue that social media technologies in online IT environments have changed some key assumptions about how knowledge creation takes place. Knowledge creation is no longer just happening within existing social circles or work places where people are interdependent and share common goals; instead, knowledge creation can involve large numbers of dispersed people around the world who are not known to each other, who do not share common interests, and who do not engage in direct dialogue with each other. In a geocaching community's portal, (www.geocaching.com), members around the world share information about the location and description of caches they have hidden in physical places. Mobile geocaching apps can be downloaded from the site to mobile devices, and the mobile device used (e.g. GPS) to provide navigation support and access to the website while players are on the move searching for a cache.

Faraj *et al.* (2011) articulate three specific affordances that facilitate knowledge collaboration in online communities: reviewability, recombinability, and experimentation. Reviewability refers to the ability to see not just the current state of knowledge but also what has transpired in the past, the paths and directions that have been taken. Reviewability links the present knowledge to its past, on the way to any future action. In the geocaching community, for example, the members discuss on the site the caches they have found and share experiences. The discussions remain visible and easily accessible to others who visit the site at a later date. The discussions can promote collaboration between the owners of the caches and the persons seeking for caches. The site supports online question–answer features. Individuals share photos and videos. All this user-generated content remains visible and reviewable to anyone accessing the site.

Recombinability refers to the ability to associate, modify, and build on others' contributions and ideas. Recombinability promotes creativity and innovation (Faraj *et al.* 2010). Recombinability can be facilitated when messages can be easily linked or connected across different venues or platforms (e.g. linking a blog to a Facebook wall) (Kane *et al.*, 2011). Majchrzak, Wagner, and Yates (2012) studied organizational wikis and found that shaping – 'the continuous revision of one's own and others' contributions to a Wiki' was critical for knowledge reuse and reconfiguration. However, recombinability is not as common affordance as might be expected even in online environments. For example, the geocaching community offers reviewability, but does not support recombinability. Initiatives such as those involving creative common licensing facilitate recombinability. The music remix site www.ccmixter.org was specifically designed to promote recombinability via its easy-to-mix file formats and reuse genealogy (Jarvenpaa & Lang, 2011).

Experimentation is the speed and ease with which ideas such as a thought or a piece of knowledge, or possibly some output or product can be shared and tested, and measured for the result. Experimentation requires openness to fresh ideas, the capacity to see value in diverse ties and connections, and the means to gather quick feedback, perhaps by empowering or enabling others to vote with a simple thumbs up/thumbs down or perhaps with more complex feedback (e.g. Facebook). Although many online sites and applications provide experimentation, this is not always the case. For example, there is little support for experimentation in the online geocaching community.

In the mobile IT literature, little discussion has been devoted so far to these knowledge processing affordances. As one example, De Reuver *et al.* (2010), in discussing a mobile wiki that contains recommendations and advice for hikers, stress that individuals must be able to see what comes from their input. This mapping to future 'conversation' is critical for reviewability and recombinability, but also in terms of providing fair rewards in the forms of social recognition and attention.

Affordances of human motivation

The mobile IT environments also need to support multidimensional human needs to render knowledge collaboration. Motivational affordances are critical for an individual to exert the necessary effort to adapt his or her behavior to productive mobile knowledge collaboration. Human motivation relates to meeting people's psychological, cognitive, social, and emotional needs. In any context, knowledge collaboration requires effort to engage in purposeful behavior, aimed toward achieving some particular goal or avoiding some particular negative situation. Motivation is critical in its influence on the direction and energy of collaboration efforts.

The literature of mobile IT and the literature of online knowledge collaboration acknowledge the importance of motivation. Faraj *et al.* (2011) underscore the importance of passion in online knowledge creation. In discussing mobile coordination, Sorensen (2011) notes the amount of human effort to maintain just connection: people need to keep batteries charged, bring along cables and connectors, and make sure firmware upgrades are completed. This level of effort ramps up quickly when individuals need to interact with others, whether on small screens or in small interaction spaces, and also deal with potentially unreliable connections to access critical data on a centralized server. Junglas et al (2009) found in their study of nurses that the use of mobile IT was dependent on meeting key human needs to acquire status and legitimacy, to bond and seek mutual assurance in the best interests of the other, to protect one's identity and defend against possible threats, and to learn.

In the information systems literature, Zhang (2008) developed the concept of motivational affordances that lead to strong, intense, and persistent behavior so that the individuals are 'attract(ed) to [the technology], really want to use [it], and cannot live without it.' Zhang based the concept of motivational affordance on five different needs: (1) autonomy and self; (2) competence and achievement; (3) social identification or social relatedness; (4) power and control; and (5) emotion and affect. Different IT design principles can influence these needs (Zhang, 2008). For example, different mobile phone ring tones can provide both autonomy and control. A particular ring tone can help an individual to determine whether to allow an incoming call to interrupt a current activity. Sorensen (2010) reports on the implications of the conflict between the need to allow for autonomy in the field versus need to ensure the centralized power of surveillance technology. The literature on mobile phone usage (Ling & Stald, 2010) and multipurpose mobile devices (Hong & Tam, 2006) found that devices need to reinforce self-determined motivation including autonomy, competence, but also promote social relatedness in cohesive small groups. The literature also suggests that individuals' needs are dependent on life-phases (Ling, 2010) and lifestyles (de Reuver & Bouwman, 2010). With mobile devices (Wakefield & Whitten, 2006; Hong & Tam, 2006) and mobile services (van der Heijden & Sorensen, 2003), not only usefulness but also playfulness is important in predicting intention to use.

Studying journalists and photographers in work settings that were using smart phones with multimedia capabilities, Vaataja (2010) found that the user experience of mobile newsmakers was dependent on meeting both instrumental and hedonic needs, and maintaining positive affect. Not only did the professionals need to be able to meet instrumental needs such as taking a photograph and writing text but also hedonic needs such as career ambitions, competence, and professional image.

Mobilizing knowledge collaboration

We argue that mobile knowledge collaboration is possible only when the situation renders all three different facets of affordances simultaneously: (1) ubiquitous interaction, (2) knowledge processing and accumulation, and (3) human motivation. The need for simultaneity of these three facets of affordances may help explain why mobile knowledge collaboration still seems rare in organizational and private lives. Mobile knowledge collaboration requires access to and availability of real-time information and communication, along with the memory of past interactions, accessible from anywhere at any time; processing and cumulative capabilities for expertise and knowledge on the move; and the motivation to connect on the move, based on multifaceted human needs (see Figure 4.1). Weaknesses or deficiencies in any of the three types of affordances make mobile knowledge collaboration unlikely, or at least unlikely on a sustained basis.

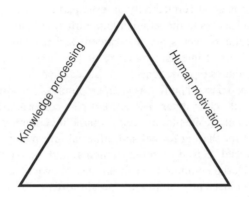

Interaction ubiquity

Figure 4.1 Mobilizing knowledge collaboration

Examples of mobile collaboration

To understand further the affordances in mobile knowledge collaboration, we studied examples from the literature. Two examples caught our attention as we initially believed that they exemplified the three sets of affordances. A closer examination proved us otherwise.

The first example is a site called arabianranta.fi, in Helsinki Finland. The site is mentioned in Sun and Poole (2010). We have expanded the example with material from the actual site, including newspaper articles and interviews. In the second example, we use material collected in a mobile social media project in Finland (Multisilta, Mäenpää & Suominen, 2010).

Example 1: Wireless Digital City www.arabianranta.fi

The Wireless Digital City is a service application where people in a certain urban area, a town, or a district of a city, can form a community and discuss their concerns and interests with those in the same local area. We focus on one such community: Arabianranta.fi. The area has recently been planned and built, even though the environment also includes older buildings and a factory. The community's proximity to the Helsinki city center and good communications make it an attractive residential area for about 10,000 people. The area, which includes educational institutions and small and medium-sized enterprises, has a relatively young population comprising primarily students and young adults. From its beginning, the Wireless Digital City was planned to be an active and creative virtual village where affordances of ubiquitous interaction, knowledge processing, and human motivation would be supported.

The local area has good connectivity. Every apartment has a broadband wireless connection and access to the Arabianranta virtual village portal. Through the portal, arts and cultural events are announced, and residents can take part in discussions on matters of interest, exchange or sell things in the virtual marketplace, and share pictures or experiences.

The portal has two parts. The first is an open portal where anyone in the whole area can interact with each other. The second part comprises closed communities/forums where only residents in a certain building complex can interact. The closed part is used for sharing formal and informal information within the building, including social activity announcements and contact information of neighbors. Every closed community or forum has its own moderator. The moderators negotiate member entry and exit. The site offers filtering and prioritized interaction to people in the same building block. Even the open portal mainly supports interaction in the local context and does not extend to remote contexts (see Luff & Heath, 1997).

A moderator in a building with 300 residents expressed his enthusiasm for the site in an interview with a local newspaper (Mykkänen, 2008). In his opinion the portal helps people get to know each other, arrange parties together, and share experiences and pictures from activities. Even mundane issues, such as coordinating the regular visits to the building's sauna, can be more efficiently handled via the site. If someone has already booked a sauna session and cannot keep the appointment, this availability might be announced on the closed part of the site so that someone else can take advantage of the opportunity. The interaction affordances seem to be well in place.

The site also meets motivational needs, particularly related to social identification and social relatedness. The area is newly built. Many of the residents did not know people in the area before they moved in, and they were socially motivated to get to know their neighbors. Those residents who do not work outside the home have become particularly active users of the portal (Mykkänen, 2008).

In the wireless community of Arabianranta, the members of the community form a stable clan, and within that environment, they take on different roles as residents, administrators, and visitors (Sun & Poole, 2010). Sun and Poole argue that the portal makes people feel more closely connected to each other because they have a greater sense of living, working, and sharing the same physical and virtual space. The sense of common context and closeness intensifies the social identification and social relatedness among community members.

Nevertheless, the site offers little evidence of mobile knowledge collaboration. The members share photos or videos, but this sharing happens primarily among rather close friends, well-known group participants, and neighbors who meet in small face-to-face groups. The discussions on the open portal are infrequent and highly temporal and, according to some residents, rather trivial in nature. The division of the site into open and closed communities might support close social relationships, but it also may limit the diversity necessary for knowledge processing, such as experimentation of new digital traffic services. The site has been important in recruiting residents, workers in nearby businesses, as well as local students to participate in living lab cases of new service development. For example, the case studies involving the development of new digital traffic and retail services had large numbers of people involved, met their goals and were generally viewed successful; however, the development and experimentation of potential services did not necessarily involve co-creation on the site and mobile IT environment.

Example 2: The pilot project on mobile social media

In the Finnish Mobile Social Media project, a specific prototype application called MoVie was developed. Compared to YouTube, the available features are less advanced, but the application has made it possible for individuals to upload videos, as well as tag (index) the content with keywords, using their mobile devices (Multisilta *et al.*, 2010).

The project was piloted during Pori Jazz Festival in the summers of 2008 and 2009. The first pilot made it possible to combine videos from different individuals and render them into a well dramatized, interesting story (Östman, 2010). The project supported both the reviewability and recombinability affordances of knowledge processing. Individuals could upload videos and combine them into different sequences with different narratives.

In the second stage of the project, in summer 2009, eight festival workers participated in a test where they were asked to produce videos, using a mobile phone, that were related to their work environment and work tasks and to share them with and communicate them to their colleagues. The videos were also produced to make it possible to store information about settings and problem situations for the coming years of festival arrangements (Haverinen, 2010).

Although knowledge processing affordances were present in the work setting of the individuals who participated, they were not fully used because of the lack of interaction and motivational affordances. Perhaps surprisingly, memorable moments were related to videos that people had personally captured, but much less emotion was expressed toward the videos of others (Östman, 2010). At the jazz festival, uploading of files was experienced as a distraction and an interference with the overall festival experience. Even inserting tags to the videos was perceived as requiring too much attention (Perttula & Suominen, 2010). The tagging and uploading were seen as secondary activities that disrupted the temporal flow of the main activity of enjoying music. At least in these examples, the affordances did not realize their potential by enabling new joint knowledge production. The lack of realization of mobile collaboration was partly because the technology did not support sufficient ubiquitous interaction particularly in a rapidly changing work setting. But perhaps even more important was the lack of collective goals for truly engaging in mobile collaboration (Haverinen, 2010). It was not sufficient that festival workers had a positive view towards using videos for collaboration in a work setting.

Conclusion

This chapter addresses the question of how well mobile IT environments afford knowledge collaboration. As information systems scholars, we are interested in learning how individuals use mobile environments to foster collaborative problem solving and joint knowledge production – termed by some as mobile collaboration or mobile collaborative problem solving (Chatterjee & Shankar, 2007). As more of the Internet-based interaction moves to mobile IT environments, will the online knowledge collaboration become mobile knowledge collaboration?

This chapter provides a three-tier affordance framework to assess the mobile collaboration possibilities in work and non-work settings. Our framework, shown in Figure 4.1, identifies the need to assess the interaction affordances of mobile IT environments, and to anticipate influences both of knowledge processing and of human motivation fulfillment. Because of the need for all these affordances, mobile knowledge collaboration is still a rare occurrence. The mobilization of knowledge collaboration requires simultaneity of all three sets of affordances working together.

The examples provided illustrate only minimal knowledge collaboration activities so far in mobile IT environments. The richest examples in the literature relate to photo and video-sharing and collaborative editing in live performances such as music or sporting events (Engström, Esbjörnsson & Juhlin, 2008). In mobile environments even where information seeking, communication, and transactions are well supported, still knowledge processing affordances are rarely supported, and even when they are, the weaknesses in interaction and motivational affordances limit what the individual can and will do in mobile environments. The affordance lens used here provides a relational perspective on an actor's action that allows us to recognize that the technology in itself is not what limits knowledge collaboration or what defines what the actor will do in a collaborative co-creation setting. Nevertheless, neither is the actor free from the limitations of the technological environment.

The examples presented in this chapter suggest that mobile collaboration is mainly limited to managing social relationships in mobile environments (Counts & Fisher, 2008). The current literature indicates little transformation of knowledge in collaborative mobile settings. Mobile knowledge collaboration is difficult to maintain because the motivational challenges are particularly great when collaboration occurs on the move. The knowledge processes are demanding in terms of effort and attention in fast-paced activities, and individuals face many competing cognitive and emotional needs particularly in work settings. The knowledge processes also require support for both human and technological meta-knowledge management.

Of course, as more work and more social activities move to the mobile Internet environment and more users tend to be digital natives, we anticipate more interest in mobile knowledge collaboration. Much of the research reported in this chapter involved 'digital immigrants' rather than digital natives. Digital immigrants (Vodanovich *et al.*, 2010) are those people who were born before the millennial generation and who learned to engage with it in their late teens or adult lives, whereas digital natives are the millennial generation who grew up in the networked world. Compared to digital immigrants, digital natives are depicted as celebrating free form agile collaboration and fundamentally believing that best ideas come from working jointly on common problems. Digital natives also demand continuous feedback and value instant recognition. Hence, the rise of the digital natives with advanced mobile IT might change the landscape of mobile knowledge collaboration. At the minimum, we anticipate that the study of mobile collaboration will attract increasing research interest in the years to come. This chapter, in the meantime, serves to introduce a few key elements of mobile knowledge collaboration.

We look forward to much additional work that can be done to understand the landscape of the phenomenon. The framework that is presented stresses the importance of more research where the support for interaction ubiquity, motivational aspects and knowledge creation processes is studied not separately but together in order to get a more realistic picture of mobile knowledge collaboration. Emergency management contexts can be a great starting point for such research. Such contexts call for support for 'emergent serenpidity' or 'agility in the surprise,' and should render high levels of psychological and social motivation for action (Majchrzak & More, 2011). Mobile IT environments are often the only possible way that knowledge collaboration can take place. Professionals in this domain have already incorporated mobile access devices into their daily work practices.

There is a need for more research on mobile collaboration in both work and non-work settings. The affordances might take different perceptual and actual forms in work and non-work settings. Studies of work settings where there is a mix of professional and amateurs should be also undertaken such as a study of collaboration between professional and amateur journalists. Research cases involving mobile collaboration using social media (e.g. collaborative content creation in virtual worlds and massive multiplayer games) in work settings would particularly add to the literature.

Acknowledgments

Tekes Fidipro Project provided financial support for the first author. Academy of Finland 3DGIS-project within the Motive program provided financial assistance for the second author.

References

Aksulu, A. & Wade, M. (2010) A comprehensive review and synthesis of open source research. *Journal of the Association for Information Systems*, 11, 576–656.

Albors, J., Ramos, J. C. & Hervas, J. C. (2008) New learning network paradigms: Communities of objectives, crowdsourcing, wikis, and open source. *International Journal of Information Management*, 28, 194–202.

Ali-Hassan, H., Nevo, D. & Nevo, S. (2010) Mobile collaboration: Exploring the role of social capital. *The DATA BASE for Advances in Information Systems*, 41, 9–24.

Arnold, M. (2003) On the phenomenology of technology: The 'Janus-faces' of mobile phones. *Information and Organization*, 13, 231–256.

Avital, M. & Te'eni, D. (2009) From generative fit to generative capacity: Exploring an emerging dimension of information systems design and task performance. *Information Systems Journal*, 19, 345–367.

Axtell, C., Hislop, D. & Whittaker, S. (2008) Mobile technologies in mobile spaces: Findings from the context of train travel. *International Journal of Human-Computer Studies*, 66, 902–915.

Chatterjee, S., Chakraborty, S., Sarker, S., Sarker, S. & Lau, F. (2009) Examining the success factors for mobile work in healthcare: A deductive study. *Decision Support Systems*, 46, 620–633.

Chatterjee, S. & Sarker, S. (2007) Revisiting 'collaboration' under conditions of 'Mobility.' *Proceedings of the 40th Hawaii International Conference on System Sciences*, 2007.

Counts, S. & Fisher, K. E. (2008) Mobile social networking: An information grounds perspective. *Proceedings of the 41st Hawaii International Conference on Systems Sciences*, IEEE Press.

Daniels, K., Lamond, D. & Standen, P. (2001) Teleworking: Frameworks for organizational Research. *Journal of Management Studies*, 38, 1151–1185.

Dennis, A. R., Rennecker, J. A. & Hansen, S. (2010) Invisible whispering: Restructuring collaborative decision making with instant messaging. *Decision Sciences*, 41, 845–886.

De Reuver, M. & Bouwman, H. (2010) Explaining mobile internet service adoption by context-of-use and lifestyle, *2010 Ninth International Conference on Mobile Business*.

De Reuver, M., Stein, F., Hampe, F. & Bouwman, H. (2010) Towards a service platform and business model for mobile participation. *2010 Global Mobility Roundtable*.

Dorn, C., Schall, D., Gombotz, R. & Dustdar, S. (2007) A view-based analysis of distributed and mobile teams. *Proceedings of the 16th IEEE international Workshops on Enabling Technologies: Infrastructure for Collaborative Enterprises*. June 18–20, pp. 198–203.

Engström, A., Esbjörnsson, M. & Juhlin, O. (2008) Mobile collaborative live video mixing, *Proceedings of MobileHCI* (September 2–5).

Er, M. (2007) Technology adoption and the mobile worker: The case of the field journalist. *Collaborative Computing: Networking, Applications and Worksharing*. Collaborate com, pp. 442–446.

Faraj, S., Jarvenpaa, S. L. & Majchrzak, A. (2011) Knowledge co-creation in online communities, *Organization Science* (forthcoming).

Fomin, V. V. (2008) Snow, buses, and mobile data services in the information age. *Journal of Strategic Information Systems*, 17, 234–246.

Gibson, J. J. (1979) *The ecological approach to visual perception*. Reading, MA: Houghton Mifflin.

Hampton, K. N., Livio, O. & Goulet, L. S. (2010) The social life of wireless urban spaces: Internet use, social networks, and the public realm. *Journal of Communication*, 60, 701–722.

Haverinen, A. (2010) Kameran edessä ja takana – Tapaustutkimus festivaalihenkilökunnan sitoutumisesta mobiilivideointiin 2009. In J. Multisilta, J. Mäenpää & Jaakko Suominen (eds), *Yhdessä ja liikkeellä: Mobiili sosiaalinen media*. CAT – Culture, Art and Technology Network. Aalto-yliopisto; Porin taiteen ja median laitos; Tampereen teknillinen yliopisto, Porin yksikkö; Turun yliopisto, kulttuurituotannon ja maiseman-tutkimuksen koulutusohjelma.

Hong, S.-Y. & Tam, K. Y. (2006) Understanding the adoption of multipurpose information appliances: The case of mobile data services. *Information Systems Research*, 17, 162–179.

Hutchby, I. (2001) Technologies, texts and affordances, *Sociology*, 35, 441–456.

Jarvenpaa, S. L. & Lang, K. R. (2005) Managing the Paradoxes of Mobile Technology, *Information Systems Management*, 22, 7–23.

Jarvenpaa, S. L. & Lang, K. R. (2011) Boundary management in online communities: Case studies of the nine inch nails and ccmixter music remix sites. *Long Range Planning*, 44, 440–457.

Junglas, I., Abraham, C. & Ives, B. (2009), Mobile technology at the frontlines of patient care: Understanding fit and human drives in utilization decisions and performance. *Decision Support Systems*, 46, 634–647.

Kakihara, M. & Sorensen, C. (2001) Expanding the 'mobility' concept. *ACM SIGGROUP Bulletin*, 22, 33–37.

Kane, G. C. (2009) It's a network, not an encyclopedia: A social network perspective on Wikipedia collaboration, *Academy of Management Annual Meeting Proceedings*, Chicago, IL: pp. 1–6.

Kane, G. C., Azad, B., Faraj, S. & Majchrzak A. (2011) Fostering innovation and intellectual capital creation· The paradoxical influence of social media affordances. Working Paper, Boston College.

Kleinrock, L. (2001) Breaking news. *Communications of the ACM*, 44, 41–45.

Landgren, J. & Bergstrand, F. (2010) Mobile live video in emergency response: Its use and consequences. *Bulletin of the American Society of Information Science and Technology*, 36, 27–29.

Landgren, J. & Nulden, U. (2007) A study of emergency response work: Patterns of mobile phone interaction. *Proceedings of the 2007 SIGCHI conference on Human Factors in computing systems CHI 2007*, ACM Press.

Ling, R. (2010) Texting as a life phase medium. *Journal of Computer-Mediated Communication*, 15, 277–292.

Ling, Rich. (2004) *The mobile connection: The cell phone's impact on society*. San Francisco: Morgan Kaufmann.

Ling, R. & Stald, G. (2010) Mobile communities: Are we talking about a village, a clan, or a small group? *American Behavioral Scientist*, 53, 1133–1147.

Luff, P. & Heath, C. (1997) Mobility in collaboration. *Proceedings of CSCW '98*, November 14–18, pp. 305–314.

Lyytinen, K. & Yoo, Y. (2002) Research commentary: The next wave of nomadic computing, *Information Systems Research*, 13, 377–388.

Majchrzak, A. & More, P. H. B. (2011) Emergency! Web 2.0 to the Rescue. *Communications of the ACM*, 54, 125–132.

Majchrzak, A., Wagner, C. & Yates, D. (2012) The impact of shaping on knowledge reuse for organization improvement with Wikis. *MIS Quarterly*, forthcoming.

Malone, T.W. (2004) *The future of work: How the new order of business will shape your organization, your management style, and your life.* Cambridge, MA: Harvard Business School Press.

McAfee, A. P. (2006) Enterprise 2.0: The dawn of emergent collaboration. *MIT Sloan Management Review*, 47, 21–28.

Markus, M. L. & Silver, M.S. (2008) A foundation for the study of IT effects: A new look at DeSanctis and Poole's concepts of structural features and spirit. *Journal of Association for Information Systems*, 9, 609–632.

Michaels, C. F. & Carello, C. (1981) *Direct perception.* Englewood Cliffs, NJ: Prentice Hall.

Morgan Stanley Research. (2010) Company reports, mobile internet ramping faster than desktop internet did, Apple leading charge, October 7.

Multisilta, J., Mäenpää, J. & Suominen, J. (2010) *Yhdessä ja liikkeellä: Mobiili sosiaalinen media, Yhdessä ja liikkeellä: Mobiili sosiaalinen media.* CAT – Culture, Art and Technology Network. Aalto-yliopisto; Porin taiteen ja median laitos; Tampereen teknillinen yliopisto, Porin yksikkö; Turun yliopisto.

Mykkänen, J. (2008) Arabianrannan asukkaat sumplivat saunavuoronsa netissä. *Helsingin Sanomat,* May 4.

Östman, S. (2010) Kun tutkijakokelas käyttäjätestauksen muistitiedoksi muutti – Pori jazz 2008 – Mobiilividekokeilujen rekonstruointia. In J. Multisilta, J. Mäenpääm & Jaakko Suominen (eds), *Yhdessä ja liikkeellä: Mobiili sosiaalinen media.* CAT – Culture, Art and Technology Network. Aalto-yliopisto; Porin taiteen ja median laitos; Tampereen teknillinen yliopisto, Porin yksikkö; Turun yliopisto, kulttuurituotannon ja maiseman-tutkimuksen koulutusohjelma.

Perttula, A. & Suominen, M. (2010) Internetin videojakelupalvelut – Älypuhelin päätelaitteena. In J. Multisilta, J. Mäenpääm & Jaakko Suominen (eds), *Yhdessä ja liikkeellä: Mobiili sosiaalinen media.* CAT – Culture, Art and Technology Network. Aalto-yliopisto; Porin taiteen ja median laitos; Tampereen teknillinen yliopisto, Porin yksikkö; Turun yliopisto, kulttuurituotannon ja maiseman- tutkimuksen koulutusohjelma.

Ransbotham, S. & Kane, G. C. (2011) Membership turnover and collaboration success in online communities: Explaining rises and falls from grace in Wikipedia. *MIS Quarterly, 2011*, 35, 613–627.

Reinsch, N. L., Jr., Turner, J. W. & Tinsley, C. (2008) Multicommunicating: A practice whose time has come? *Academy of Management Review*, 33, 391–403.

Shen, Z., Yoo, Y. & Lyytinen, K. (2005) Temporal implications of information technology for work practices: Organizing in and for time in an emergency department. *Proceedings of the 39th Hawaii Conference on System Sciences (HICCS).*

Sorensen, C. (2010) Cultivating interaction ubiquity at work. *The Information Society*, 4, 276–287.

Sorensen, C. (2011a) Mobile IT. In R.D. Galliers and W. Currie (eds), *The Oxford handbook of management information systems: Critical perspectives and new directions.* Oxford: Oxford University Press.

Sorensen, C. (2011b) *Enterprise mobility: Tiny technology with global impact on work.* Hampshire: Palgrave Macmillan.

Sun, J. & Pool, M. S. (2010) Beyond connections: Situated wireless communities. *Communications of the ACM*, 53, 121–125.

Tamaru, E., Hasuike, K. & Tozaki, M. (2005) Cellular phone as a collaboration tool that empowers and changes the way of mobile work: Focus on three fields of work. *Proceedings of the Ninth European Conference on Computer-Supported Cooperative Work*, September 18–22, pp. 247–264.

Tilson, D., Lyytinen, K. & Sorensen, C. (2010) Digital infrastructures: The missing IS research agenda. *Information Systems Research*, 20, 748–759.

Vaataja, H. (2010) User experience evaluation criteria for mobile news making technology: Findings from a case study. *Proceedings of OZCHI 2010.*

Van der Heijden, H. & Sørensen, L. S. (2003) Measuring attitudes towards mobile information services: an empirical validation of the HED/UT scale. *Proceedings of the European Conference of Information Systems*, Naples, Italy.

Van Osch, W. & Avital, M. (2010) Generative collectives. *Proceedings of the International Conference on Information Systemsi,* St. Louis, MO.

Vodanovich, S., Sundaram, D. & Myers, M. (2010) Digital natives and ubiquitous information systems, *Information Systems Research*, 21, 711–723.

Wakefield, R. L. & Whitten, D. (2006) Mobile computing: A user study on hedonic/utilitarian mobile device usage. *European Journal of Information Systems*, 15, 292–300.

Yuan, Y., Archer, N., Connelly, C. E., Zheng, W. (2010) Identifying the ideal fit between mobile work and mobile work support. *Information & Management*, 47, 125–137.

Zammuto, R. F., Griffith, T. L., Majchrzak, A., Dougherty, D .J. & Faraj, S. (2007) Information technology and the changing fabric of organization. *Organization Science*, 18, 1–14.

Zhang, P. (2008) Motivational affordances. Reasons for ICT design and use. *Communications of ACM*, 51, 145–147.

5 Knowledge, skills, abilities and other characteristics (KSAOs) for virtual teamwork

Stefan Krumm and Guido Hertel

Due to the ongoing globalization and digitalization of business processes, digital media are becoming the default communication and collaboration channel in modern business organizations (Axtell, Fleck & Turner, 2004; Golden & Raghuram, 2010). A recent survey by the Institute for Corporate Productivity showed that 80% of companies with more than 10,000 employees considered or employed virtual forms of collaboration (Perry, 2008). The most prominent form is 'virtual teams', i.e. teams that consist of two or more persons who collaborate interactively to achieve common goals, while at least one of the team members works at a different location and/or time; additionally, communication and coordination are predominantly based on digital communication media (e-mail, phone, online chat, web- or video conference, etc.; cf. Hertel, Geister & Konradt, 2005).

By employing virtual teams, companies can capitalize on the expertise of different individuals without bringing them physically together. This is particularly relevant for organizations with geographically dispersed centers of expertise. Microsoft, for example, has recently established three strategic Research & Development (R&D) centers in India, China, and Israel. Virtual forms of collaboration can be used to assemble employees from all three sites, thereby aiming at synchronizing research efforts. Creating innovation is another potential advantage of virtual teams because diversity and creativity due to multiple perspectives is more easily realized (e.g. van Knippenberg & Schippers, 2007). Moreover, virtual teams facilitate rapid adoption of new knowledge (e.g. about diverse markets, see Siebdraht, Hoegl & Ernst, 2009) and can help to reduce overall business costs. Quite a few global companies reacted to the 2008 economic crisis with increased virtual collaboration. As a consequence, some of these companies were able to cut their travel expenses by around 20% (Reuters, 2010).

But virtual teams do not only provide benefits at the company level. At the level of the individual worker, virtual teams – as compared to traditional teams – provide more autonomy and flexibility to adopt work conditions to individual needs (job crafting). Moreover, high levels of autonomy granted by the company might be perceived as indicators of high trust in the employee (Hertel *et al.*, 2005). Simultaneously, job strain due to frequent traveling (jet-lag, delays, etc.)

can be avoided. Thus, virtual teamwork offers solutions for the multiple challenges aligned to the current globalization, both at the individual worker's and at the company's level.

However, the potential benefits of virtual teams come along with various challenges, again both for organizations and individual workers. Challenges particularly relevant in virtual teams are: how to promote efficient and errorless work flows around the globe; how to monitor and lead team members who can only be contacted with digital communication media; how to create high team spirit and commitment in a team with globally dispersed team members; how to manage conflicts among team members across distance, acknowledging differences in cultural background (cf. Ebrahim, Ahmed & Taha, 2009; Furst, Reeves, Rosen & Blackburn, 2004). During the last two decades, growing research effort has been devoted to addressing these challenges. This research either focused on technology-related challenges (e.g. what are the differences between face-to-face and computer-mediated collaboration, how to effectively use technology in virtual teams; e.g. Driskell, Radtke & Salas, 2003), task-related challenges (e.g. which task types can be dealt with in virtual teams; e.g. Hertel *et al.*, 2005), or challenges related to interpersonal processes (e.g. which variables affect the adoption of group decision support systems, or how to create trust and a sense of belongingness in virtual teams; e.g. Jarvenpaa & Leidner, 1998; Montoya-Weiss, Massey & Song, 2001). However, people-related issues have been largely neglected so far, i.e. what are crucial knowledge, skills, abilities, and other characteristics (KSAOs) for virtual teamwork, and how to select people for virtual teams?

The aim of this chapter is twofold. First, we review the existing research on KSAOs relevant for traditional and virtual teamwork. Second, we propose a systematic approach of identifying KSAOs in virtual teams, which considers KSAO clusters both for traditional and for virtual teamwork, the interaction between these KSAO clusters, and theoretically derived moderators of the relationship between KSAOs and virtual teamwork. Finally, we discuss implications of this model for further research and for applied issues.

KSAOs for traditional and for virtual teamwork: what we know so far

KSAOs for traditional teamwork

Teamwork is certainly one of the core occupational competencies in the 21st century (Barton, 2007). Accordingly, quite a few researchers examined KSAO-based taxonomies for teamwork (Cannon-Bowers, Tannenbaum, Salas & Volpe, 1995; Hoegl & Gemuenden, 2001; Loughry, Ohland & Moore, 2007; Stevens & Campion, 1994).[1] Although the KSAOs presented by these authors differ to some extent, a substantial overlap can be identified. Table 5.1 provides a (non-exhaustive) overview of teamwork KSAO taxonomies as proposed by different researchers. The following KSAOs are considered unanimously relevant for traditional teamwork: willingness to contribute to the team's work, interacting with team-mates, keeping the team on track, expecting quality and goal setting, planning and task coordination, and interpersonal relations. Please note that these labels define higher-order dimensions of teamwork KSAOs and are further qualified by first-order factors (e.g. Stevens & Campion, 1994). According to these dimensions, a good team-player is willing to do a fair share of the team's work, communicates relevant information effectively, has a good understanding of the overall team goals and monitors the team's progress towards these goals, has high performance standards, has an overview of other team members' tasks, can coordinate task completion appropriately, and, finally, is well accepted by the other team members (cf. Table 5.1).

Table 5.1 Teamwork KSAO in different taxonomies

	Loughry *et al.* (2007)	Stevens & Campion (1994)	Cannon-Bowers *et al.* (1995)	Hoegl & Gemuenden (2001)
Contributing to the team's work	x	x	x	x
Interacting with team-mates	x	x	x	x
Keeping team on track	x	x	x	x
Expecting quality and goal setting	x	x	x	
Planning and task coordinating		x	x	x
Interpersonal relations			x	x
Relevant taskwork KSAOs	x			
Conflict resolution		x		
Adaptability			x	
Situational awareness			x	
Effort				x

Note: KSAOs printed in bold are shared by most of the authors.

Although all the aforementioned teamwork KSAOs are intuitively plausible, it is neither clear whether this list is exhaustive, nor whether this list includes unique or at least important KSAOs for teamwork. For instance, KSAOs such as effort (Hoegl & Gemunden, 2001) or task-related expertise (Loughry *et al.*, 2007) are also relevant for non-teamwork (cf. the differentiation between taskwork and teamwork skills used by Stevens and Campion, 1994). In order to identify teamwork KSAOs, a common approach in the past was to select a broad set of KSAOs based on existing literature (at the time), create items to measure these KSAOs, determine the dimensionality of the item set, and consider the resulting dimensions to be relevant teamwork KSAOs (see Loughry *et al.*, 2007 for a good example of such an approach). In some cases (e.g. Miller, 2001), the relevance of the identified KSAOs is further examined by regressing these KSAOs on individual and team performance criteria. Although such an approach provides a good starting point, the resulting KSAOs taxonomies partly depend on the initial set of KSAOs that are considered. Relevant KSAOs that might (unintentionally) have been overlooked in the initial set will not be included in the final taxonomy. On the other hand, over-represented KSAOs of a certain domain (e.g. communication) influence the factorial solution (see Horn, 1967 for typical problems in factor-analyses). The latter is particularly likely when researchers draw their initial set of KSAOs from existing literature as research on evolving themes often concentrates on specific topics in the beginning (see for instance the focus on trust in the beginning of virtual team research).

An interesting next step in research on teamwork KSAOs might be a *multi-method approach* that empirically identifies crucial teamwork requirements in a bottom-up fashion (critical-incident technique, qualitative in-depth interviews etc.), thereby avoiding biases due to existing research trends. Moreover, integrating *generic frameworks of KSAOs*, such as the Great Eight competency model (Bartram, 2005), might also contribute to achieve a complete picture. According to our knowledge, such an approach is still rare in research on teamwork KSAOs.

KSAOs for virtual teamwork

Systematic empirical research on KSAOs for virtual teams is hard to find. The majority of existing literature on KSAOs for virtual teamwork employs theoretical or case-study based comparisons either between traditional and virtual teams (e.g. Arnison & Miller, 2002), or between successful and unsuccessful virtual teams (e.g. Siebdraht *et al.*, 2009). An overview of the variety and plentitude of potentially relevant KSAOs for virtual teamwork as proposed by different authors is depicted in Figure 5.1 ('KSAO-cloud'). Duarte and Snyder (2001), for instance, stress that virtual team members need to develop trust and feelings of cohesion over distance. Unlike traditional teams, members of virtual teams cannot meet casually during lunch breaks or chit-chat in between tasks (Arnison & Miller, 2002) so that developing trust and cohesion should be more difficult (Jarvenpaa & Leidner, 1998). Moreover, communication is often asynchronous and digitalized. As a consequence, team members need to employ more effort to communicate effectively (Shin, 2004). Usually, virtual team members are less closely monitored and receive less feedback (e.g. Harvey, Novicevic & Garrison, 2004). Hence, higher demands are imposed on self-management skills (Hertel *et al.*, 2006). Finally, virtual teams are often culturally diverse (e.g. Ellingson & Wiethoff, 2002) and less stable as teams are often specifically composed for concrete projects and are dissolved after project completion. Therefore, team members have to frequently adapt to new circumstances and to deal with ambiguity.

Figure 5.1 The KSAO-cloud: virtual teamwork KSAOs as proposed by different authors

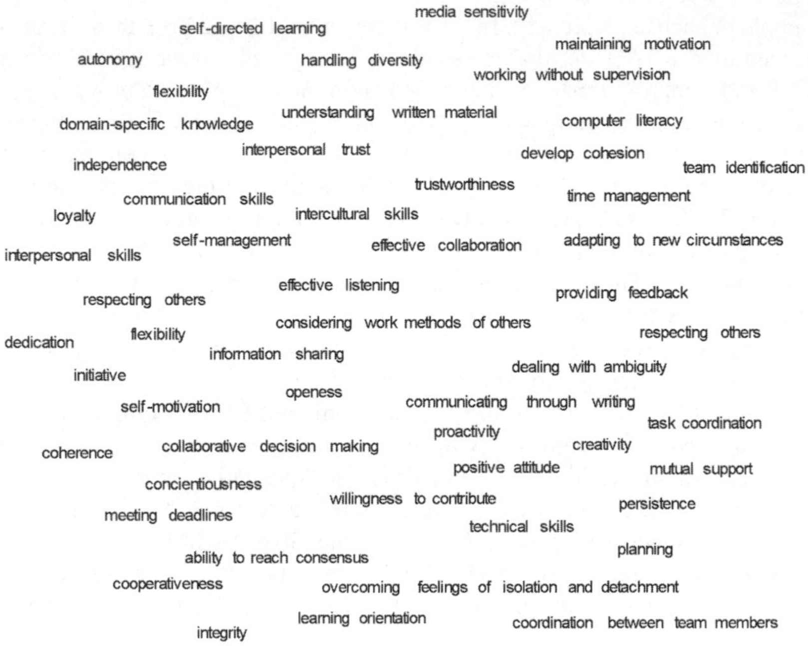

media sensitivity
self-directed learning
maintaining motivation
autonomy   handling diversity
working without supervision
flexibility
domain-specific knowledge   understanding written material   computer literacy
interpersonal trust
independence   develop cohesion
team identification
trustworthiness
communication skills   time management
loyalty   intercultural skills
self-management   effective collaboration   adapting to new circumstances
interpersonal skills
effective listening
respecting others   providing feedback
considering work methods of others
dedication   flexibility   respecting others
information sharing
initiative   dealing with ambiguity
openess
self-motivation   communicating through writing
proactivity   task coordination
coherence   collaborative decision making   creativity
concientiousness   positive attitude   mutual support
willingness to contribute   persistence
meeting deadlines
technical skills
ability to reach consensus   planning
cooperativeness   overcoming feelings of isolation and detachment
learning orientation   coordination between team members
integrity

Notes: KSAOs were proposed by Anawati & Craig (2006), Cordery, Morrison, Wright, & Wall
(2010), Hertel *et al.* (2006), Hertel, Deter, & Konradt (2003), Siebdraht *et al.* (2009),
Kirkman, Rosen, Gibson, Tesluk, & McPherson (1995), Newman (2005), Shin (2004),
Harvey *et al.* (2004); Kirkman *et al.*, 2004; Shin (2004) or added by the authors of this book
chapter

Although these assumptions are plausible, empirical examinations are rare.
Moreover, similar as with KSAOs for traditional teamwork, there is a lack of
systematic bottom-up job analyses that would reduce potential theoretical biases
and enable researchers to identify unique virtual teamwork KSAOs. Initial information in this respect might be found in research comparing computer-mediated
and face-to-face collaboration. However, the vast majority of this work has
focused on technology-related issues (e.g. how to design group decision support
systems) or task-related questions (e.g. ideal levels of task complexity in
computer-mediated collaboration tools; e.g. Fjermestad & Hiltz, 1998, 2000),
which are difficult to apply to individual KSAOs. Explicit examinations of
required KSAOs so far are rather neglected in research on computer-mediated
collaboration.

Nevertheless, empirically demonstrated differences between computer-
mediated and face-to-face teamwork might still allow initial suggestions of
KSAOs required for virtual teams. For instance, studies have shown that mutual

trust among team members is more difficult in virtual as compared to traditional teamwork (e.g. Jarvenpaa & Leidner, 1998; Rocco, 1998; Wilson, Straus & McEvily, 2006). Among the various reasons is the lower level of media richness and shared social context during collaboration (e.g. Cramton, 2002; Handy, 1995). At the same time, virtual teams that successfully develop and maintain trust seem to have various benefits. For instance, trust helps to manage the higher uncertainty in virtual teams by reducing the amount of effortful control behaviors (e.g. checking whether the others are also working). Moreover, trust helps virtual teams to deal with higher risks of misunderstandings by expecting positive intentions of team partners as default value. Hence, KSAO to develop trust and to be trustworthy seem to be crucial in virtual teams. Another KSAO possibly derived from the computer-mediated collaboration literature is *proactivity*. Münzer and Holmer (2009) examined the effects of different media characteristics of computer-mediated communication and found that team members in highly asynchronous communication conditions needed to be more proactive, for instance, by actively contacting different sources and asking for needed information (similar results are reported by Konradt, Schmook, Wilm & Hertel, 2000, for teleworkers in different business companies). Hofner Saphiere (1996) examined communication processes in global business teams. According to the results, productive global business teams used significantly more *non-task related communication* as compared to unproductive teams. Thus, it seems to be essential for virtual teams to value non-task related communication that provides the socio-emotional 'glue' to keep the team members connected. In a similar approach, Siebdraht *et al.* (2008) surveyed 80 global software development teams. Their main finding was that high-performing virtual teams were characterized by higher team member *effort*, better *coordination* between team members, and higher mutual task-related *support*. Additionally, the authors report that high dispersion is associated with higher social instability, thus suggesting need or willingness for *team identification* as another potential KSAO for virtual teams. Finally, Hoegl, Ernst, and Proserpio (2007) report a significant interaction between teamwork quality and team member dispersion in product development teams, suggesting that teamwork KSAOs increase in importance when geographical dispersion of the team increases. Among the teamwork KSAOs considered, the authors in particular stress *communication skills*, *coordination skills*, mutual *support*, and *effort*. Thus, typical KSAOs for traditional teamwork are also considered relevant for virtual teams.

Although these studies are helpful to draw inferences concerning relevant KSAOs, they do not provide direct tests of the relevance of individual differences in KSAOs. For instance, the fact that effective virtual teams coordinate tasks appropriately does not necessarily imply that members of successful virtual teams need to possess high levels of coordination KSAOs. It might just as well be that successful virtual teams are guided by clear leadership principles or self-administered guidelines and rules how to coordinate tasks, and thus each team member simply needs to comply with these standards. Or put differently, the situational demand in some environments might be very strong and override individual differences (cf. Mischel, 2004). Hence, KSAOs which are pivotal to successful performance in virtual teams might be better identified by relating individual characteristics to performance criteria (instead of relating characteristics of the team to performance criteria).

Additionally, the developmental phase of each team (Furst *et al.*, 2004; Marks, Mathieu & Zaccaro, 2001) has to be considered. Imagine a research specialist being hired for a well-managed R&D team with good intra-team relationships, explicit rules and norms, and high cohesion. Most likely, the new employee will find it easy to adapt to the new team. Undisputedly, the relevant KSAOs in such a situation differ from the KSAOs necessary in a newly built team with little or no established rules and low cohesion. Beyond that, it is necessary not only to consider either the team or the individual level, but both levels at the same time (e.g. by using multi-level analysis).

So far, only a few studies have assessed individual differences in KSAOs related to performance indicators at the team or at the individual team member level. In an initial attempt, Hertel, Konradt, and Voss (2006) developed a model of virtual teamwork competencies based on a theoretical review of the existing literature. The resulting model (see Figure 5.2) comprised three main levels of KSAOs: Taskwork-related KSAOs, teamwork-related KSAOs, and telecooperation-related KSAOs. Additionally, cognitive abilities and professional expertise / technical training were considered as predictors of team effectiveness. Telecooperation-related KSAOs covered persistence, willingness to learn, creativity, independence, interpersonal trust, and intercultural skills. Hence, this KSAO cluster consisted of several aspects outlined in the previous paragraph together with supplementary KSAOs. Their conceptually broad approach enabled the authors to assign each KSAO to the respective layer of the model according to its predominant relevance. For example, self-management KSAOs are frequently considered in taxonomies of traditional teamwork (e.g. Stevens & Campion, 1994). However, when comparing their relevance to both, traditional and virtual teams, self-management skills seem to be particularly important when supervisory and peer control are reduced (Harvey *et al.*, 2004). Consequently, self-management KSAOs (independence, persistence, learning orientation, and creativity) was assigned to the telecooperation-related KSAO cluster. Similarly, aspects of trustworthiness and reliability were considered taskwork-related KSAOs, as these aspects were shown to be generally related to performance (e.g. Schmidt & Hunter, 1998). Based on this model the authors created the *Virtual Team Competency Inventory* (VTCI; Hertel *et al.*, 2006).

The relevance of the VTCI subscales was tested in a sample of 258 members of 22 virtual teams. Concurrently, supervisory ratings of their team managers were gathered. Hertel *et al.* (2006) assessed the validity of the subscales on the individual and the team level. Results yielded a significant contribution of the VTCI subscales in predicting altogether 24% of team member performance variance. However, only taskwork-related KSAOs (conscientiousness, integrity, and loyalty) and teamwork-related KSAOs (cooperativeness) proved to be significant predictors of individual performances whereas telecooperation-related KSAOs

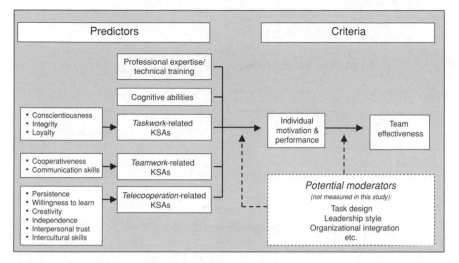

Figure 5.2 KSAs/KSAOs in the virtual team competency inventory

did not. At the team level, however, telecooperation-related KSAOs such as creativity, learning orientation and independence turned out to be significant or at least marginally significant predictors of team performance in addition to taskwork-related and teamwork-related KSAOs. (Please note that the team level sample size was only $n = 22$.)

Taken together, although the study conducted by Hertel *et al.* (2006) synthesized the existing literature and carefully selected KSAOs that seem to be relevant in virtual teams (i.e. telecooperation-related KSAOs, see Figure 5.2), their results indicated traditional teamwork and taskwork KSAOs to be most relevant. Based on these findings and considering that the Hertel *et al.* (2006) study was the first approach in this vein, we preliminary draw the following conclusions: (a) research on virtual teamwork KSAOs needs to consider traditional teamwork KSAOs and taskwork-related KSAOs, (b) results from analyses and theoretical considerations at the team level cannot be simply transferred into requirements of individual team members' KSAOs. In order to summarize the aforementioned theoretical considerations, comparisons between face-to-face and computer-mediated communication, case studies, and empirical examinations in an initial classification, we assigned the potentially relevant KSAOs to the respective Great Eight dimensions (Bartram, 2005). Interestingly, the vast majority of KSAOs that might be relevant in virtual teams can be assigned to only three Great Eight dimensions: Supporting and Cooperating, Organizing and Executing, as well as Creating and Conceptualizing (cf. Figure 5.3).

The Supporting and Cooperating dimension covers trust (e.g. Jarvenpaa & Leidner, 1998), proactivity (e.g. Konradt *et al.*, 2000), coordination between team

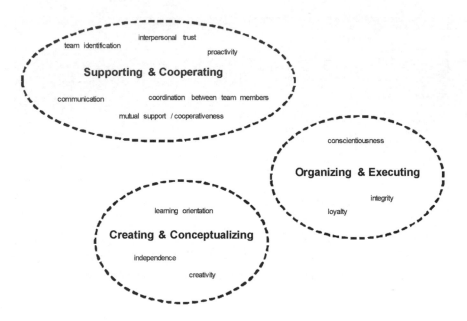

Figure 5.3 Preliminary summary of KSAOs that are relevant in virtual teams

members (e.g. Siebdraht *et al.*, 2008), communication (e.g. Hofner Saphiere, 1996) as well as mutual support (e.g. Siebdraht *et al.*, 2008) and cooperativeness (e.g. Hertel *et al.*, 2006). The Organizing and Executing dimension includes the teamwork-related KSAOs that provided predicted validity in Hertel *et al.*'s (2006) study: conscientiousness, integrity, and loyality. Finally, the Creating and Conceptualizing dimension comprises telecooperation related KSAOs that were found to be relevant for performances on the team level (cf. Hertel *et al.*, 2006): creativity, learning orientation, and independence.

A systematic approach of identifying KSAOs in virtual teams

In this section, we develop a systematic approach to deepen our understanding of KSAOs that are unique to virtual teams. An overview of this approach is depicted in Figure 5.4. We also present a research agenda aligned to our systematic approach that has the potential to provide more insights in the future regarding KSAOs in virtual teams. In our opinion, more concrete statements concerning relevant KSAOs that exceed those in our preliminary summary (cf. Figure 5.3) can only be made after applying such a systematic approach.

Individual differences in team performances. A core presumption of research aiming at identifying unique virtual teamwork KSAOs is that individual differences in performances of low virtuality teams do not perfectly determine individual differences in performances of high(er) virtuality teams. If individuals work simultaneously in two teams which differ in one or more dimensions of team virtuality, their performances should not correlate perfectly. In other words, the best team players in a traditional team might not automatically be the best team player in a virtual team. Please note that this presumption is a precondition to assume unique variance of high virtuality teams that can be explained by unique KSAOs. Hence, a main presumption in our systematic approach (see Figure 5.4) is that team member performances in high virtuality teams are not perfectly predicted by team member performances in low virtuality teams (path a in Figure 5.4). To the best of our knowledge, no studies so far have examined the performance of the same individual in two teams (within-subjects design) which only differ in their level of (one or more dimensions of) virtuality. The importance of such analyses is illustrated by the following example. Let us assume that we are examining individuals that work in a traditional and a virtual team at the same time. This situation is not unusual; consider, for example, team members that work in their local R&D team as well as in a global (virtual) R&D team. Let us further assume that team members' performance in the traditional and in the virtual team (supervisory ratings) can be measured with a reliability of .70 (this is an optimistic example, the reliability of supervisory ratings is usually much lower, see Viswesvaran, Ones & Schmidt, 1996). Hence, the upper threshold of the correlation between both performances is $\sqrt{.70 \times .70} = .70$ (i.e. 70% of true variance in the overall variance). Further, imagine that the bivariate observed correlation between both performances is .60 (i.e. 36% shared variance). As a consequence, only 34% of unique virtual teamwork variance (70% true overall variance minus 36% shared teamwork variance) remains to be predicted by unique KSAOs related to virtuality. Given this presumption, 24% of explained variance reported by Hertel *et al.* (2006) is remarkable. However, to date we do not know whether team member performance in traditional and virtual teams in fact correlates at .60. Hence, future (laboratory and field) research is needed to examine the correlation between performances in tasks that differ only in terms of their virtuality (separately for different virtuality dimensions) in order to identify the uniqueness of team member performance in virtual teams.

KSAOs predicting unique virtual teamwork performance. Our proposed model (see Figure 5.4) considers four different KSAO domains which are organized in two KSAO clusters. In line with other authors (e.g. Hertel *et al.*, 2006; Stevens & Campion, 1994), taskwork-related KSAOs and teamwork-related KSAOs comprise the traditional teamwork KSAO cluster. Hence, this cluster includes predictors of performance in traditional teams. Predictors of performance in teams scoring high in one or more dimensions of team virtuality, on the other hand, are subsumed in the virtual teamwork KSAO cluster. In contrast to existing solutions, our model also differentiates between taskwork and teamwork KSAOs within the virtual team domain. In fact, we argue that taskwork-related and teamwork-related KSAOs within both traditional and virtual teamwork clusters only partly overlap. The reason is that taskwork and teamwork in virtual teams as compared to traditional teams differ even if the same problem is tackled. Consider for example a team member delivering a presentation in a web meeting. Besides

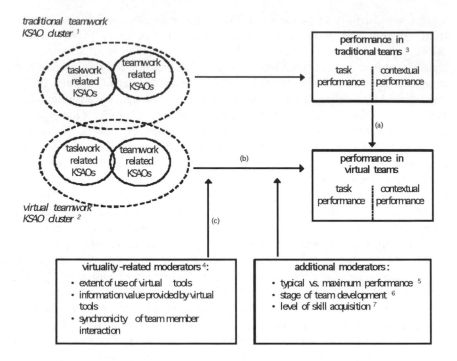

Figure 5.4 A systematic approach of identifying KSAOs in virtual teams

Notes: 1 Stevens & Campion (1994), 2 Hertel, Konradt, & Voss (2006),
    3 Borman & Motowidlo (1993), 4 Kirkman & Matthieu (2005),
    5 Sackett, Zedeck, & Fogli (1988), 6 Tuckman (1965), 7 Ackerman & Cianciolo (2000)

the taskwork which is required in a face-to-face presentation, additional tasks emerge such as setting up the web meeting technically, inviting the participants electronically and sending information needed in advance, and using web-based tools to guide interactively through the presentation. Moreover, task-related processes have to be organized more thoughtfully and in line with requirements of virtual teamwork (Siebdraht *et al.*, 2009). Similarly, teamwork KSAOs in virtual teams can be qualitatively and quantitatively different from teamwork KSAOs in traditional teams. Some of the teamwork KSAOs in the virtual team-work cluster may be similar to those in the traditional teamwork cluster, but are possibly even more important to effective teamwork. Hoegl *et al.* (2007), for example, report that effective coordination and mutual support becomes more important as team member dispersion increases. Other teamwork-related KSAOs may predominantly apply to virtual teamwork (Hertel *et al.*, 2006). Plausible examples of such KSAOs are learning orientation or independence. On the other hand, teamwork KSAOs such as active listening techniques or the strict adherence to rules and procedural guidelines seem to be less relevant or even obstructive in virtual teams (Hertel *et al.*, 2006).

Given the crucial differentiation between traditional and virtual teamwork, future research is desirable to decide whether KSAOs are (a) only relevant in traditional teams, (b) relevant in both traditional and virtual teams but to a different degree, or (c) only relevant in virtual teams. This can be done by separately assessing each individual's performance in traditional forms of teamwork and in (comparable) virtual forms of teamwork as criterion measures. KSAOs from both the traditional and the virtual teamwork KSAO cluster may be applied to both criteria as well as to the residual virtual teamwork performance after controlling for traditional teamwork performance. Such an approach would enable researchers to employ a broad set of potentially relevant KSAOs and examine their predictive value for (a) traditional teamwork, (b) traditional and virtual teamwork, (c) exclusively virtual teamwork.

The moderating effects of dimensions of virtuality. Although general definitions of virtual teams (e.g. Hertel *et al.*, 2005) provide a first orientation, the variety of existing virtual teams in organizations indicates that the mentioned defining elements of space, time, and communication technologies can vary independently of each other. Some teams predominantly communicate over digital media but are located in the same building; other teams are geographically dispersed but regularly arrange face-to-face meetings. Consequently, more recent research considers different *dimensions* of team virtuality.

For instance, Kirkman and Mathieu (2005) define three dimensions of team virtuality that may vary gradually and independently of each other: (a) extent of use of digital media ('virtual tools' in the diction of Kirkman & Mathieu, 2005), (b) information value provided by digital media, and (c) synchronicity of team member interaction. In our systematic approach, we posit that the dimensions of team virtuality moderate the KSAO – performance relationship (see Figure 5.4, path c). Next, these dimensions are described and illustrated with examples.

Extent of use of digital media refers to the amount of interaction which is conducted by the means of digital media. Teams which extensively rely on digital communication media during interaction are considered to have a high level of team virtuality. For example, teams responsible for turning around passenger aircraft at airports work in close proximity in and around the aircraft and are engaged in several sequential activities (e.g. passenger de-boarding, refueling, unloading luggage, cleaning the aircraft, passenger boarding, etc.), but the major part of their coordination is done by digital means of communication (computer software, portable radio devices, etc.).

Information value provided by digital media as a dimension of team virtuality denotes the extent to which digital media convey information that is needed for the team to be effective. This dimension is similar but not identical to the concept of media richness (see Griffith, Sawyer & Neale, 2003, for a definition of team virtuality drawing on media richness). Kirkman and Mathieu (2005) reason that less rich media are sometimes more effective for a team to solve a task than richer media. For example, architect teams who convey spatial relationships of objects by mutually working on 3-dimensional computer simulations benefit more from computer simulations than video-conference meetings (the latter would be considered richer media). The more information value provided by digital media in use, the lower the virtuality level of the team. Examples for high virtuality in this dimension can be found in Web-based instruction and training: instructors have to rely on participants' written feedback and thus, might find it difficult to gather precise information about their feelings and emotions.

Synchronicity of team member interaction describes the extent of synchronous information exchange between team members. Synchronous exchange (e.g. online chat systems) takes place in real-time, whereas asynchronous exchange (e.g. e-mail) denotes time-displaced communication. According to Kirkman and Mathieu (2005), the more asynchronous the communication between team members, the more virtual is the team. A team of researchers co-authoring a book chapter often communicates in a time-displaced fashion as team members over-look each other's draft, engage in several other tasks in between, then comment on the draft, and send a revised version back and forth.

These examples illustrate that virtuality is a multi-facet construct, with some teams scoring high on one dimension of virtuality but, at the same time, low on other dimensions. Please note that these dimensions denote objective characteristics of a team and, thus, cannot be equated with individual characteristics. However, these dimensions place specific demands on members of virtual teams: Teams interacting in a highly asynchronous manner by using media with high information value require different KSAOs as compared to teams which only occasionally rely on virtual tools, but if they do, they use media with low information value. Thus, we argue that the KSAOs for virtual teamwork should be aligned to the proposed dimensions of team virtuality, thereby providing a conceptual framework for virtual teamwork KSAOs.

Especially in later phases of the team life cycle, i.e. when high virtuality has already been established, it seems likely that organizations impose virtual team-work requirements on team members rather than adapting the virtuality of the team to the level of team member KSAOs. Moreover, the globalization of markets and organizational processes forces several teams to adopt a certain level of virtuality. As a consequence, team members need to adapt to these circumstances. However, these circumstances may be rather different depending on the virtuality dimension of the team. As mentioned earlier, high use of digital tools is likely to impose other demands on team members as compared to low synchronicity of team member interaction. Hence, we posit that specific dimensions of team virtuality moderate the relationship between specific KSAOs and team performance (path c in Figure 5.4). Below, initial assumptions concerning the moderating role of each dimension of team virtuality are suggested.

The *extent of using virtual tools* (digital media) as one aspect of team virtuality might moderate the relevance of computer and media literacy. This is in line with findings showing that the individual level of comfort with communication media is influenced by the individual KSAO to use these media (Trevino, Lengel & Daft, 1987; see also Hertel, Schroer, Batinic & Naumann, 2008). Flexibility in media use was also found to be relevant for effective performance (Rice, 1992). Thus, one can presume that the frequency of digital media use is associated with the importance of individuals' flexibility in media use and media sensitivity. The latter is reflected in appropriate media choice as a function of task requirements. The extent of using virtual tools might also moderate the relevance of trust in virtual teams: According to findings reported by several authors (e.g. Jarvenpaa & Leidner, 1998; Rocco, 1998; Shin, 2004; Wilson *et al.*, 2006), members of virtual teams who rarely meet face-to-face, i.e. extensively use digital tools, are especially required to develop trust. Likewise, overcoming feelings of isolation and detachment (Kirkman *et al.*, 1995) is pivotal if team members predominantly use virtual tools. Moreover, the relevance of working independently and without supervision might by enhanced (Hertel *et al.*, 2006).

If teams predominantly communicate with digital media that provide low information value, team members are required to deal with ambiguity (see Siebdraht *et al.*, 2009). Additionally, team members might be forced to proactively search information which was not communicated in the first place. Therefore, initiative (Siebdraht *et al.*, 2009), proactive information sharing (Steege, 2003) and persistence (Hertel *et al.*, 2006) are especially relevant if this virtuality dimension is high. Moreover, one might assume that deep domain-specific knowledge (Shin, 2004) helps to fully and immediately understand communication even if information value is low. Kirkman and Mathieu (2005) highlight that informational value as a virtuality dimension is similar but not identical to the concept of media richness. Drawing from the media richness literature, one can speculate, however, that computer and media literacy is a relevant KSAO if information value is low: Carlson and Zmud (1999) found that higher experience with communication media was associated with higher perceived media richness. Therefore computer and media literacy might enable team members to fully exploit the possibilities of the given media even if the level of richness or information value is low.

Synchronicity of team member interaction is likely to moderate the role of planning and task coordinating KSAOs (Hertel *et al.*, 2006; Kirkman *et al.*, 2004). The more asynchronous a team member interaction and the lower the opportunities to adapt team processes in between, the more important is a thorough planning and task coordination in advance. Moreover, higher asynchrony might imply that problems cannot be solved immediately. Instead, team members might put certain tasks aside, occupy themselves with other tasks, switch media and communication partner (Su & Mark, 2008), and only get back to the initial task when a (remote) team member replies to their request. Hence, asynchronous interactions should impose higher demands on time management and multitasking (Wasson, 2004), as well as on working memory as various tasks need to be held mentally present (cf. Bühner, König, Pick & Krumm, 2006). First evidence for these assumptions is provided by Münzer and Holmer (2009) who showed that individuals working under asynchronous conditions experienced more mental effort in integrating relevant information than did individuals in synchronous conditions. Please note that this result is not trivial as one could also assume higher mental effort under synchronous conditions since many different processes have to be handled simultaneously. Münzer *et al.* (2009) further reported that asynchronous communication hindered the coherence of the group discussion, thereby potentially attenuating mutual understanding. Thus, mutual understanding and coherence might be especially important in teams with asynchronous communication. Additionally, less synchronous interactions might require team members to show higher self-management (Hertel *et al.*, 2006), because the relevant information and feedback is not immediately accessible.

Besides considering dimensions of virtuality separately, it seems also plausible to consider *interactions between combinations of the three dimensions of virtuality*. To date, we can only speculate about potential interaction effects. One might assume that extensively using virtual tools with low information value might enhance the requirement to overcome feelings of isolation and detachment. Likewise, highly asynchronous communication with low information media could imply that team members need to be very high in autonomy to complete their tasks. Certainly, more research providing substance to these and similar assumptions is needed.

The moderating effects of other variables. Our model depicted in Figure 5.4 additionally considers moderating variables that are not directly linked to dimensions of virtuality. For instance, the *stage of team development* needs to be considered (e.g. Furst *et al.*, 2004; Marks *et al.*, 2001; Maznevski & Chudoba, 2000). At early stages and or planning phases of the team project, asynchronous communication and low information value of the applied media might be quite challenging for the team members. However, if tasks and roles are clear for a project sequence and not much coordination is needed (work phases), obviously high degrees of virtuality are particularly efficient (for examples see Alge, Wiethoff & Klein, 2003; Hertel, Konradt & Orlikowski, 2004; Maznevski & Chudoba, 2000). Another example is the level of skill acquisition that requires different KSAOs (Ackerman & Cianciolo, 2000). For instance, Ackerman and Cianciolo (2000) used air-traffic control tasks to examine required KSAOs at different levels of skill acquisition. Task performance in initial phases of skill acquisition was predominantly associated with general mental ability, whereas later phases required perceptual and motor speed. Notably, similar tasks are frequently administered in studies on teams (e.g. distributed dynamic decision making simulation, Miller, Young, Kleinmann & Serfaty, 1998). Thus, the level of skill acquisition in teams should be assessed and considered when examining KSAOs in virtual (and traditional) teams.

Initial suggestions for a research agenda. Our proposal for a research agenda is closely linked to the model presented here. First, research should provide evidence that individual differences in performances in virtual teams can be separated from individual differences in performance in traditional teams, as well as non-teamwork. Second, a set of potentially relevant KSAOs needs to be established. Supplementing theoretical considerations and case studies, this can be done by using systematic methods of job analyses (critical-incident technique, standardized job analyses questionnaires and observation instruments, etc.). Moreover, the initial set of KSAOs should be aligned to generic competency models, such as the Great Eight competency model (Bartram, 2005), in order to ensure content validity. Third, these KSAOs can be assessed and applied as predictors of team member performances and team performances (multi-level analyses). In order to ensure that the variance predicted is unique to virtual teams, the corresponding performances in traditional teams need to be controlled for. Finally, the proposed dimensions of team virtuality together with aspects of time (stages of team development, levels of skill acquisition) might be considered as important moderators of the relationship between individual KSAOs and team performances. Understanding virtuality as a multi-faceted construct (e.g. Mathieu & Kirkman, 2005) renders different KSAOs to be important, depending on the dimension(s) of virtuality. Such an approach might also help to integrate seemingly contradicting results of the past. For instance, whereas the importance of trust has been stressed in early work on virtual teams both theoretically and empirically (e.g. Rocco, 1998; Jarvenpaa & Leidner, 1998), subsequent work found trust to be rather unrelated to virtual team performance (e.g. Hertel, Niedner & Herrmann, 2003; Hertel *et al.*, 2004). Thus, instead of relating specific KSAOs unambiguously to virtual teams, it might be more fruitful to adopt a differentiated perspective that considers the specific levels of team virtuality separately for the different dimensions. For instance, trust-related KSAOs might be particularly relevant in virtual teams when virtuality is connected to high exploitability of individual team members. Consider, for example, collaboration in open source software development projects such as Mozilla or Linux (e.g. Hertel *et al.*, 2003). Given that participants in such communities often develop software for their own purpose anyway, additionally sharing of such a product does not imply many additional costs that might be exploited. In contrast, if these software developers are part of a virtual R&D team in a business company, with both salary and career being determined by the team success, sharing of individual work becomes much more exploitable, and mutual trust in the reciprocity of effort much more crucial.

Summary and conclusion

If leaders of virtual teams ask for guidance in staffing their team or developing their team members, what would we tell them? Summarizing this chapter, we feel that in addition to existing approaches and instruments (e.g. Duarte & Snyder, 2001; Hertel *et al.*, 2006) the following concrete recommendations apply in many settings:

a) do not simply derive individual KSAOs from analyses and theoretical considerations at the team level;
b) consider traditional teamwork KSAOs in virtual teams as well, such as communication skills (cf. Hofner Saphiere, 1996), cooperativeness and conscientiousness (Hertel *et al.*, 2006);
c) complement initial suggestions and existing approaches of general KSAOs required in virtual teams (cf. Figure 5.3) by checking established KSAO taxonomies (cf. Figure 5.2);
d) conduct systematic research based on requirement analyses (cf. Figure 5.4) considering the different dimensions of virtuality and their related demands for members of virtual teams.

Although many organizations already employ virtual forms of cooperation, many practitioners are still looking for advice when employing virtual teams. Therefore, research should be especially concerned with the production and translation of practically relevant knowledge, in order to avoid the typical practitioner–researcher divide we see in many areas (Shapiro, Kirkman & Courtney, 2007). Research along the lines of the model proposed in this book chapter might provide further insights into crucial KSAOs for virtual teamwork.

Note

1   For personality-based assessments of the member–team effectiveness relationship see for example Barrick, Stewart, Neubert, and Mount (1998).

References

Ackerman, P. & Cianciolo, A. T. (2000) Cognitive, perceptual-speed, and psychomotor determinants of individual differences during skill acquisition. *Journal of Experimental Psychology: Applied*, 6, 259–290.

Alge, B. J., Wiethoff, C. & Klein, H. J. (2003) When does the medium matter? Knowledge-building experiences and opportunities in decision-making teams. *Organizational Behavior and Human Decision Processes*, 91, 26–37.

Anawati, D. & Craig, A. (2006) Behavioral adaptation within cross-cultural virtual teams. *IEEE Transactions on Professional Communication*, 49, 44–56.

Arnison, L. & Miller, P. (2002) Virtual teams: A virtue for the conventional team. *Journal of Workplace Learning*, 14, 166–173.

Axtell, C. M., Fleck, S. J. & Turner, N. (2004) Virtual teams: Collaborating across distance. *International Review of Industrial and Organizational Psychology*, 19, 205–248.

Barrick, M. R., Stewart, G. L., Neubert, M. J. & Mount, M. K. (1998) Relating member ability and personality to work-team processes and team effectiveness. *Journal of Applied Psychology*, 83, 377–391.

Barton, P. E. (2007) What about those who don't go? *Educational Leadership*, 64, 26–27.

Bartram, D. (2005) The great eight competencies: A criterion-centric approach to validation. *Journal of Applied Psychology*, 90, 1185–1203.

Borman, W. C. & Motowidlo, S. J. (1993) Expanding the criterion domain to include elements of contextual performance, in N. Schmitt & W. C. Borman (eds), *Personnel selection in organizations*. San Francisco, CA: Jossey Bass, pp. 71–98.

Bühner, M., König, C., Pick, M. & Krumm, S. (2006) Working memory dimensions as differential predictors of the speed and error aspect of multitasking performance. *Human Performance*, 19, 253–275.

Cannon-Bowers, J. A., Tannenbaum, S. I., Salas, E. & Volpe, C. E. (1995) Defining competencies and establishing team training requirements, in R. A. Guzzo & E. Salas (eds), *Team effectiveness and decision making in organizations*. San Francisco: Jossey-Bass, pp. 333–381.

Carlson, J. R. & Zmud, R. W. (1999) Channel expansion theory and the experimental nature of media richness perceptions. *Academy of Management Journal*, 42, 153–170.

Cordery, J. L., Morrison, D., Wright, B. M. & Wall, T. D. (2010) The impact of autonomy and task uncertainty on team performance: A longitudinal field study. *Journal of Organizational Behavior*, 31, 240–258.

Cramton, C. D. (2002) Attribution in distributed work groups. In P. J. Hinds & S. Kiesler (eds), *Distributed work*. Cambridge, MA: MIT Press, pp. 191–212.

Driskell, J. E., Radtke, P. H. & Salas, E. (2003) Virtual teams: Effects of technological mediation on team performance. *Group Dynamics: Theory, Research, and Practice*, 7, 297–323.

Duarte, D. L. & Snyder, N. T. (2001) *Mastering virtual teams: Strategies, tools, and techniques that succeed*. San Francisco: Jossey-Bass.

Ebrahim, N. E., Ahmed, S. & Taha, Z. (2009) Virtual teams: A literature review. *Australian Journal of Basic and Applied Sciences*, 3, 2653–2669.

Ellingson, J. E. & Wiethoff, C. (2002) From traditional to virtual: Staffing the organization of the future today, in R. Heneman & D. Greenberger (eds), H*uman resource management in virtual organizations*. Greenwich, CT: Information Age, pp. 141–177.

Fjermestad, J. & Hiltz, S. R. (1998) An assessment of group support systems experimental research: methodology and results. *Journal of Management Information Systems*, 15, 7–149.

Fjermestad, J. & Hiltz, S. R. (2000) Group support systems: A descriptive evaluation of case and field studies. *Journal of Management Information Systems*, 17, 113–157.

Furst, S., Reeves, M. E., Rosen, B. & Blackburn, R. S. (2004) Managing the life cycle of virtual teams. *Academy of Management Executive*, 18, 6–20.

Golden, T. D. & Raghuram, S. (2010) Teleworker knowledge sharing and the role of altered relational and technological interactions. *Journal of Organizational Behavior*, 31, 1061–1085.

Griffith, T. L., Sawyer, J. E. & Neale, M. A. (2003) Virtualness and knowledge: Managing the love triangle of organizations, individuals, and information technology. *Management Information Systems Quarterly*, 27, 265–287.

Handy, C. (1995) Trust and the virtual organization. *Harvard Business Review*, 73, 40–50.

Harvey, M., Novicevic, M. M. & Garrison, G. (2004) Challenges to staffing global virtual teams. *Human Resource Management Review*, 14, 275–294.

Haywood, M. (1998) *Managing virtual teams: Practical techniques for high-technology project managers*. Boston: Artech House.

Hertel, G., Deter, C. & Konradt, U. (2003) Motivation gains in computer-mediated work groups. *Journal of Applied Social Psychology*, 33, 2080–2105.

Hertel, G., Geister, S. & Konradt, U. (2005) Managing virtual teams: A review of current empirical research. *Human Resource Management Review*, 15, 69–95.

Hertel, G., Konradt, U. & Orlikowski, B. (2004) Managing distance by interdependence: Goal setting, task interdependence, and team-based rewards in virtual teams. *European Journal of Work and Organizational Psychology*, 13, 1–28.

Hertel, G., Konradt, U. & Voss, K. (2006) Competencies for virtual teamwork: Development and validation of a web-based selection tool for members of distributed teams. *European Journal of Work and Organizational Psychology*, 15, 477–505.

Hertel, G., Niedner, S. & Herrmann, S. (2003) Motivation of software developers in open source projects: An internet-based survey of contributors to the Linux kernel. *Research Policy*, 32, 1159–1177.

Hertel, G., Schroer, J., Batinic, B. & Naumann, S. (2008) Do shy people prefer to send e-mail? Personality effects on communication media preferences in threatening and non-threatening situations. *Social Psychology*, 39, 231–243.

Hoegl, M. & Gemuenden, H. G. (2001) Teamwork quality and the success of innovative projects: A theoretical concept and empirical evidence. *Organization Science*, 12, 435–449.

Hoegl, M., Ernst, H. & Proserpio, L. (2007) How teamwork matters more as team member dispersion increases. *Journal of Product Innovation Management*, 24, 156–165.

Hofner Saphiere, D. M. (1996) Productive behaviors of global business teams. *International Journal of Intercultural Relations*, 20, 227–259.

Horn, J. L. (1967) On subjectivity in factor analysis. *Educational and Psychological Measurement*, 27, 811–820.

Jarvenpaa, S. L. & Leidner, D. E. (1998) Communication and trust in global virtual teams. *Journal of Computer-Mediated Communication*, 3, 1–36.

Kirkman, B. L. & Mathieu, J. E. (2005) The dimensions and antecedents of team virtuality. *Journal of Management*, 31, 700–718.

Kirkman, B., Rosen, B., Gibson, C., Tesluk, P. & McPherson, S. (1995) Five challenges to virtual team success: Lessons from Sabre. *Academy of Management Executive*, 16, 67–79.

Kirkman, B. L., Rosen, B., Tesluk, P. E. & Gibson, C. B. (2004) The impact of team empowerment on virtual team performance: The moderating role of face-to-face interaction. *Academy of Management Journal*, 47, 175–192.

Konradt, U., Schmook, R., Wilm, A. & Hertel, G. (2000) Health circles for teleworkers: Selective results on stress, strain, and coping styles. *Health Education Research*, 15, 327–338.

Latham, G. P. & Locke, E. A. (2007) New developments in and directions for goal-setting research. *European Psychologist*, 12, 290–300.

Loughry, M. L., Ohland, M. W. & Moore, D. D. (2007) Development of a theory-based assessment of team member effectiveness. *Educational and Psychological Measurement*, 67, 505–524.

Marcus, B., Goffin, R. D., Johnston, N. G. & Rothstein, M. G. (2007) Personality and cognitive ability as predictors of typical and maximum managerial performance. *Human Performance*, 20, 275–285.

Marks, M. A., Mathieu, J. E. & Zaccaro, S. J. (2001) A temporally based framework and taxonomy of team processes. *The Academy of Management Review*, 26, 356–376.

Maznevski, M. L. & Chudoba, K. M. (2000) Bridging space over time: Global virtual team dynamics and effectiveness. *Organization Science*, 11, 473–492.

Miller, D. L. (2001) Reexamining teamwork KSAs and team performance. *Small Group Research*, 32, 745–766.

Miller, D. L., Young, P., Kleinman, D. & Serfaty, D. (1998) *Distributed dynamic decision-making simulation: Phase I. Release notes and user's manual.* Woburn, MA: Aptima.

Mischel, W. (2004) Toward an integrative science of the person. *Annual Review of Psychology*, 55, 1–22.

Montoya-Weiss, M. M., Massey, A. P. & Song, M. (2001) Getting it together: Temporal coordination and conflict management in global virtual teams. *Academy of Management Journal*, 44, 1251–1262.

Münzer, S. & Holmer, T. (2009) Bridging the gap between media synchronicity and task performance: Effects of media characteristics on process variables and task performance indicators in an information pooling task. *Communication Research*, 36, 76–103.

Newman, L. V. (2005) Building effective virtual teams using selection interviews and peer assessments. *18th Annual Conference on Distance Teaching and Learning, University of Wisconsin.*

Perry, G. (2008) Virtual teams now a reality. Retrieved January 12, 2010 from www.pr.com/press-release/103409 .

Reuters (2010) Cisco expected to unveil affordable telepresence. Retrieved December 22, 2010 from www.channelinsider.com/c/a/Cisco/Cisco-Expected-to-Unveil-Affordable-Telepresence-361710/

Rice, R. E. (1992) Task analyzability, use of new media, and effectiveness: A multi-site exploration of media richness. *Organization Science*, 3, 475–500.

Rocco, E. (1998) Trust breaks down in electronic contexts but can be repaired by some initial face-to-face contact. *Proceedings of ACM CHI Conference on Human Factor in Computing Systems*. New York: ACM Press, pp. 496–502.

Sackett, P. R., Zedeck, S. & Fogli, L. (1988) Relations between measures of typical and maximum job performance. *Journal of Applied Psychology*, 73, 482–486.

Schmidt, F. L. & Hunter, J. E. (1998) The validity and utility of selection methods in personnel psychology: Practical and theoretical implications of 85 years of research findings. *Psychological Bulletin*, 124, 262–274.

Shapiro, D. L., Kirkman, B. L. & Courtney, H. G. (2007) Perceived causes and solutions of the translation problem in management research. *Academy of Management Journal*, 50, 249–266.

Shin, Y. (2004) A person-environment fit model for virtual organizations. *Journal of Management*, 30, 725–743.

Siebdraht, F., Hoegl, M. & Ernst, H. (2009) How to manage virtual teams. *MIT Sloan Management Review*, 50, 63–68.

Steege, T. (2003) *How mature are your virtual team processes*. Wayne, PA: Transformations Strategies.

Stevens, M. J. & Campion, M. A. (1994) The knowledge, skill, and ability requirements for teamwork: Implications for human resource management. *Journal of Management*, 20, 503–530.

Su, N. M. & Mark, G. (2008) Communication chains and multitasking. *Proceedings of the ACM Conference on Human Factors in Computing Systems, Italy*, pp. 83–92.

Trevino, L. K., Lengel, R. K. & Daft, R. L. (1987) Media symbolism, media richness and media choice in organizations. *Communication Research*, 14, 553–574.

Tuckman, B. W. (1965) Developmental sequence in small groups. *Psychological Bulletin*, 63, 384–399.

Van Knippenberg, D. & Schippers, M. C. (2007) Work group diversity. *Annual Review of Psychology*, 58, 515–541.

Viswesvaran, C., Ones, D. S. & Schmidt, F. L. (1996) Comparative analysis of the reliability of job performance ratings. *Journal of Applied Psychology*, 81, 557–574.

Wasson, C. (2004) Multitasking in virtual meetings. *Human Resource Planning*, 27, 47–60.

Wilson, J. M., Straus, S. G. & McEvily, B. (2006) All in due time: The development of trust in computer-mediated and face-to-face teams. *Organizational Behavior and Human Decision Processes*, 99, 16–33.

Part 2
Gaming and online tests

6 Games-work interaction

The beneficial impact of computer games on work behaviors

Despoina Xanthopoulou and Savvas Papagiannidis

What do computer games have to do with how individuals function at work? These two activities seem unrelated at first, particularly if one considers the stereotypical player profile, who is male, relatively young, and a socially maladapted person. Contrary to this stereotypical view, recent studies on massively multiplayer online role-playing games (MMORPGs; Yee, 2006c; Williams, Yee & Caplan, 2008) suggest that the largest concentration of gamers are people in their 30s, who are highly educated, mainly male (80%), and who spend about 25 hours per week playing. Importantly, about half of them are employed full-time. These findings suggest that a significant number of employees spend a great deal of their time after work on online games. The increasing popularity of online games as a leisure activity of the members of the workforce emphasizes the importance of examining the potential impact of games on players' behavior at work.

The central aim of this chapter is to analyze the interplay between online games and work in determining employee behavior and job performance. We choose to focus on online games and not other forms of computer or traditional (e.g. chess) games, because these seem to be extremely popular and influential among workers (Reeves, Malone & O' Driscoll, 2008). Online games that are developed in three-dimensional, virtual spaces constitute an immersive environment that may highly resemble a real-life environment. Consequently, online games can potentially exert a stronger impact on real-life behaviors than more traditional games, which explains the focus of the present chapter.

We propose two parallel psychological processes that are initiated by online gaming as a leisure activity during non-working hours. The first process suggests that the environment of online games makes it possible to manifest and practice certain behaviors that may be transferred to the real work environment. We integrate psychological spillover models (Edwards & Rothbard, 2000; Westman, 2001) and game literature (Yee & Bailenson, 2007) in order to explain how behaviors that are exerted in the game (active learning, leadership, and collaboration) may spill over directly or indirectly to the work domain, and impact on employee performance. In this context, the role of specific mediators (e.g. self-efficacy) and moderators (e.g. game performance) is discussed. According to the second process, spending time after work on playing games online may help employees to recover from work and recharge their batteries. Specific leisure activities (e.g. physical or social activities) have been found to contribute to employee recovery (Sonnentag & Natter, 2004; Rook & Zijlstra, 2006). Online games are often promoted as virtual environments, where users have unique experiences that allow them to escape after coming home from work (Yee, 2006b). Nevertheless, games have not been previously considered as an activity that may help employees to distance themselves from work, and return to their base-line energy levels. This chapter extends this line of reasoning by considering online gaming as a recovery activity that contributes to employee unwinding from work-related demands, and consequently to optimal functioning at work.

The main purpose of this chapter is to put together an overall theoretical framework that explains the potential favorable impact of online games for employees. Despite the fact that the games-to-work spillover process and the recovery process concern different psychological mechanisms, we focus on these because they are significant for understanding work-related behaviors. Taking time spent on online games as a starting point, we discuss how these two processes evolve and interrelate in explaining employee well-being and enhanced performance.

By focusing on games-to-work facilitation, we do not intend to question the potential detrimental effects of excessive gaming, which may cause difficulties with managing one's off-game life (Caplan, Williams & Yee, 2009). Increased participation in games was found to relate positively to violent and aggressive thoughts, feelings and behavioral tendencies, while it was also found to decrease prosocial behavior (Anderson & Bushman, 2001). Although male adolescents are at higher risk of developing addictions, game addiction is not unique to any particular demographic of users (King, Delfabbro & Griffiths, 2010a). The most typical characteristics of game addiction are psychological withdrawal symptoms (e.g. irritability, frustration), lack of sleep, and problems in social life (Charlton & Danforth, 2007). Next to these, Shotton (1989) in her seminal work on computer dependency found that extreme computer use may result in strain injuries or muscle pains, which can be problematic for employees).

There is a large body of research on the negative effects of computer games for individuals that could harm – among others – their functioning at work. If one considers the variety of online games, it is evident that games have the potential to both psychologically harm and benefit players (Ryan, Rigby & Przybylski, 2006). Despite the fact that the literature on the negative effects of games is quite rich, the theorizing on potential positive effects of gaming is scarce (cf. King *et al.*, 2010a). As such, in this chapter we focus solely on the beneficial impact of online games on employee behavior, over and above their addictive potential. That is, the theoretical assumptions that we propose concern employees who play games as a hobby and not in those who play instead of going to work or who work in virtual worlds. Related to this, in the study of Griffiths, Davies, and Chappell (2004), only 7.3% of the 452 adult players of *Everquest* reported that they sacrificed work or education in order to play.

We begin by introducing the reader into the world of metaverses (i.e. the electronic space that hosts online games). We present certain features of online games, as well as individuals' motivations in participating in online games. We explain the psychological mechanisms underlying the spillover and the recovery processes that may be initiated by online games as a leisure activity. The chapter ends with an overall discussion of the proposed theoretical framework for studying games-work facilitation.

Metaverses: extending our physical world

Technological advances have resulted in significant changes to our work and social environment, fundamentally changing the landscape we have got to know. Initially, this was reflected by the advent of the 'electronic space' which intertwined with the space and place of our physical world (Li, Whalley & Williams, 2001). The electronic space in the form of the Internet became the pervasive conduit for changes that significantly affected the way we live, work, communicate, learn, and play (Li, 2007). Actually, now, we have an even more complex landscape to which various metaverses have been added.

Metaverses are usually three-dimensional extensions of the 'traditional' electronic space. Whilst the electronic space is primarily a representation of the physical world, the virtual worlds are primarily computer-simulated, synthetic worlds that are more detached from the physical world, and some of them operate under very different rules (Li, Papagiannidis & Bourlakis, 2010). This does not imply that they are completely detached, which is why we refer to them as synthetic to highlight that they are products of human actions (Malaby, 2006). Castronova's (2005) analogy of the porous membrane is a vivid way of presenting this. Accordingly, 'we find human society on either side of the membrane, and since society is the ultimate locus of validation for all of our important shared notions – value, fact, emotion, meaning – we will find shared notions on either side as well' (pp. 147–148). To an extent, the membrane separates the real from the virtual space, but this separation does not confine actions and reactions within the boundaries of each space. Lehdonvirta (2010) concludes that several caveats have to be made when choosing to view online games as virtual worlds standing apart from 'the real world.' For instance, the space the virtual world occupies is not clearly distinguishable: its inhabitants' identities cannot be equated with avatars (i.e. the representation of the user in the virtual world); the social relationships are not bounded by its limits; the outside norms and institutions regulate behavior within it, while its economies, laws and politics are shaped by outside processes.

The above illustrates how blurred the boundaries are, and as a result how difficult it is to disentangle what is 'virtual' and what is 'real.' Thus, the real and the virtual are strongly interconnected and events in one space can affect the other. Put differently, behavior in one space is not just a function of the space's characteristics and an avatar's identity, but also a function of factors originating from other spaces, and vice versa. In this chapter, we solely focus on the impact of online games on behaviors outside the game membrane, namely in the work context. Nevertheless, it is evident that the reverse is also possible. In order to understand how games facilitate real work, it is important first to discuss why online games are so attractive, and what the motives of players are.

Online games: features and players' motivations

Metaverses are often wrongly considered just as games. It may be the case that they do host the MMORPGs and that their first end-goal is typically to provide entertainment. However, such a simplistic approach ignores their rich and diverse features, which often change dramatically from case to case. For example, one may slay dragons in *War of Warcraft*, before entering *Second Life* to socialize and indulge in virtual purchases. Once the user craves more action again, he or she could go back to fighting or trading in *Star Wars Galaxies* or *Entropia Universe*. Online games, even those 'simple' ones that a user may play on social networking sites, support multi-user interactions. Users by definition assume a role while playing and immersion may be the result of the engagement with the game. Metaverses enable full immersion and typically do not confine the user's behavior. There may be a goal, but how the user achieves this goal is up to the user to decide. This suggests that there is a much wider scope for decision making and identity development of the avatar, and subsequently of the user behind the avatar. As Dickey (2007) emphasizes, MMORPGs are open-ended environments: there is no end which players strive to achieve, and there is not only one way to play the game, while the feedback that is provided allows players to improve constantly. In short, the design of online games allows players choice, collaboration, challenge, achievement and a continuous opportunity to progress and learn.

Following King, Delfabbro, and Griffiths' (2010b) taxonomy of video games, the main characteristics of online games can be distinguished as a) social (e.g. communication and social networking); b) manipulation and control (i.e. the way the player can interact with and control in-game properties that create a sense of mastery over the game); c) narrative and identity (i.c. the opportunity to take on an identity and become a part of a storytelling experience); d) reward and punishment (i.e. the way in which the gamers are reinforced for skillful play and punished for losing); and e) presentation (i.e. the looks and sounds of the game). In the study of Wood, Griffiths, Chappell, and Davies (2004), 76% of the 382 self-selected video game players reported that 'exploring new areas' was the most important game feature for them. Also, 68.1% recognized 'skill development,' 67.1% 'sophisticated artificial intelligence interactions', 65.3% 'finding things,' and 45.4% 'solving time-limited problems' as important game characteristics.

Taking into account the main features of online games, the motivation for entering each metaverse may differ from user to user. Bartle (1996) recognized the *Achievers*, who are motivated by setting goals and working vigorously to meet them, the *Explorers*, whose drive is to find as much as they can about the world they have entered and how it works, and the *Socializers*, who want to role-play, meet and interact with other players. In a similar vein, Yee's (2006a) survey among 30000 MMORPG players over a three-year period revealed a five-factor model of user motivation. The relationship factor refers to users' desire to interact with others and to form meaningful and supportive relationships. The achievement factor measures the desire to become powerful through the achievement of in-game goals, while the manipulation factor refers to how inclined a user is to manipulate the game environment for his/her personal gains and satisfaction. The immersion factor refers to the enjoyment provided by being in a fantasy world, and finally the escapism factor concerns being in the virtual environment in an attempt to forget about and escape from real-life stress and problems.

The drive to enter a specific online game seems to resemble the needs that people seek to fulfill with their real-life employment. For instance, Van den Broeck, Vansteenkiste, de Witte, and Lens (2008) applied Deci and Ryan's (1985) self-determination theory (SDT), and showed that occupations that satisfy employees' basic psychological needs for autonomy (i.e. freely chosen and volitional behavior), competence (i.e. to feel effective when pursuing activities), and relatedness (i.e. human striving for close and meaningful relationships and the feeling of belonging), are intrinsically motivating and enhance employee well-being. Ryan and colleagues (2006) applied SDT in explaining player motivation in (video and online) gaming contexts. They hypothesized and showed that games are primarily motivating to the extent that they satisfy gamers' needs of autonomy, competence and relatedness. Namely, it is the satisfaction of basic psychological needs that makes gaming 'fun.' Given that participation in games is nearly always voluntary, in-game autonomy is typically high. The need for competence is also likely to be satisfied, because online gaming provides ongoing challenges and immediate performance feedback. Finally, online gaming generates the feeling of connectedness in players, because success in MMORPGs by definition requires active and constant interaction with others.

The roles and identities assumed in each game, as well as gamers' motivations, call for certain skills that the user must possess, as well as certain behaviors that need to be manifested in order to progress and become successful in the game (Bartle, 1996). For example, if a player wants to organize and lead a clan of warriors in order to collaboratively meet a target, he or she should be able to work effectively with other players, and communicate clear goals to them. Similarly, players should possess strong negotiation skills during trading agreements with other players, who may have different motives and overall strategies. These examples suggest that many of the skills and behaviors that are common in online games are not fundamentally different from skills and behaviors manifested in real work environments. This is particularly true for metaverses that have an embedded economic model, as many of the user activities are often business oriented (e.g. managing and leading, recruiting players, organizing production, transacting, etc.).

The similarity between the motives and activities pursued in metaverses and in real work environments together with Castronova's (2005) assumption that virtual spaces may have significant consequences because events inside and outside them cannot be isolated from one another, imply that in-game behaviors may impact on work. The avatars have their own human and social capital associated with them (Papagiannidis, Bourlakis & Li, 2008), which can be developed further in the game, potentially affecting the user's real human and occupational capital. In this context, we propose that certain behaviors that are manifested and developed by players in the game may spill over to their real occupational context.

Spillover from online games to work

Spillover takes place when experiences in one life domain are transferred to another life domain, generating similarities between domains (Edwards & Rothbard, 2000; Westman, 2001). Put differently, spillover is a within-person mechanism that links various areas of everyday life in a way that psychological states and their behavioral manifestations transfer from one domain to another. In this chapter, we are interested in positive spillover, namely the transfer of behaviors from games to work that promote role performance.

Edwards and Rothbard (2000) suggest that behavioral spillover is either direct or indirect. In the first case, behaviors in one domain (e.g. games) directly influence behaviors in another domain (e.g. work) in the form of mimicking. This is the case when role requirements in the two domains are highly similar. In the case of indirect spillover, behaviors in one life domain influence behaviors in other life domains because they become ingrained as habits, scripts or styles. Spillover is most likely to take place when both conditions apply: when skills and behaviors have been internalized and there is similarity across domains (Edwards & Rothbard, 2000). Finally, spillover can be unintentional for habitual behaviors or intentional, when the person thinks that certain behaviors may help him/her to meet role expectations in another life domain. Taking into consideration the main features of online games, it could be argued that the spillover of in-game behaviors to work can occur, first because there is a substantial similarity in terms of the activities undertaken across domains (e.g. trying to fulfill collaboratively set goals), and secondly because online games facilitate continuous practicing of behaviors. As a result, these may easily become habitual, and may be applied to work if they are perceived to facilitate successes.

The literature on training transfer suggests that small differences in one domain may lead to negative transfer, because the behaviors that are learned in the first domain are of no use in the other domain (Sanders, 1998). However, the central argument that supports the game-to-work positive spillover is that in-game and work tasks and behaviors are highly similar. More specifically, all three conditions that according to Sanders are critical for a successful transfer apply. First, both game and work environments require the same type of skills. For example, interacting with other individuals in order to decide upon a strategy change is a common situation both in games and at work, and requires the same type of skills, irrespective of the environment. The second issue, according to Sanders, concerns the extent to which there are similar stimuli-response sequences in both environments. The study of Ryan and colleagues (2006) suggests that this is the case. Their findings showed that psychological theories that have been developed in order to explain specific S-R relationships at work are successful in explaining the same relationships in game environments. Finally, the third concern relates to the prediction of performance, which may be problematic because in any context performance is determined both by intentions and by random factors. To counteract this concern, it is important to note that simulation from game to work is likely to take place because in both contexts performance is determined by similar contextual (e.g. support) and personal (e.g. self-efficacy) factors, while random effects are likely to occur. One needs to keep in mind, that virtual worlds are not experimental spaces, where exogenous variables are easily controlled for.

The games-to-work spillover is further explained by Yee and Bailenson's (2007) Proteus effect. Following Bem's (1972) self-perception theory (which states that people infer their own attitudes from observing their behavior as an outsider), these authors suggested that users make inferences about their expected states based on their avatars' characteristics and then conform to these expected behaviors (see also Yee, Bailenson & Ducheneaut, 2009). To test this proposition, Yee and Bailenson performed a series of experimental studies and showed that individuals are likely to alter their behavior in order to resemble that of their avatar. For instance, participants with taller avatars negotiated more aggressively with a confederate than users with shorter avatars, while participants given taller avatars negotiated more aggressively in subsequent face-to-face interactions as well (see Yee *et al.*, 2009).

It is clear from the above that in-game behaviors can spill over into other life domains. We will discuss game-to-work spillover with regard to three specific behaviors that are commonly manifested in online games: active learning, leadership, and collaboration. Although these are not the only behaviors that may be transferred from games to work, they correspond to three of the main motives for gaming. Active learning satisfies individuals' need to explore. Effective leadership satisfies the need to achieve goals, while collaboration satisfies players' need to socialize with others. Also, these behaviors contribute to optimal performance both in the game and at work.

Active Learning refers to behaviors that offer mastery experiences of competence and proficiency, which challenge individuals without overtaxing them (Sonnentag & Fritz, 2007). Online games promote active learning in various ways. First, the look and characteristics of the virtual world enhance several aspects of visual processing, which may contribute significantly to active learning by making users more sensitive to external stimuli. Green and Bavelier (2006, 2007) showed that action gaming enhances visuospatial attention throughout the visual field (i.e. gamers exhibited an increase in attentional resources), as well as spatial resolution. Second, online games are open-ended environments, where users face many different choices and challenges (Dickey, 2007). For example, a player may repeat the same mission by adopting different strategies – based on the feedback received and the past knowledge – until the task is completed successfully. According to Dickey, declarative knowledge may be practiced in games that require a player to help another player (i.e. by teaching or assisting others), while procedural knowledge may be enhanced in games where players collect items from different places, manipulate these items and then deliver them in a different form. Finally, games, where the player has to defeat a character, provide the opportunity to plan actively and enhance strategic knowledge.

Garris, Ahlers, and Driskell's (2002) input-process-output game model helps understanding the games-work spillover of active learning. Online games trigger a cycle that incorporates user judgments or reactions (e.g. interest), user behaviors (e.g. active search for information or task persistence), and system feedback. This cycle enhances users' engagement in the game, which results in specific learning outcomes. The debriefing process that is embedded in the game (i.e. analysis of events that occur in the game, recognition of mistakes and corrective actions) allows learning to occur. This acquired knowledge is linked to knowledge and behavior in the real world, and particularly to those areas of life in which this knowledge is useful. Thus, online gamers, when facing challenging situations at work, are likely to apply similar active learning behaviors that have been practiced in games (e.g. make better use of their performance feedback or be more analytical). This may have additional beneficial outcomes for the employee, since general cognitive ability and job knowledge have been found to relate positively to job performance (for a review see Hunter, 1986).

Leadership is practiced in online games, even by players who do not have an official leadership role. Players often face organizational and strategic challenges that require users to engage in leadership roles such as creating clans, recruiting new players, assessing, motivating, encouraging loyalty, rewarding talented team members, setting missions and goals for the future, organizing resources, and analyzing constantly changing and often incomplete data in order to make decisions (Yee, 2006 a; 2006c). Reeves *et al.* (2008) called MMORPGs online labs for leadership, implying that game elements can make leadership easier. In their study among 135 employees who had led both business teams and teams in MMORPGs, the majority of participants reported that factors within the online games could enhance leadership effectiveness in an organization. Also, half of them said that playing games improved their real-world leadership capabilities. Similarly, in Yee's (2006a) cross-sectional survey, 10% of the participants reported that they learned a lot about motivating team members, persuading others, and becoming better leaders at work while playing.

Taking into account that game and work environments share similar qualities, and that activities in MMORPGs resemble activities in occupational settings, we argue that effective leadership in the game may be transferred to work as a habitual behavior that is expressed under similar situational cues (e.g. when trying to reach a goal; Edwards & Rothbard, 2000). To test this hypothesis, we have performed a two-wave study with a one-month interval, and recruited 79 employees who were also active MMORPGs players (Xanthopoulou & Papagiannidis, 2012). Analyses showed that those individuals, who acted in a transformational manner (e.g. encouraged and motivated their game mates, set clear goals and plans for the future) in the game, reported acting in a transformational manner at work, one month later. Employees may benefit further from behaving as effective leaders at work. Empirical studies have shown that leaders who, for instance, clarify expectations and rewards when these expectations are met are not only more effective, but also perform better (for a meta-analysis see, Judge & Piccolo, 2004).

Collaboration in the game relates strongly to exercising effective leadership. In online games, players typically get to collaborate closely in order to accomplish tasks and reach goals, while most often they join long-term associations, the so-called 'guilds.' Within these guilds, players interact intensively, create new relationships and manage existing ones (Caplan, Williams & Yee, 2009). Players need each other to survive and progress in the game, thus collaboration becomes an imperative course of action. As Yee (2006c) explains, in battle-oriented games, users form groups of 4–8 players to overcome challenges. These groups are composed of players with a balanced combination of roles, who must communicate effectively following a predetermined group strategy. During a crisis situation, players should communicate opinions and decisions (over typed chat) that determine the group performance. Further, in games like *Star War Galaxies,* where production and transactions of goods are user-driven, players need to communicate effectively and develop their own product strategy, which feels 'more like a second job than entertainment' (Yee, 2006c, p. 68).

Due to the substantial similarity among the roles that are assumed in MMORPGs and the roles individuals need to fulfill as members of the workforce, a spillover of collaborative behaviors is likely to take place. Collaborative systems promote trust, cohesion, and mutually supportive behaviors among the team members, which consequently facilitates performance (Ivancevich & Matteson, 1999). Based on SDT (Deci & Ryan, 1985), we further argue that collaboration satisfies individuals' need for belonging, and as a result intrinsic motivation is enhanced and performance requirements are met.

Potential moderators of the spillover process

Active learning, leadership and collaboration are common in-game behaviors that may spill over directly to work. The strength of this spillover depends on the type of game. For instance, the spillover of collaboration and leadership will be stronger in games that promote these behaviors, such as *War of Warcraft* or *Everquest*. Next to this, there are other factors that may boost the spillover effect of learning, leadership and collaboration from games to work. Two of these factors are game performance and flow in the game.

We propose that when in-game behaviors co-occur with enhanced performance in the game, the behavioral spillover will be stronger. In contrast, when in-game behaviors coexist with bad performance, spillover is not likely to occur. That is, individuals are more likely to transfer in-game behaviors to work, when these behaviors are combined with successes. This is quite possible because work is a context where effectiveness is highly significant. In line with the SDT (Deci & Ryan, 1985), outperforming in the game suggests that the user has satisfied his/her need to be competent. When certain behaviors like collaboration or active learning are combined with the satisfaction of basic needs, these behaviors are valued, and thus people tend to mimic them outside the game environment. Indeed, the results of the 2-wave study among employees who were active gamers showed that game performance moderated the spillover of active learning and transformational leadership from online games to work over the period of one month (Xanthopoulou & Papagiannidis, 2012). Specifically, it was particularly under conditions of enhanced game performance that learning and leadership behaviors were transferred to work. Interestingly, active learning behaviors combined with bad game performance led to avoiding these behaviors at work.

Flow while playing may also moderate the spillover of active learning, leadership, and collaboration from games to work. According to Csikszentmihalyi (1975), flow is the 'holistic sensation that people feel when they act with total involvement' (p. 4). The flow experience is characterized by three core elements: enjoyment (i.e. feelings of happiness), total absorption in the activity (i.e. the feeling that 'time flies'), and intrinsic motivation (i.e. activities are undertaken regardless of external rewards or costs; Bakker, 2008). As such, flow may be experienced during any activity in everyday life, including games. Indeed, Hsu and Lu (2004) defined in-game flow as 'an extremely enjoyable experience, where an individual engages in an on-line game activity with total involvement, enjoyment, control, concentration and intrinsic interest' (p. 857). According to Chen, Wigand, and Nilan (1999), in order for a person to experience flow online, the activity should provide immediate feedback, should offer clear rules and goals to pursue, should provoke enough complexity (which should not be easily exhausted), and must create dynamic challenges. Taking into account the main features of MMORPGs it is evident that they satisfy all of these prerequisite conditions.

We suggest that being in flow while playing facilitates the positive spillover from games to work. According to Fredrickson's (2001) broaden-and-build theory, positive affective states share the ability to *broaden* people's momentary thought-action repertoires and *build* their enduring personal resources. Hence, flow, as a peak affective experiential state, *broadens* players' thought-action repertoires by prompting exploratory behaviors, such as flexibility and/or creativity. The state of flow activates players to make use of those features in the game that allow them to learn new things, which may strengthen the transfer of such active behaviors outside the game membrane. Similarly, those gamers who are high (vs. low) in flow *build* accurate maps of what is good or threatening in the environment, which helps them manage any challenges. Thus, when in a state of flow, players are better able to act in a collaborative manner or to motivate others in the game, which makes the spillover of these behaviors to real life more likely.

Potential mediators of the spillover process

We have explained the direct spillover from games to work, as well as potential moderators that may boost this spillover effect. What about the indirect spillover process? Which psychological states transfer behaviors exerted in the game to work? According to Edwards and Rothbard (2000), in the case of indirect spillover, behavioral manifestations in one domain become internalized as habits or behavioral styles, and in turn are transferred to other domains. In what follows, we discuss two mechanisms that may be of significance in explaining the games-work spillover: game performance, and self-efficacy.

According to Festinger (1942), transfer of motivation takes place in situations where motivational processes and outcomes on one task determine a subsequent, distinct task. In this context, Quintela and Donovan (2008) suggested that motivational processes in one task are affected by previous successes or failures in a distinct, yet similar task. Within this theoretical framework, we suggest that meeting performance goals in the game may be the mediating mechanism that explains games-to-work spillover. Players who actively look for new knowledge and experiences in the game, who set clear goals, motivate others, and work collaboratively towards these goals, are likely to perform well in the game because they are intrinsically motivated (Dickey, 2007). As a result, these behaviors spill over to other areas of life when facing similar challenges, because they are found to be successful.

Self-efficacy (i.e. the belief that one has what it takes to control one's environment effectively, Bandura, 1997) may be enhanced – among other things – through the enactment of mastery experiences. By now it is clear that the virtual environments of online games facilitate learning. Learning new things, effectively collaborating with and motivating others to reach common goals in the game are likely to increase gamers' self-efficacy beliefs. When the users are aware of all aspects and procedures of a specific virtual environment, they are more likely to believe themselves to be able to control and impact upon this environment successfully. Thus, active learning, leadership and collaboration are considered as effective behaviors in a highly demanding environment because they contribute significantly to controlling this environment. As a result, these behaviors are likely to be developed in a similar, and equally demanding environment, that of work. Put differently, game-related self-efficacy may be the mechanism that shows to users that certain in-game behaviors contribute to controlling the environment, and consequently that these should be applied to other areas of life. Hence, the user will try to learn all aspects and procedures in his/her real life environment as an attempt to control this environment better. This suggestion is in line with the theory of planned behavior (Ajzen, 1991), where perceived behavioral control predicts behavior both directly and indirectly, via intention.

Up to this point, we have explained how certain beneficial in-game behaviors may spill over (directly or indirectly) to the real work life of an employee, and consequently benefit his/her job performance. Nevertheless, this positive spillover process is not the only mechanism that explains how online games may benefit employee behavior at work. In what follows, we will discuss online games as facilitators of recovery from work-related demands.

Online games as recovery experiences

Seen as an entertaining activity that may be pursued during leisure hours, we argue that online games may contribute to employee recovery from work. According to Meijman and Mulder's (1998) effort-recovery model, the required energy expenditure during work depletes employees' emotional and energy resources and results in feelings of fatigue at the end of the working day. During leisure hours, employees need to take a rest from their work-related demands, in order to replenish their resource reservoir (Zijlstra & Sonnentag, 2006). Recovery is the process during which used-up resources are refilled, and employees' functional systems return to baseline (Meijman & Mulder, 1998; Sonnentag & Fritz, 2007).

Lack of recovery on a daily basis has detrimental effects on employee well-being and job performance (for a review, Demerouti, Bakker, Geurts & Taris, 2009). Inadequate or incomplete recovery may result in fatigue accumulation, and consequently in physical and psychological complaints (e.g. chronic fatigue). Additionally, employees' inability to replenish the resource reservoir may prevent them from reaching performance standards. In contrast, a state of enhanced well-being after successful recovery has been found to relate positively to various work behaviors including engagement and proactive behavior (Sonnentag, 2003). Further, Binnewies, Sonnentag, and Mojza (2009a) found that employees who started a new workday feeling recovered reported higher task performance, personal initiative, and organizational citizenship behavior (i.e. behavior that is not directly recognized by the formal reward system, but which promotes organizational effectiveness; Organ, 1988). Moreover, Binnewies, Sonnentag, and Mojza (2009b) in a longitudinal study with an interval of 6 months showed that employees who recovered during leisure time manifested better task performance over time.

The recovery process relates closely to the type of activities pursued during non-working hours. For instance, Sonnentag (2001) in her study among Dutch teachers found that low-effort social and physical activities pursued after work related positively to well-being before going to sleep. In a similar vein, the diary study of Rook and Zijlstra (2006) found that spending time on physical activities after work is beneficial for recovery. According to Hobfoll's (1998) conservation of resources theory, in order to restore used-up resources, one needs to invest in other available resources. Thus, the type of resources that are invested during leisure activities determines the level of recovery. Consequently, recovery is more likely to occur when leisure activities do not require resources similar to that of work-related activities.

In this context, it is difficult to establish how online games facilitate employee recovery. Considering that very often the activities pursued in the game closely resemble work-related activities, one may argue that MMORPGs are more likely to inhibit rather than promote recovery and work-related well-being. Both environments are often characterized by the same types of demands, and thus they require the investment of similar types of resources. For example, if one needs to invest cognitive resources in order to solve a difficult problem at work, one is unlikely to recover when playing an online game that requires one to spend cognitive resources to solve a difficult problem in the virtual world. In this context, as Yee (2006b) states MMORPGs 'are advertised as worlds to escape to after coming home from work, but they too make us work and burn us out' (p. 70).

Although this may be true, we argue that the negative consequences of online games for employee recovery are more likely to take place under two specific circumstances: total addiction to games (which falls outside of the scope of this chapter), and individually-oriented, competitive games. Such games may enhance feelings of antagonism in individuals, which change the core of the game that is to be an entertaining activity. In contrast, virtual environments that facilitate sociability or cooperation are more likely to replenish users' resources and be beneficial for recovery. In this context, Bakker and Gorgievsky (2010) conducted a diary study among 41 employees who were also enthusiastic gamers. It was hypothesized that gaming may call upon the same functional systems as work, and thus playing competitive (vs. cooperative) games in the evening relates nega-tively to the following morning's recovery and well-being, and on next day's flow at work. Their results showed that the type of game creates differential effects on recovery. Competitive games were found to drain users' energy and undermine recovery and flow at work. In contrast, cooperative games facilitated day-to-day recovery. This study emphasizes that certain types of games may actually enhance and not overtax employee well-being.

Recently, recovery researchers suggested that the type of activity that employ-ees engage in is not the most important for recovery. Rather, the degree to which this activity contributes to individuals' recovery experiences is much more crucial. Sonnentag and Fritz (2007) recognize four recovery experiences: psycho-logical detachment from work, relaxation, mastery, and control. *Psychological detachment* refers to being physically and mentally away from work or switching off from work. Detachment implies that one is taking a break – physically and psychologically – from work-related demands. *Relaxation* is a state of low acti-vation and enhanced positive affect that results from deliberately chosen activities. The significance of relaxation activities for recovery lies in the fact that these limit the prolonged activation of the functional system and undo the effects of negative emotional states. *Mastery experiences* (e.g. taking a language course) concern activities that take attention away from the job because they offer oppor-tunities to learn new things and to face new challenges. Finally, being in *control* of your time implies that you may spend your time freely, which, consequently, may result in gaining additional resources.

We argue that online games have certain functions that contribute to recovery experiences. Despite the fact that for some authors problematic online gaming is explained by the need of players to be immersed in the real world and escape from their real life problems in an attempt to alleviate negative moods (e.g. to relieve stress; Caplan *et al.*, 2009), the opportunity to forget about the real-world prob-lems may be actually profitable, if considered in relation to the recovery process. Online games offer an environment that helps users to forget about their real-life worries and relax either by exploring the virtual world or by socializing with their online co-players. In the study of Yee (2006c), a significant number of players reported that MMORPGs help them to temporarily avoid, forget about, and escape from real-life stress and problems. The fact that there are no external limi-tations to the users' behavior, while certain activities can be very easily pursued in the game, though these may not even be possible in real life (e.g. flying), makes games extremely entertaining environments that may help them detach from work and recover.

Furthermore, online games contribute to recovery because they offer mastery experiences to users. In virtual environments, players have the opportunity to learn new things or face new challenges. For instance, entering a virtual world, where it is possible to fly from one place in the world to another and get to know different civilizations, may enhance recovery via mastery. As Sonnentag and Fritz (2007) point out, despite the fact that mastery experiences are not effortless (i.e. they may put additional demands on individuals), they contribute to recovery because they help employees to gain additional resources (e.g. to acquire new skills and competences, or enhance positive moods). Finally, the fact that in MMORPGs failure to fulfill a goal is seen more as a learning opportunity than anything else strengthens their role as recovery activities that enhance mastery experiences. Indeed, we have conducted a study among 299 employees who were active gamers in their free time (with a particular preference for achievement-oriented games) which showed that time spent on MMORPGs related positively to mastery experiences in the game (Xanthopoulou & Papagiannidis, 2009). Interestingly, it was not time spent on the game that related positively to psychological detachment and relaxation, but flow in the game. Being in flow while playing related positively both to psychological detachment and relaxation. These findings underline the significance of the quality of the leisure activity for recovery.

Online games and recovery: the moderation of in-game flow

As explained above, the type of MMORPG may determine the degree to which the time spent on online games results in recovery experiences. Another, psychological, factor that may function as a moderator is flow in the game. Despite the fact that being in flow may increase the time spent on games, flow is not related to game addiction, which may be detrimental for recovery. Wan and Chiou (2006) in their studies among Taiwanese online gamers found that flow related negatively to addictive inclination, while addicts' flow state was significantly lower than non-addicts. Being in flow while playing means that one enjoys the activity, while being addicted in gaming means that one is irritated and frustrated when not playing (see also, Lafrenière, Vallerand, Donahue & Lavigne, 2009).

When flow is high (vs. low), gamers live an extremely enjoyable experience (Hsu & Lu, 2004). When MMORPG players engage in an online activity with total involvement, control, concentration and intrinsic interest, the time spent on the game is more likely to boost recovery experiences like psychological detachment or mastery. When gamers are totally involved, they are more likely to spend their time in MMORPGs engaging in learning activities that help them recover from work-related demands. Similarly, time spent on online games combined with positive feelings of enjoyment is more likely to increase relaxation in the game, because non-working hours are spent easily without many complications. In any case, flow in the game seems to boost the recovery potential of MMORPGs, which consequently may enhance employee well-being (e.g. energy) before going to bed and performance the next day at work.

Discussion and practical implications

The main purpose of this chapter was to put forward an overall theoretical framework to examine games-to-work facilitation. To this end, we have analyzed two parallel processes that may be initiated by playing online games and may contribute to employees' optimal functioning at work. These processes are depicted on Figure 6.1.

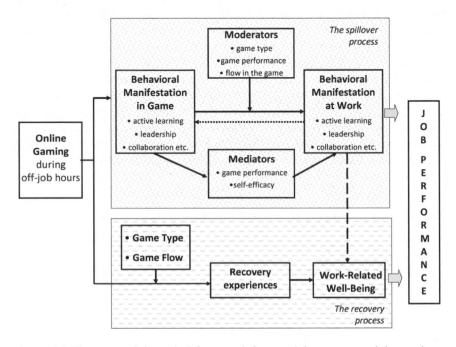

Figure 6.1 The proposed theoretical framework for examining games-work interaction

According to the spillover process, active learning, leadership and collaborative behaviors that are commonly manifested in online games may be transferred – directly or indirectly (via game performance and/or self-efficacy) – to work, and in turn enhance job performance. This spillover effect is particularly strong for games that facilitate these behaviors, and under conditions of enhanced game performance and flow in the game. According to the recovery process, spending non-working time on online games may initiate recovery experiences (e.g. psychological detachment, mastery), which may impact on individuals' job performance via the enhancement of employee well-being. Employees who are immersed in the world of games after work are likely to detach themselves from work-related demands, acquire new knowledge and experience new things. Put differently, what people do in the game may foster their recovery experiences. As a result, their fatigue levels return to base-line and vigor is increased while resources are refilled (Meijman & Mulder, 1996). This is particularly the case for cooperative games, and when gaming is combined with high levels of flow.

The model presented in Figure 6.1 suggests that either via the spillover of favorable behaviors or through the mechanism of recovery, online games may facilitate enhanced job performance. Despite evolving in parallel, these two processes may also interrelate in explaining work behaviors. Organizational psychology literature suggests that active learning, effective leadership, and collaboration relate to employee well-being. For instance, the job demands-control model (Karasek & Theorell, 1990) proposes that jobs that are designed to enhance active learning in employees protect them from strain and may enhance their well-being. Similarly, Arnold, Turner, Barling, Kelloway, and McKee (2007) in a series of studies found transformational leadership to relate to employee well-being (i.e. positive affect, and general health). Interestingly, this effect was mediated by the meaning that employees ascribe to their work. It may be argued that, when behaving in a transformational and cooperative manner or when learning new things at work, employees are more likely to perceive work as meaningful, which makes them feel capable of meeting their goals and, in turn, they outperform. The relationship between favorable behaviors and well-being is also depicted in Figure 6.1 (i.e. dotted lines connecting the two processes).

Furthermore, although our focus was on the path from games to work, it does not mean that the reverse is not possible. For instance, it could be argued that employees who encourage their colleagues to perform better or who are able to collaborate well in order to reach a work goal are likely to exert similar behaviors in the game. In other words, a continuous feedback loop between games and work may take place that may amplify the spillover phenomenon. This reciprocal effect is also depicted in Figure 6.1 (i.e. dotted lines in the spillover process). To this end, we propose that the use of advanced methodologies (e.g. repeated-measured or diaries) that allow capturing game and work episodes close to their occurrence may yield interesting insights into the bi-directional spillover process by recording the dynamic relationship between games and work.

From a practical point of view, our theoretical analysis suggests that the features of online games may prove useful for the flourishing of both employees and organizations, presupposing that playing games is not addictive. First, MMORPGs, when seen as an entertaining activity, may contribute to recovery by helping employees to be detached psychologically from work-related demands and by facilitating mastery. Second, the new generation of employees, which is actively occupied in online games, is likely to transfer game-influenced behaviors as the best ways to learn, lead or collaborate. In this context, Sharritt (2010) performed a qualitative analysis on how game interface designs may encourage real-life learning. He found that engagement and learning in the game is particularly enhanced when there is a proper balance between feelings of boredom and difficulty in interactions. Boredom or feelings of frustration in the game interface often led users to abandon in-game tasks. However, frustration during goal achievement often led to re-negotiation of in-game strategies, which indicates engagement. These findings suggest that certain features of online games could be adopted by organizations in an attempt to make work more motivating and fulfilling.

In a similar vein, Beck and Wade (2004) suggested that MMORPGs may be an effective way of developing business skills like bold but measured risk taking, multitasking abilities, and leadership skills. For instance, the British Open University tested whether Second Life and virtual role-play could be an effective alternative to real-life role play for staff development (Broadribb & Carter, 2009). An intervention was developed in Second Life that allowed participants to practice in giving and receiving feedback. Three groups were compared in three distinct types of skill practice: scriptwriting, traditional real-life role-play, and role-play in the virtual environment. In the 'virtual condition' each group used their avatar to provide feedback to another avatar that was controlled by a learning professional. Participants reported that Second Life helped them put theory into practice, and described this as a very motivational experience. Additionally, analyses revealed that all members of the virtual group showed an increase in their level of confidence in providing and receiving feedback.

However, the adoption of game practices in real world environments requires a change in organizational culture. As Reeves *et al.* (2008) correctly note, failure to achieve a goal is considered a learning experience in online games and allows 'reattempting with new knowledge' (p. 9). This is often an impossible practice in current organizational life. Perhaps the most important contribution of online games for organizations is the perception that errors are a natural, instructive part of the process towards goal achievement because they facilitate learning. In this context, it could be argued that games enhance participants' learning-goal orientation (Locke & Latham, 2002). Individuals high in learning-goal orientation seek challenging tasks and the opportunity to develop, which boosts their self-efficacy and contributes significantly to goal attainment and task performance.

Although this chapter offers a theoretical framework to test the beneficial impact of games on work behaviors, it is not an extensive analysis of all the potential ways that online games may facilitate work-related behaviors. Nevertheless, we do hope that it will constitute an inspiring context to guide researchers in the – still unexplored – area of the interplay between virtual game environments and real work experiences.

References

Ajzen, I. (1991) The theory of planned behavior. *Organizational Behavior and Human Decision Processes*, 50, 179–211.

Anderson, C. A. & Bushman, B. J. (2001) Effects of violent video games on aggressive behavior, aggressive cognition, aggressive affect, physiological arousal and prosocial behavior: A meta-analytic review of the scientific literature. *Psychological Science*, 12, 353–359.

Arnold, K. A., Turner, N., Barling, J., Kelloway, K. E. & McKee, M. C. (2007) Transformational leadership and psychological well-being: The mediating role of meaningful work. *Journal of Occupational Health Psychology*, 12, 193–203.

Bakker, A. B. (2008) The work-related flow inventory: Construction and initial validation of the WOLF. *Journal of Vocational Behavior*, 72, 400–414.

Bakker, A. B. & Gorgievsky, M. (2010) Computer games, recovery, and work: A diary study. *Erasmus University Rotterdam, the Netherlands.*

Bandura, A. (1997) *Self-efficacy: The exercise of control.* New York: Freeman.

Bartle, R. (1996) Hearts, clubs, diamonds, spades: Players who suit MUDs. Retrieved April 5, 2010 from http://www.mud.co.uk/richard/hcds.htm

Beck, J. C. & Wade, M. (2004) *Got game: How the gamer generation is reshaping business forever.* Boston: Harvard Business School Press.

Bem, D. (1972) Self-perception theory, in L. Berkowitz (ed.), *Advances in experimental social psychology (Vol. 6).* New York: Academic Press.

Binnewies, C., Sonnentag, S. & Mojza, E. J. (2009a) Daily performance at work: Feeling recovered in the morning as a predictor of day-level job performance. *Journal of Organizational Behavior*, 30, 67–93.

Binnewies, C., Sonnentag, S. & Mojza, E. J. (2009b) Feeling recovered and thinking about the good sides of one's work. *Journal of Occupational Health Psychology*, 14, 243–356.

Broadribb, S. & Carter, C. (2009) Using second life in human resources development. *British Journal of Educational Technology*, 40, 547–550.

Caplan, S., Williams, D. & Yee, N. (2009) Problematic Internet use and psychosocial well-being among MMO players. *Computers in Human Behavior*, 25, 2009.

Castronova, E. (2005) *Synthetic worlds: The business and culture of online games.* Chicago: University of Chicago Press.

Charlton, J. P. & Danforth, I. D. W. (2007) Distinguishing addiction and high engagement in the context of online game playing. *Computers in Human Behavior*, 23, 1531–1548.

Chen, H., Wigand, R. T. & Nilan, M.S. (1999) Optimal experience of web activities. *Computers in Human Behavior*, 15, 585–608.

Csikszentmihalyi, M. (1975) *Beyond boredom and anxiety: Experiencing flow in work and play.* San Francisco, CA: Jossey-Bass.

Deci, E. L. & Ryan, R. M. (1985) *Intrinsic motivation and self-determination in human behavior.* New York: Plenum.

Demerouti, E., Bakker, A. B., Geurts, S. A.E. & Taris, T. W. (2009) Daily recovery from work-related effort during non-work time, in S. Sonnentag, P. L. Parrewé & D. C. Ganster (eds), *Current perspectives on job-stress research in occupational stress and well being*, 7, 85–123. Bingley, UK: Emerald.

Dickey, M. D. (2007) Game design and learning: A conjectural analysis of how massively multiple online role-playing games (MMORPGs) foster intrinsic motivation. *Educational Technology Research Development*, 55, 253–273.

Edwards, J. R. & Rothbard, N. P. (2000) Mechanisms linking work and family: Clarifying the relationship between work and family constructs. *Academy of Management Review*, 10, 76–88.

Festinger, L. (1942) Wish, expectation, and group standards as factors influencing level of aspiration. *Journal of Abnormal and Social Psychology*, 37, 184–200.

Fredrickson, B. L. (2001) The role of positive emotions in positive psychology: The broaden-and-build theory of positive emotions. *American Psychologist*, 56, 218–226.

Garris, R., Ahlers, R. & Driskell, J. E. (2002) Games, motivation, and learning: A research and practice model. *Simulation & Gaming*, 33, 441–467.

Green, C. S. & Bavelier, D. (2006) Effect of action video games on the spatial distribution of visuospatial attention. *Journal of Experimental Human Perceptual Performance*, 32, 1465–1478.

Green, C. S. & Bavelier, D. (2007) Action-video-game experience alters the spatial resolution of vision. *Psychological Science*, 18, 88–94.

Griffiths, M. D., Davies, M. N. O. & Chappell, D. (2004) Online computer gaming: A
comparison of adolescent and adult gamers. *Journal of Adolescence*, 27, 87–96.

Huh, S. & Bowman, N. D. (2008) Perception and addiction to online games as a function
of personality traits. *Journal of Media Psychology*, 13.

Hsu, C-L. & Lu, H-P. (2004) Why do people play on-line games? An extended TAM with
social influences and flow experience. *Information & Management*, 41, 853–868.

Hunter, J. E. (1986) Cognitive ability, cognitive aptitudes, job knowledge, and job
performance. *Journal of Vocational Behavior*, 29, 340–362.

Hobfoll, S. E. (1998) *Stress, culture, and community: The psychology and physiology of
stress*. New York: Plenum.

Ivancevich, J. M. & Matteson, M. T. (1999) *Organizational behavior and management*, 5th
edn. Boston: McGraw-Hill.

Judge, T. A. & Piccolo, R. F. (2004) Transformational and transactional leadership: A
meta-analytic test of their relative validity. *Journal of Applied Psychology*, 89,
755–768.

Karasek, R. A. & Theorell, T. (1990) *Healthy work: Stress, productivity, and the recon-
struction of working Life*. New York: Basic Books.

King, D. L., Delfabbro, P. H. & Griffiths, M. (2010a) Recent innovations in video game
addiction and theory. *Global Media Journal-Australian Edition*, 4.

King, D. L., Delfabbro, P. H. & Griffiths, M. (2010b) Video games structural characteristics: A new psychological taxonomy. *International Journal of Mental Health and
Addiction*, 8, 90–106

Lafrenière, M-A. K., Vallerand, R. J., Donahue, E. G. & Lavigne, G. L. (2009) On the costs
and benefits of gaming: The role of passion. *CyberPsychology & Behavior*, 12,
285–290.

Lehdonvirta, V. (2010) Virtual worlds don't exist: Questioning the dichotomous approach
in MMO studies. *Journal of Technology, Learning, and Assessment*, 10.

Li, F. (2007) *What is e-Business? How the Internet transforms organisations*. Oxford:
Blackwell.

Li, F., Papagiannidis, S. & Bourlakis, M. (2010) Living in 'multiple spaces': Extending our
socio-economic environment through virtual worlds. *Environment & Planning D:
Space and Society*, 28, 425–446.

Li, F., Whalley, J. & Williams, H. (2001) Between the electronic and physical spaces:
Implications for organisations in the networked economy. *Environment and Planning
A*, 33, 699–716.

Locke, E. A. & Latham, G. P. (2002) Building a practically useful theory of goal setting
and task motivation: A 35-year odyssey. *American Psychologist*, 57, 705–717.

Malaby, T. (2006) Parlaying value: Capital in and beyond virtual worlds. *Games &
Culture*, 1, 141–162.

Meijman, T. & Mulder, (1998) Psychological aspects of workload. In P. J. D. Drenth & H.
Thierry (eds), *Handbook of work and organizational psychology*, 2, 5–33. Hove:
Psychology Press.

MMOGChart.com. (2009) Total active MMOGs subscriptions. Retrieved September 26,
2009 from http://www.mmogchart.com/Chart4.html.

Organ, D. W. (1988) *Organizational citizenship behavior: The good soldier syndrome*.
Lexington, MA: Lexington.

Papagiannidis, S., Bourlakis, M. A. & Li, F. (2008) Making real money in virtual worlds:

MMORPGs and emerging business opportunities, challenges and ethical implications in metaverses. *Technological Forecasting and Social Change*, 75, 610–622.

Quintela, Y. & Donovan, J. J. (2008) A model of motivational spillover. In K. Kiefer (ed.), *Applied psychology research trends*. New York: Nova Science Publishers, pp. 141–159.

Reeves, B., Malone, T. W. & O' Driscoll, T. (2008) Leadership's online labs. *Harvard Business Review*, 86, 58–66.

Ryan, R. M., Rigby, C. S & Przybylski, A. (2006) The motivational pull of video games: A self-determination theory approach. *Motivation & Emotion*, 30, 347–363.

Rook, J. W. & Zijlstra, F. R. H. (2006) The contribution of various types of activities to recovery. *European Journal of Work & Organizational Psychology*, 15, 218–240.

Sanders, A. F. (1998) *Elements of human performance: Reaction processes and attention in human skills*. Mahwah, NJ: Lawrence Erlbaum.

Screen Digest.com (2009) There's life beyond World of Warcraft. Retrieved September 26, 2009 from http://www.screendigest.com/press/releases/pdf/PR-LifeBeyond WorldOfWarcraft-240309.pdf

Sharritt, M. (2010) Designing game affordances to promote learning and engagement. *Cognitive Technology*, 14, 43–57.

Shotton, M. A. (1989) *Computer Addiction? A Study on Computer Dependency*. Basingstoke: Taylor & Francis.

Sonnentag, S. (2001) Work, recovert activities, and individual well-being: A diary study. *Journal of Occupational Health Psychology*, 6, 196–210.

Sonnentag, S. (2003) Recovery, work engagement, and proactive behavior: A new look at the interface between nonwork and work. *Journal of Applied Psychology*, 88, 518–528.

Sonnentag, S. & Fritz, C. (2007) The recovery experience questionnaire: Development and validation of a measure for assessing recuperation and unwinding from work. *Journal of Occupational Health Psychology*, 12, 204–221.

Sonnentag, S. & Natter, E. (2004) Flight attendants' daily recovery from work: Is there no place like home? *International Journal of Stress Management*, 11, 366–391.

Van den Broeck, A., Vansteenkiste, M., de Witte, H. & Lens, W. (2008) Explaining the relationships between job characteristics, burnout, and engagement: The role of basic psychological need satisfaction. *Work & Stress*, 22, 277–294.

Westman, M. (2001) Stress and strain crossover. *Human Relations*, 54, 717–751.

Wan, C-S. & Chiou, W-B. (2006) Psychological motives and online games addiction: A test of flow theory and humanistic needs theory for Taiwanese adolescents. *CyberPsychology & Behavior*, 9, 317–324

Williams, D., Yee, N. & Caplan, S.E. (2008) Who plays, how much, and why? Debunking the stereotypical gamer profile. *Journal of Computer-Mediated Communication*, 13, 993–1018.

Wood, R. T. A., Griffiths, M. D., Chappell, D. & Davies, M. N. O. (2004) The structural characteristics of video games: A psycho-structural analysis. *CyberPsychology & Behavior*, 7, 1–10.

Xanthopoulou, D. & Papagiannidis, S. (2009) Massively multiplayer online role-playing games as a recovery activity. Erasmus University Rotterdam, the Netherlands.

Xanthopoulou, D. & Papagiannidis, S. (2012) Playing online, work better? Spillover of active learning and transformational leadership. *Technological Forecasting & Social Change*, 79, 1328–1339.

Yee, N. (2006a) The demographics, motivations and derived experiences of users of massively multi-user online graphical environments. *PRESENCE: Teleoperators and Virtual Environments*, 15, 309–329.

Yee, N. (2006b) The labor of fun: How video games blur the boundaries of work and play. *Games & Culture*, 1, 68–71.

Yee, N. (2006c) The psychology of massively multi-user online role-playing games: Motivations, emotional investment, relationships, and problematic usage. In R. Schroeder & A-S., Axelsson (eds), *Avatars at work and play: Collaboration and interaction in shared virtual environments*. Dordrecht: Springer, pp. 187–207.

Yee, N. & Bailenson, J. (2007) The Proteus effect: The effect of transformed self-representation on behavior. *Human Communication Research*, 33, 271–290.

Yee, N., Bailenson, J. N. & Ducheneaut, N. (2009) The Proteus effect: Implications of transformed digital self-representation on online and offline behavior. *Communication Research*, 36, 285–312.

Zijlstra, F. R. H. & Sonnentag, S. (2006) After work is done: Psychological perspectives on recovery from work. *European Journal of Work and Organizational Psychology*, 15, 129–138.

7 Serious gaming @ work

Learning job-related competencies using serious gaming

Hans Korteling, Anne Helsdingen and
Nicolet C. M. Theunissen

In our rapidly changing society, formal training alone cannot meet the need for development of working individuals. For this reason, serious games increasingly are gaining interest as a potentially valuable, efficient, and effective alternative for conventional training at work. Serious gaming for application in labor organizations can capture many characteristics and processes of the job. It can be used to train many relevant competencies of workers in a realistic, attractive and challenging manner. Serious gaming fits with recent theories of learning and instruction that promote a form of learning through experience, by doing, such as discovery learning (i.e. Gerven, 2003), action learning (i.e. Smith & O'Neil, 2003), and experiential learning (i.e. Jiusto & DiBiasio, 2006). Such theories advocate an active, central role for the learner and use authentic (realistic, practical, job-related) learning environments that require educators to adopt more supportive rather than directive roles (Johnston & McCormick, 1996; Salter, 2003). Although game-based learning builds on the 'learning through experience' tradition, in itself it is a relatively new learning technology. In this chapter, our discussion on the value of serious games for the workplace will borrow from three intersecting knowledge domains: Learning, Modeling & Simulation (M&S), and Play. Figure 7.1 shows that serious gaming can be positioned at the heart of these domains. From each domain, we will present those issues that are most relevant for serious gaming. On the basis of this presentation, we will show the possibilities and limitations of serious gaming for professional learning and training objectives and how gaming can play a *serious* role in training and development at the workplace.

Learning

The potential of games for education and job-related training can be partly ascribed to the opportunities that games offer for providing different and, from a didactical perspective, better ways of learning, education, and training. Therefore this paragraph discusses the potential benefits and limitations of using serious games, from the perspective of learning and didactics. In addition, it will present the basic principles of a training approach that capitalizes on the didactic possibilities provided by games.

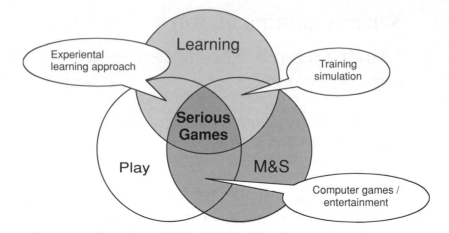

Figure 7.1 Three knowledge domains defining learning, modeling and simulation
(M&S), and play

A flexible and innovative economy requires permanent adaptations of knowledge, skills and attitudes, also called 'competencies.' Competencies are indivisible clusters of skills, knowledge, conduct, attributes and notions (e.g. 'Able to cooperate with people from other organizations' or 'Uses ICT systems to collect information and knowledge quickly.')

They are context dependent, connected to activities and tasks, but also flexible in time (Van Merriënboer, Van der Klink & Hendriks, 2002). Another characteristic of competencies is that they can be acquired through training and experience. Competencies can be valuable to match individual performance and career planning with organizational job needs (Whan, Marko & Savickas, 1998).

Games may create dynamic, and interactive learning environments that offer the opportunity to practice job-related competencies, for instance, by introducing functionally relevant professional tasks. However, not all serious games that have been designed or used for educational purposes seem to live up to their potential. Hays (2005) has reviewed 48 empirical research articles on the effectiveness of 'instructional' games. Hayes' report also includes summaries of 26 other review articles and 31 theoretical articles on instructional gaming. For the present purposes, we will suffice ourselves with the major conclusions and recommendations of their report in Table 7.1.

These conclusions and recommendations of Hays (2005) especially emphasize the significance of a sound didactical plan for implementation of serious games. Sitzmann (2011) draws similar conclusions concerning the role of instructional support. She also deduces that trainees learn more, relative to comparison groups, when instructional games convey content actively, rather than passively and when trainees could access the game as many times as desired.

Table 7.1 Major conclusions and recommendations of Hays (2005)

Conclusions

1   The empirical research on the instructional effectiveness of games is fragmented, filled with ill-defined terms, and plagued with methodological flaws.

2   Some games provide effective instruction for some tasks some of the time, but these results may not be generalizable to other games or instructional programs.

3   No evidence exists that games are the preferred instructional method in all situations

4   Instructional games are more effective if they are embedded in instructional programs that include debriefing and feedback.

5   Instructional support during play increases the effectiveness of instructional games.

Recommendations

1   The decision to use a game for instruction should be based on a detailed analysis of learning requirements and tradeoffs among alternative instructional approaches.

2   Games should be used as adjuncts and aids, not as stand-alone instruction, therefore instructor-less approaches (e.g. web-based applications) must include all 'instructor functions.'

Serious gaming didactics

Games *par excellence* provide the opportunity to model realistic environments and tasks that reflect the relevant functional aspects of the to-be-performed job. This helps learners to practice job-related competencies; stimulates them to learn to coordinate constituent skills; and facilitates transfer of what is learned to new realistic problem situations (Korteling & Sluimer, 1999; Merrill, 2002; Van Merriënboer & Kirschner, 2007). Furthermore, the rich learning environments of many serious games represent those features that help to encode new information or serve as retrieval cues for subsequent remembering of this information (Smith & Vela, 2001).

A didactical approach that specifically capitalizes on gaming and *authentic learning* is the Job Oriented Training (JOT) approach (Stehouwer *et al.*, 2005, 2006; Van der Hulst *et al.*, 2008). Authentic learning tasks create a challenging and integrated task training that is motivating for learners, but sometimes real-life tasks are too difficult for learners. Ideally, the sequencing of learning tasks and feedback should create a level of 'desirable difficulty' for the learner (Bjork, 1994) or practice in the zone of 'proximal development' (Vygotsky, 1978) to enhance learning and transfer. Instead of part task training to practice all constituent skills separately, different modeling approaches can be used to adapt task difficulty to the competence level of the learner. This can, for instance, be done by using worked-out examples (Renkl, 1997; Renkl & Atkinson, 2007) or software models (artificial intelligence, virtual agents) to scaffold the whole learning tasks. In many games, the difficulty level is usually selected by the players themselves, and if the game does not allow for scripted sequencing of levels, learners should be instructed as to what constitutes the right level for them. In the

JOT-approach, the focus on teaching such self-regulating skills to learners makes learners active managers of their own learning process and progress. This also enables them to select an adequate difficulty level.

Apart from sequence of game levels, the sequencing of learning tasks can also greatly contribute to learning and transfer. First, practice variability – that is, practice involving many parameter variations of a task – is supposed to lead to better post-training performance and transfer, compared to practice following only one or a limited number of parameter variations. This counts even for performance on criterion tasks that only involve that one, or a limited set of parameters. The benefit of practice variability has been found in motor tasks (Donovan & Radosevich, 1999) and similar results have been found with cognitive tasks as well (Goode, Geraci & Roediger III, 2008; Taylor & Rohrer, 2010). Second, random sequencing of different task variations, as opposed to blocked presentations of one variation per block, leads to better transfer (Helsdingen, Van Gog & Van Merriënboer, 2011; Magill & Hall, 1990; Van Merriënboer, De Croock & Jelsma, 1997). Game-based JOT, with its authentic learning tasks offers such practice variability in random sequence and thus provides an adequate learning experience.

It is important that learners self-regulate their learning. In this context, the concept of self-directed learning is often mentioned and intensively discussed. Self-directed learning implicates that the learner has control over all educational decisions. In interaction with the environment, social and physical, the learner decides what he needs to learn and how he can achieve this (Percival, 1996). According to a review study of Stubbé and Theunissen (2008), a learning solution that supports self-directed learning needs to help the learner: (1) to get insight in his/her own development; (2) to manage and monitor his/her own learning process; (3) to collaborate in learning; (4) to relate the learning to 'real life' needs; and (5) to take control over educational decisions. This has profound implications for the way instructors interact with learners (Zimmerman, 1990). The JOT approach advocates this notion: rather than a very directive role, instructors have to act as expert coaches merely guiding the practice sessions, and stimulate reflection (Stehouwer *et al.*, 2005, 2006). This means that in the absence of a directive instructor providing feedback, JOT requires a *meaningful* learning environment that provides the learner with adequate feedback on the appropriateness of his/her actions. Games are very suitable to present such an environment. Paramount for learning and transfer, especially in such an unguided approach, is that learners are stimulated to reflect on their learning and self-explain their strategies afterwards (Aleven & Koedinger, 2002; Chi, 2000; Schworm & Renkl, 2007).

The JOT approach for game-based training has been implemented and evaluated in several military training courses. An example is the training of new platoon squad leaders of the Royal Netherlands Army: In this training program, the game Virtual Battle Space 1[1] is implemented and used according to JOT principles. Learners play several scenarios in multiple sessions over multiple days. Reactions of the learners and training staff were very positive and enthusiastic (Hulst *et al.*, 2008). Recently, a more quantitative validation study with positive results has been carried out in the training program of operators of submarine mine sweepers (Stubbé & Oprins, 2011). Students reported high scores for the quality of the courses and took more control over their own learning process during these courses. All students passed the courses with high scores on practical exam, initiative, pro-activity, independence, motivation, and working as a team.

The conception of the learner as an active agent managing his/her own learning process and progress, as described above, is also consistent with what we know about the basics of neuronal development and the functioning of the brain (e.g. Hebb, 1949; Korteling, 1994; McClelland, McNaughton & O'Reilly, 1995; Meltzoff, Kuhl, Movellan & Sejnowski, 2009). Contemporary cognitive neuroscience states that knowledge and skills are embodied in the way neurons in the brain are connected and interact with one another. Learning then, is the acquisition and development of memories, behavior and skills by the constant refinement and expansion of this neuronal (or cognitive) framework. These processes are similar to what Piaget (1950) called *assimilation* (fitting into cognitive framework) and *accommodation* (reframing). On micro-level, this existing neuronal (or cognitive) framework is very idiosyncratic and unique for each individual. Therefore, only when the learners are *actively* involved in the process of integrating new knowledge (Büchel, Coull & Fristel, 1999) they can adequately link new information to their own personal neuronal/cognitive framework, that is: build new or refined neuronal connections. This forms the neuroscientific basis for the constructivistic conception that individuals construct new knowledge from their experiences. Serious games provide those experiences from which new knowledge can be actively created.

Modeling and simulation

In the domain of Modeling and Simulation (M&S), an elaborate research agenda has been dominated by questions regarding those characteristics that determine the value of models and synthetic environments to be used for different purposes (Farmer *et al.*, 1999; Lathan *et al.*, 2002, Liu, Machiarella & Vicenzi, 2008). Therefore, in the current paragraph, we will focus on training value, or transfer of training, borrowing from the domain of M&S. We introduce the key concepts and present information about possibilities and limitations and potential advantages of game-like PC-based (or desktop) training simulations.

In the domain of M&S, the concepts of training effectiveness and efficiency are captured in the term transfer. Transfer denotes the ability to flexibly apply (parts of) what has been learned to new tasks and/or new situations, i.e. real world tasks (see e.g. Detterman & Sternberg, 1993; Mayer & Wittrock, 1996). In line with similar definitions provided by Baldwin and Ford (1988) and Gielen (1995) for Transfer of *Training*, we define Transfer of *Gaming* (ToG) to the workplace as:

> The degree to which knowledge, skills and attitudes that are acquired by playing a game can be used effectively in the real workplace.

Empirical transfer studies are complex and sometimes even impossible because it is often difficult to determine what exactly is learned with respect to the (real) task or job for which the training is intended. In addition, job situations do not always easily allow for the objective measurement of performance of former learners. And even when these real world measures can be collected, it remains questionable to what respect the (confounding) training has contributed to that performance level, and to what respect performance effects can be attributed to other factors. However, it is possible to get a reasonable insight in the ToG, or training value of games, by means of smart experimental studies. Numerous studies over the past years have already documented that PC-based or desktop simulation environments can offer effective training for certain types of tasks (e.g. Jentsch & Bowers, 1998, Fisher *et al.*, 2002). For example, in a study of cockpit crew training, an experimental group trained on a PC-based simulator was compared to a control group. Detailed crew resource management (CRM) proficiency data as well as self-reports showed that the experimental group performed better on many skills, such as task management, communication, and crew coordination (Nullmeyer *et al.*, 2006). The evidence in favor of games, however, is less strong although positive results have been reported for example in academic achievement (Blunt, 2007) in aviation training (Proctor, *et al.*, 2004), and education of small unit tactics (Proctor, *et al.*, 2002). Rosser *et al.* (2007) showed that completion time in laparoscopic surgery was faster for surgeons when they had game experience in a learning environment that was specifically designed for this kind of surgery, than for non-gaming surgeons. These gaming surgeons also made fewer errors. In the previously discussed literature review of Hays (2005) on instructional games, he concluded that empirical research thus far on the effectiveness of games is rather fragmented. Besides, in her meta-examination of the instructional effectiveness of computer-based games, Sitzmann (2011) provides evidence of publication bias in this research area. In this respect, it is interesting to focus on what constitutes a game's potential training value and what factors are involved in determining transfer to task performance in the real world.

Key concepts

It is generally conjectured that *similarity* between a simulated world used for training and the real world results in transfer; that is: higher degrees of similarity lead to more transfer (Korteling & Sluimer, 1999). The degree of *physical* similarity between a synthetic environment and reality is called *physical fidelity* (Baum *et al.*, 1982). Fidelity denotes to what extent a simulation mimics the real equipment and environment in terms of physical measurable characteristics i.e. does a game steering set mimic the real world vehicle in such a way that the forces experienced during game play are the same as in the real vehicle? For most simple PC-based simulations and games, the physical environment in which a person has to work does not match that of the real world. It is therefore said that the fidelity of games is relatively low compared to simulators on which, for instance, realistic mock-ups are used to mimic real world operator environments. However, it is not easily defined to what extent the fidelity of the elements of a simulation contribute to the experience of realism (Roza, 2005). The graphics and animations of a simulation, for example, may be very realistic; however, if the behavior of the entities is not realistic, the game may not 'convince' or attract the player. This points at two other major constructs determining transfer. First, *functional fidelity* defined as the degree to which the simulation acts like the operational equipment in reacting to the operations that are performed by the trainee (Allen *et al.*,1986). While expensive simulators can recreate visual cues and precise instrument operation (i.e. physical fidelity), comparatively inexpensive gaming technologies may be very effective in recreating interactivity (i.e. functional fidelity) across a range of applications (Lewis & Jacobson, 2002). Second, *psychological fidelity* is the degree to which the simulation replicates the relevant psychological phenomena, such as stress or mental load, which are also experienced in the real-world environment. This will affect and engage the trainee in the same manner as the actual job environment and tasks would in the real world (Kaiser & Schroeder, 2003). Taking into account all these aspects of fidelity, the issue of the relationship between realism, or similarity and transfer remains complicated. Ultimately, the issue concerns the degree to which a simulation or game fulfills its intended use, which is termed *validity*. Next to learning and training, this use may include a variety of purposes, such as entertainment, research and development, health care, providing information, etc. When placed in a training program the intended purpose of a simulation is the obtainment of specific training objectives. As long as those training objectives are obtained that are *intended* to be trained, a simulation is valid. Hence, in a training context, validity is always coupled to the training objectives to be acquired. These training objectives are usually described as knowledge, skills, or competencies. Validity, in a game-training context, can therefore be defined in terms of transfer, i.e. the degree to which competencies learned by gaming are similar to those needed for real-task performance. This 'transfer of gaming' can be objectively and quantitatively measured by various types of experimental studies (Roscoe & Williges, 1980; Korteling & Sluimer, 1999; Korteling *et al.*, 2011).

Transfer of gaming

As will be clear now, not all tasks, competencies or types of jobs, can be effectively or efficiently trained using simple desktop simulations or games. When designing simulation-based training, job and training analyses should identify the types of (sub)tasks and related competencies that have to be trained as well as instructional support. These analyses specify the necessary input, task-features (visual, auditory, procedural, cognitive, motor), and instructional support (instructions, performance monitoring, and feedback), that are critical for the training goals, i.e. the competencies that have to be learned. These critical features need to be present in the game scenarios to realize an adequate training environment. Whether or not a simulation or game may be adequate for a specific job training program thus depends on whether or not the critical task features *can be represented adequately* in a game environment. This can be decided on the basis of general knowledge on human performance (e.g. Fleishman, 1972; Proctor *et al.*, 2002, 2004) and learning processes (Van Merriënboer, 1997; Van Merriënboer, Jelsma & Paas, 1992). Based on this knowledge, it is possible to identify classes or types of tasks that are better suited to train using a typical desktop simulation or training game, and types of tasks that seem unfit for this kind of training. A typical game, in this respect, constitutes a PC game configuration with standard commercial software, a flat screen and simple manual controls. In collaboration with four training and simulation experts we have developed a *Competence Taxonomy* (see Table 7.2) for this purpose and estimated the degree of transfer for each type of skill, expressed in +++, ++, +, –, – –, – – – meaning excellent, good, reasonable, little, very little and no transfer, respectively). Estimated degrees of transfer thus are global and do not count for each specific game and/or for each skill to be trained. In addition, it should be noted that we considered as equal all other factors that may affect the effectiveness and efficiency of simulation and gaming, such as the instructional support, didactical approach, or factors that may influence the motivation of learners. In other words the Competence Taxonomy, represented below, shows potential transfer of training, assuming that the standard PC game has been well designed and developed to represent and practice the listed types of competences.

The estimated amount of transfer of training is then determined by the *physical*, *functional*, and *psychological fidelity* that may be obtained by typical PC gaming consoles. In combination, these three kinds of fidelity determine the degree to which activities, attitudes, emotions, knowledge, skills, and/or processing operations competences that are included in the game may call upon the same (type of) underlying competences that are required in the real world (validity).

On a physical, level (i.e. physical fidelity) the look and feel of the standard PC gaming environment may differ substantially from operational environments in which people process information and operate. However, for most kinds of tasks (except primarily for perceptual motor tasks) these differences do not necessarily affect or degrade realistic interactivity (functional fidelity), and/or the realism of social, emotional or cognitive behaviors to be trained (psychological fidelity). In other words: for the transfer of job-related competences, the degree of similarity between game and real task – such as exact forms, sounds, motion or colors – often is relatively less important (e.g. Woodman, 2006).

As can be seen above, we expect TOG to be generally limited with respect to *perceptual-motor* task components (Woodman, 2006). This is not the case when the game (and especially its user-interface) is specially developed to train a specific perceptual motor task (e.g. laparoscopic surgery games). The reason for this is that perceptual-motor training requires that the specific characteristics of the physical task environment (e.g. control devices, visual cues) are represented with high physical and functional fidelity. Since most games are typically played on a PC or game console with a small flat screen, a keyboard and/or simplified game controllers, such a high level of fidelity is usually lacking. The differences

Table 7.2 Competence taxonomy with potential transfer of training estimations for typical PC games (PC, standard commercial software, flat screen, simple manual controls)

	Transfer
Attitudes	
Initiative	+++
Motivation	++
Integrity	+
Honesty	+
Courage	–
Knowledge	
Rules (regulations, guiding principles)	+++
Procedures (if…, then…, fixed action sequences)	+++
Job-specific facts (background, context, goals, conditions)	++
Mental models, schemata (e.g. functionality of interfaces)	+/–
Social skills	
Communication (primarily verbal)	+++
Collaboration, cooperation	+++
Leadership	+++
Emotional skills	
Stress coping, resilience	+++
Self-efficacy	++
Empathy	++
Non-verbal communication	+/–
Cognitive skills	
(Contingency) planning	+++
Calculation, problem solving, (strategic) decision making	+++
Interpretation	++
Self reflection	++
Perceptual-motor and physical skills	
Physical fitness	++
Perception (different modalities)	+/–
Operation	+/–
Searching	–
Detection	–
Motor performance	– –

between typical game displays/controls and the real equipment have a large impact on sensory input and motor output and thus make perceptual-motor transfer impossible.

Although game- – or PC – based simulation training may not be as effective or efficient as training in real, on-the-job, training settings, this does not necessarily mean that this training has little or no added value for training, or that it is of little use. Gaming- – or low – cost training simulation can still be efficient or valuable for various other reasons:

- It may be *very cheap* relative to training with real equipment and/or under real training conditions.
- It may provide an alternative training solution when training with real equipment under real task conditions is *dangerous* or restricted due to regulations.
- It may be preferred because of *environmental and sustainability* issues.
- It offers the possibility of training under certain relevant conditions that *rarely occur* at the working place, such as emergency situations.
- It can be done in *leisure* time, which may make it very cost-effective.
- It still may *save on the cost* of instruction personnel.
- It may awake or encourage people for new initiatives or *stimulate interest* for new tasks or knowledge areas.

In conclusion, we argue that, despite large superficial or physical differences between playing games and real tasks, serious gaming may allow people to learn many kinds of relevant skills. This, however, does not generally count for the training of most perceptual-motor skills, generic, and academic skills or for experienced learners (Korteling *et al.*, 2011).

Play

In the previous sections on Learning and M&S, aspects of learning motivation, flow, and engagement, and their relation to serious gaming have not yet been discussed. In this section it will be the main focus. Only when these aspects of *play* are purposefully combined with learning and M&S, *serious gaming* emerges. In the present paragraph we discuss why play should be included when one intends to enrich a training simulation program, what function may be ascribed to it, and what factors should be taken into consideration.

There has been a longstanding debate on the function of play, and more specifically, the role of play in learning (see e.g. Christie, 2001; Eifermann, 1971; Ortlieb , 2010; Pepler & Rubin, 1982; Singer, Golinkoff & Hirsh-Pasek, 2006), and the current debate surrounding 'serious gaming' shows a similar complexity. Some authors seem to suggest that games will provide the solution for all learning problems (e.g. Prensky, 2001; Rieben, 1996; Stapleton and Taylor, 2003), whereas others argue that gaming can never provide real learning experiences (e.g. 'I would not like to be a passenger in an airplane with a pilot that learned flying in Microsoft Flight Simulator,' Cannon-Bowers, 2005). Therefore, in this paragraph, we will analyze the potential value of play in serious games in learning for the work place. For this purpose, we will first ask ourselves the question why we play in the first place. This question may have two answers (Chick, 1998). The first is that people play because there are certain endogenous or environmental stimuli that trigger playful behavior. Play is fun, engaging, triggers 'flow' (Csikszentmihayli, 1999), and it can be competitive and inspiring, as will be argued in the next section. The second answer is related to development and evolution: play may exist because playful behavior has somehow evolutionary benefits to the species (e.g. Lewis, 1982; Poirier, 1982; Smith 1982).

The function of play

Play is often seen as an activity of minimally scripted, open-ended exploration in which the participant is absorbed in the spontaneity of the experience (Ortlieb, 2010). Evolutionary biologists have attributed numerous functions to play (Bekoff, 1997; Bekoff & Beyers, 1981; Fagen, 1981; Smith, 1982, 1995) and numerous studies indicate that these various forms of guided and unguided play give children the opportunity to practice motor skill (Pellegrini, 1987; Pellegrini & Smith, 1998), important social behaviors (e.g. Connolly & Doyle, 1984; Howes & Matheson, 1992), acquire academic (e.g. Kagan and Lowenstein, 2004; Ramani & Sigler, 2008) and cognitive skills (e.g. Elias & Berk, 2002; Lloyd & Howe, 2003). Play thus seems to aid educational, developmental and evolutionary goals. The evolutionary explanation for the function of play also offers an explanation for the *non-goal directed* behavior in play: i.e. a key process generating random variation in behavior (Gregory, 1987, p. 239). The non-goal directed aspects of play may be useful to explore and possibly extend the behavioral envelope (e.g. a monkey may not be able to think through the cracking effect of a stone thrown on a nut, but may stumble upon this effect when 'just playing around' with some stones). This newly discovered strategy may be refined and/or generalized by 'useless' repetitions. So, playing may be considered as an important aspect in the development of higher organisms. This is supported by the finding that play behavior peaks during periods of maximal cortical development (Chick, 1998; van Lawick-Goodall, 1968).

Nevertheless, there are also researchers who advocate a more prudent attitude towards the value of play for learning, especially when it concerns academic or cognitive skill. As Christie and Johnson (1983) state: 'why use play as a training medium for producing outcomes that are not playful?' They conclude that for some of the desired learning goals, other means may be more efficient. Also, Piaget (1951) questioned the developmental function of play after reaching a more advanced cognitive state, and although his views with respect to the function of play have been questioned since then (e.g. Meyers, 1999; Sutton-Smith, 1998), studies by Pellegrini and Galda (1982) as well as by Udwin (1983) have found that the effectiveness of guided play for developing academic skills may be lower for older participants than for younger participants. Careful consideration of such factors as age, or expertise that may decrease the effectiveness of play for learning is thus paramount when implementing playful activities to reach learning goals.

Motivation

Games and playful activities can be fun, engaging, satisfying, exciting or challenging and thus *motivate* the player to continue their playful activities without any external values or real-world goals. Such motivation, without any external demands is called *intrinsic* motivation (Deci & Ryan, 2002). Several studies have shown that the immersion in a fantasy game world where players can try out different roles contributes to this intrinsic motivational quality (Yee, 2006). Nevertheless, there are also games that do not immerse the player in a rich virtual world with many different opportunities: for example, the games Patience or Tetris, although very simple, are just as engaging as the more sophisticated PC games. Interesting in this respect are extensive survey studies by Yee (2006, 2007), that have shown that players are motivated to play multiplayer online games for achievement, immersion, and social reasons, with achievement as the strongest predictor of playing time. Yee describes achievement as the desire to become powerful in the context of the virtual environment through the achievement of goals and accumulation of items that confer power. It incorporates competition as well as advancement and development.

To continue activities without any external goals, just for the sake of the activity, means that the person is intrinsically motivated. Csikszentmihalyi (1999) calls this characteristic *flow*. Flow is described as a state of deep concentration and involvement in an activity. It is one of the most enjoyable experiences, and people report feeling active, alert, happy, strong, concentrated and creative during the experience (Seligman & Csikszentmihalyi, 2000). Flow is supposed to occur when challenge (or difficulty) of a task is in balance with an individual's capacities to cope. Because of the intense, alert and concentrated nature of flow, it may be expected that, when a subject is in a state of flow, his/her brain is actively showing a high degree of metabolism. Since environmental stimulation and the resulting brain activity lead to precise and selective changes in structural neuronal interaction patterns and connectivity (e.g. Abbott & Nelson, 2000; Blakemore & Cooper, 1970; Churchland & Sejnovski, 1992; Hebb, 1949; Hirsch & Spinelli, 1970), we may suppose that flow enhances learning. Flow can be experienced during many activities, such as work, play, car driving, or exercise. The experience of flow will be most likely when a person experiences an environment containing high enough opportunities for action (or challenges), that are in balance with the person's own capacities. That is: the person is capable of mastering the challenges, but not without too much effort.

Other theoretical approaches to intrinsic motivation such as the cognitive evaluation/self-determination theory (Deci and Ryan, 2002) or the eudemonistic theory (Waterman, 1990) also recognize the importance of balancing the (relatively high) challenge of an activity and the skill level of the individual (Schwarz & Waterman, 2006). These theories also posit self-determination (i.e. the fact that an individual perceives the activity as chosen) and self-realization (activity of people to strive to realize their best potential) as additionally important predictors of intrinsic motivation. Interpersonal events and structures (e.g. rewards, communication, feedback) that lead toward feelings of competence and autonomy will enhance motivation.

However, when considering the intrinsic motivation to play games for learning purposes, we also have to take into account that in several studies a negative correlation between achievement and enjoyment has been found. Apparently, students often like the instructional approaches from which they learn the least, i.e. that pose the lightest workload (Clark, 1982; Bjork & Bjork, 2010). Thus, serious games that are really entertaining may not always be optimal for learning, i.e. they sometimes do not pose the 'desirable level of difficulty' as Bjork (1994) states, or the 'level of proximal development' (Vygotski, 1978). It seems that enjoyment and workload experiences have to be balanced to create an optimal learning result. This balancing may be done by placing *external* demands on the individual: e.g. define a goal that needs to be attained, prescribe a performance standard, set a difficulty level, or include a competitive element that challenges the learner to put more effort into their game.

Although intrinsic motivation is clearly important, demands, resources or rewards externally motivate most of the activities people do: i.e. activities done to attain some separable outcome. Similar to some of the effects of feedback, these external goals may have detrimental effects on peoples' intrinsic motivation for an activity. A meta-analysis confirms that virtually every type of expected tangible reward, but also threats, deadlines, directives and competition, undermine intrinsic motivation (Ryan, Koestner & Deci, 1999) because people experience them as controllers of their behavior. Rewards or directives are supposed to shift the locus of control from internal to external, which may have detrimental effects on self-determination and hence intrinsic motivation. Ryan and Deci (2000) view extrinsic motivation as a continuum ranging from *external regulation* to *integration*. Externally regulated behavior depends on the demand and control of other people, the environment and other extrinsic factors. The other side of the continuum is the most autonomous form of extrinsic motivation: integration. This occurs when identified regulations have been fully assimilated to the self through self-examination and bringing external regulations and demands into congruence with one's own values and needs. This type of behavior shares many of the qualities with intrinsic motivation, such that a person feels self-determined and engaged. The difference, however, is that the behavior is undertaken to reach an external goal.

Considering successful games we can thus reason why people feel motivated to play. These games pose a challenge for skilled gamers (achievement and flow), they let the gamer control the course of actions (self-direction) and also through Web-based fora it is possible for gamers to compete and compare with others and build a social network (self-realization, social reasons, achievement). However, when we choose to apply games for job-training purposes, we may place external goals and demands on the players, thereby diminishing their intrinsic motivation. It is then important to focus on minimizing the detrimental effects of external demands on the one hand, while still obtaining learning goals on the other. This can be accomplished by designing a game where the goals are similar to the learning objectives. In that case, the rules of the game reflect the learning content and the external demands on the player can be minimal. Furthermore, instructional strategies such as self-reflection may facilitate integration of the external demands, thus creating an environment where the individual feels self-determined despite the external demands placed upon him/her.

Conclusions and research questions

Games may provide meaningful and valuable learning environments if they are embedded in a training program that optimally exploits their opportunities and offers an educational approach that is congruent with the game features. This includes the focusing on integrated, authentic, self-initiated practice, and collaborative reflection. According to this approach, the control over instructions, interventions and performance assessment, shifts from instructional agents (e.g. coach, instructor, teacher, computer system) to the learner and his/her peers. Serious games may provide sufficiently realistic, meaningful, and adaptive learning environments, to facilitate this self-regulated or self-directed learning of job related competencies. However, games for educational purposes can only be successfully implemented if instructional personnel learn to become more of a non-directive *coach* than a *teacher* in the traditional sense of the word. Their main objective should be to guide the learner through their experiences and guard the quality of the learning experiences in the classroom (Hulst *et al.*, 2008). He/she should ask questions, prevent stagnations or mental overload, encourage an active and explorative disposition, challenge students, and instigate reflection and interaction. Still, some research may be required to develop an adequate theory of education for game-based learning. Other typical related research questions will be: how to enhance meta cognition, self-efficacy and self-regulation with serious games; what degree of (automated) instructional support is needed, how this support should be incorporated to foster the learning process, and how interaction and active participation, and peer-to-peer learning with serious games should be enhanced.

Next to adequate instruction and coaching, game-based training requires good curricula, carefully chosen training scenarios, relevant performance measures, and adequate feedback. In addition, the synthetic world of the game should resemble the real working environment on key physical and psychological aspects of the specific task and competencies to be trained. The task-taxonomy can be used to help game designers start the development of games for specific kinds of training objectives, or to analyze which kinds of tasks can be included in a specific serious game. Expert-scores on this taxonomy indicated that except for many perceptual-motor skills, most other types of competences may be effectively acquired on a typical PC game configuration with standard commercial displays and controls. We suppose that what gaming primarily contributes here is *interactivity*, *meaning*, and *context* instead of 'look and feel' and physics. From an M&S point of view, an interactive and meaningful job-context is provided by a synthetic task environment that includes a high amount of ambient information and feedback to actively practice and learn. Interactivity, meaning and context are embedded in a mission or story-line with goals, (other) actors, obstacles, and events that are relevant for the job. It should be noted, however, that serious gaming will only be an efficient training aid when the trainee *needs* to have this explicit presentation of rich contextual and ambient information and meaning in order to learn. This is for example the case with novices lacking contextual knowledge and experience. In contrast, when experienced professionals are confronted with serious gaming, we may hear statements like: 'this seems a waste of time, just give me a textbook and . . . '. This also means that gaming will not be very effective for further development of academic knowledge or higher-order generic skills (such as academic writing or people management), as far as these are relatively, generic, abstract, and independent of job context. This may also be part of the explanation why gaming especially seems to attract young people, who are (often) less experienced and lack generic competencies. Future research will have to establish for which kinds of tasks and target groups gaming is most beneficial, and how a game should be optimally designed to obtain its training goals. Typical research questions will then be: what the relative contribution to transfer of gaming of physical, functional, and psychological fidelity should be. More specifically, this involves questions regarding the amount of required interactivity, meaning, context, immersion, and authenticity and how to obtain these. Finally, how can this be embedded in a plausible, relevant and attractive storyline including job-relevant scenarios offering the required learning experiences?

This latter question relates already to our final main issue, i.e. play and its effects on motivation. In general, the elements of play in serious gaming make this technology most preferable in situations where motivation is a crucial factor determining behavior of learners. Based on its possible evolutionary utility, play is *internally* triggered and supported by rewarding experiences, like fun and flow. Competence, autonomy and self-realization are three major influences in the internal motivation of people to undertake or like activities that are enjoyable or entice flow. If the play or game environment elicits behaviors that are relevant or needed for the development of the individual's job-related competencies, gaming may thus motivate and encourage learning. This is especially relevant when the learning process itself requires extra effort that may not always be perceived as enjoyable. Therefore, enjoyment and workload experiences have to be balanced to create an optimal learning result. Learning effort may also be stimulated by placing *external* demands, resources or rewards that may motivate the individual. However, external motivators may negatively affect a person's feeling of autonomy and competence, and thereby *internal* motivation; it is then important to strive at minimizing the detrimental effects of external demands on the one hand, while still obtaining learning goals on the other. One way this can be accomplished is by designing a game in which the goals of the game are similar to the learning objectives. In conclusion: when considering the application of gaming for educational and training purposes, it is important to address internal and external motivators in relation to workload and effort, taking into consideration the necessary didactical prescriptions that restrict the extent of playful behavior. Future research questions will then have to ask how games should be designed to maximize intrinsic motivation, when and how to use external rewards or competition to motivate learning, how to increase engagement, enjoyment and flow, how these emotional phenomena contribute to learning, and how to balance them with effort in a restricted and structured, didactic setting. Finally, future research questions may concern factors such as the individual's age, educational and professional level, and experience. These factors may substantially affect the added value of play and the possibilities and optimal design of a serious game.

In summary, in the design and application of serious gaming with maximal transfer of training to the workplace, one has to consider many factors such as: training program and instructional features, serious gaming didactics, fidelity, validity, types of tasks and competences, target groups, learning goals, and intrinsic and extrinsic aspects of motivation. We conclude that games and play can have a valuable role in schooling and job training; not to fully replace traditional training methods, but to substantially enrich existing training curricula, and to inspire and challenge learners.

Acknowledgments

This research has been supported by the GATE project, funded by the Netherlands Organization for Scientific Research (NWO) and the Netherlands ICT Research and Innovation Authority (ICT Regie).

Note

1   Virtual Battle Space is published by Bohemia Interactive Studios.

References

Abbott, L. F. & Nelson, S. B. (2000) Neuronal plasticity: Taming the beast. *Nature Neuroscience*, 3, 1178–1183.

Aleven, V. & Koedinger, K. R. (2002) An effective metacognitive strategy: Learning by doing and explaining with a computer-based Cognitive Tutor. *Cognitive Science*, 26, 147–179.

Allen, J. A., Hays, R. T. & Buffordi, L. C. (1986) Maintenance training, simulator fidelity, and individual differences in transfer of training. *Human Factors*, 28, 497–509.

Baldwin, T. T. & Ford, J. K. (1988) Transfer of training: A review and directions for future research. *Personnel Psychology*, 41, 63–105.

Baum, D. R., Riedel, S., Hays, R. T. & Mirabella, A. (1982) *Training effectiveness as a function of training device fidelity: Current ARI research* (Technical Report 593).

Alexandria, VA: US Army Research Institute for the Behavioral and Social Sciences (Defense Technical Information Center No. ADA133104).

Bekoff, M. (1997) Playing with play: What can we learn about cognition, negotiation, and evolution? in D. Cummins & C. Allen (eds), *The evolution of mind*. New York: Oxford University Press.

Bekoff, M. & Beyers, J. A. (1981) A critical re-analysis of the ontogeny and phylogeny of mammalian social and locomotor play: An ethological hornet's nest. Im K. Immelmann, G. Barlow, M. Main & L. Petrinovich (eds) *Behavioural development*. Cambridge: Cambridge University Press, pp. 296–337.

Bjork, R. A. (1994) Memory and metamemory considerations in the training of human beings. In J. Metcalfe & A. Shimamura (eds), *Metacognition: Knowing about knowing*. Cambridge, MA: MIT Press, pp. 185–205.

Bjork, E. L. & Bjork, R. A. (2011) Making things hard on yourself, but in a good way:

Creating desirable difficulties to enhance learning, in M. A. Gernsbacher, R. W. Pew, L. M. Hough & J. R. Pomerantz (eds), *Psychology and the real world: Essays illustrating fundamental contributions to society.* New York: Worth Publishers, pp. 56–64.

Blakemore, C. & Cooper, G. F. (1970) Development of the brain depends on visual environment. *Nature,* 288, 477–478.

Blunt, R. (2007) Does game-based learning work? Results from three recent studies. In Interservice/Industry Training, Simulation & Education Conference (I/ITSEC). Orlando, FL: NTSA.

Buchel, C., Coull, J. T. & Fristel, K. J. (1999) The predictive value of changes in effective connectivity for human learning, *Science,* 283, 1538.

Cannon-Bowers, J. A. & Salas, E. (eds) (1998) *Making Decisions Under Stress: Implications for Individual and Team Training.* Washington, DC: American Psychological Association.

Case, D. A. (2003) *Antecedents and Outcomes of End User Computing Competence,* Air Force Inst of Tech Wright-Patterson Afb OH School of Engineering and Management, ADA415162.

Chi, M. T. H. (2000) Self-explaining expository texts: The dual processes of generating inferences and repairing mental models, in R. Glaser (ed.), *Advances in Instructional Psychology.* Mahwah, NJ: Erlbaum, pp. 161–238.

Chick, G. (1998) Games in culture revisited: A replication and extension of Roberts, Arth, and Bush (1959). *Cross-Cultural Research,* 32, 185–206.

Christie, J. (2001) Play as a learning medium, in S. Reifel (ed.), *Theory in context and out,* 3, 358–365. Westport, CT: Ablex.

Christie, J. & Johnsen, E. P. (1983) The role of play in social-intellectual development. *Review of Educational Research,* 53, 93–115.

Churchland, P. S. & Sejnowski, T. J. (1992) *The computational brain.* Cambridge, MA: MIT Press.

Clark, R. E. (1982) Antagonism between achievement and enjoyment in ATI studies. *Educational Psychologist,* 17, 92–101.

Connolly, J. A. & Doyle, A. B. (1984) Relations of social fantasy play to social competence in preschoolers. *Developmental Psychology,* 20, 797–806.

Csikszentmihalyi, M. (1999) If we are so rich, why aren't we happy? *American Psychologist,* 54, 821–827.

Csikszentmihalyi, M. & Csikszentmihalyi, I. S. (eds) (1988) *Optimal experience: Psychological studies of flow in consciousness.* New York: University of Cambridge Press.

Deci, E. L., Koestner, R. & Ryan, R. M. (1999) A meta-analytic review of experiments examining the effects of extrinsic rewards on intrinsic motivation. *Psychological Bulletin,* 125, 627–668.

Deci, E. L. & Ryan, R. M. (2002) *Handbook of self-determination research.* Rochester, NY: University of Rochester Press.

Detterman, D. K. & Sternberg, R. J. (eds) (1993) *Transfer on trial: Intelligence, cognition, and instruction.* Norwood, NJ: Ablex Publishing.

Donovan, J. J. & Radosevich, D. J. (1999) A meta-analytic review of the distribution of practice effect. *Journal of Applied Psychology,* 84, 795–805.

Elias, C. L. & Berk, L. (2002) Self-regulation in young children: Is there a role for sociodramatic play? *Early Childhood Research Quarterly,* 17, 216–238.

Fagen, R. (1981) *Animal Play Behavior.* New York: Oxford University Press.

Farmer, E., Jorna, P., Moraal, J., Rooij, J. van & Riemersma, J. B. J. (1999) *Handbook of*

Simulator-based Training. Brookfield, USA: Ashgate; Cambridge, GB: University Press.

Fisher, D. L., Laurie, N. A., Glaser, R., Connerney, K., Pollatsek, A., Duffy, S. A. & Brock, J. (2002) Use of a fixed-base driving simulator to evaluate the effects of experience and PC-based risk awareness training on drivers' decisions. *Human Factors*, 44, 287–302.

Fleishman, E. A. (1972) On the relation between abilities, learning, and human performance. *American Psychologist*, 27, 1017–1032.

Galda, L. (1982) Assuming the spectator stance: An examination of the responses of three young readers. *Research in the Teaching of English*, 16, 1–20.

Ghatala, E. S. (1986) Strategy-monitoring training enables young learners to select effecive strategies. *Educational Psychologist*, 21, 43–54.

Gerven, P. van (2003) Het onderste uit de kan: efficiente leerstrategieën voor ouderen. *Neuropraxis*, 7, 54–58.

Gielen, E. W. M. (1995) *Transfer of training in a corporate setting* (doctoral thesis). Enschede; Universiteit Twente.

Goode, M. K., Geraci, L. & Roediger, H. L. (2008) Superiority of variable to repeated practice in transfer on anagram solution. *Psychonomic Bulletin & Review*, 15, 662–666.

Gregory, R. L. (ed.) (1987) *The Oxford Companion to the Mind.* Oxford: Oxford University Press.

Hays, R. T. (2005) *The Effectiveness of Instructional Games: A Literature Review and Discussion.* Technical Report 2005–004. Naval Air Warfare Training Systems Division. Orlando, FL.

Hebb, D. O. (1949) *The Organization of Behavior: A neuropsychological theory.* New York: Wiley.

Helsdingen, A. S., Van Gog, T. & Van Merriënboer, J. J. G. (2011) The effects of practice schedule on learning a complex judgement task. *Learning and Instruction*, 21, 126–136.

Hirsch, H. V. B. & Spinelli, D. N. (1970) Visual experience modifies distribution of horizontally and vertically oriented receptive fields in cats. *Science*, 168, 869–871.

Hulst, A. van der, Muller, T., Besselink, S. & Coetsier, D. (2008) Bloody serious gaming – experiences with job oriented training. *Proceedings of the Interservice/Industry, Training, Simulation, and Education Conference.* Orlando, FL: I/ITSEC 2008.

Howes, C. & Matheson, C. C. (1992) Sequences in the development of competent play with peers: Social and social pretend play. *Developmental Psychology*, 28, 961–974.

Jentsch, F. & Bowers, C. A. (1998) Evidence for the validity of PC-based simulations in studying aircrew coordination. *International Journal of Aviation Psychology*, 8, 243–260.

Jiusto, S. & DiBiasio, D. (2006) Experiential learning environments: Do they prepare our students to be self-directed, life-long learners? *Journal of Engineering Education*, 95, 195–204.

Johnston, S. & McCormack, C. (1996) Integrating information technology into university teaching: Identifying the needs and providing the support. *International Journal of Educational Management*, 10, 36–42.

Kagan, S. L. & Lowenstein, A. E. (2004) School readiness and children's play: Contemporary oxymoron or compatible option? In E. F. Zigler, D. G. Singer & S. J. Bishop-Josef (eds), *Children's play: The roots of reading.* Washington, DC: ZERO TO THREE Press, pp. 59–76.

Kaiser, M. K. & Schroeder, J. A. (2003) Flights of fancy: The art and science of flight simulation, in Michael A. Vidulich & Pamela S. Tsang (eds), *Principles and Practice of Aviation Psychology.* Mahwah, NJ: Lawrence Erlbaum Associates, pp. 435–471.

Korteling, J. E. (1994) *Multiple-task performance and aging*. Dissertation: University of Groningen/TNO Human Factors, Soesterberg, the Netherlands, ISBN 90-9006920-8.

Korteling, J. E., Helsdingen, A. S., Sluimer, R. R., Emmerik, M. L. & Kappe, B. (2011) *Transfer of Gaming: Transfer of Training in Serious Gaming* (Report: TNO-DV 2011 B142). Soesterberg, the Netherlands: TNO Human Factors Research Institute.

Korteling, J. E. & Sluimer, R. R. (1999) *A critical review of validation methods for man-in-the-loop simulators* (Report: TM-99-A023). Soesterberg, The Netherlands: TNO Human Factors Research Institute.

Lathan, C. L., Tracey, M. R., Sebrechts, M. M., Clawson, D. M. & Higgins, G. A. (2002) Using virtual environments as training simulators: Measuring transfer. In K. M. Stanney (ed.), *Handbook of Virtual Environments: Design, Implementation, and Applications*. Mahwah, NJ: Lawrence Erlbaum, pp. 403–414.

Lawick-Goodall, J. van (1968) The behaviour of free-living chimpanzees in the Gombe Stream Reserve. *Animal Behaviour Monographs*, 1, 161–311.

Lewis, M. (1982) Play as whimsy. *Behavioral and Brain Sciences*, 5, 139–184.

Lewis, M. & Jacobson, J. (2002) Game engines in scientific research. *Communications of the ACM*, 45, 27–31.

Liu, D., Machiarella, N. D., Vincenzy, D. A. (2008) Simulation fidelity, in D. A. Vincenzy and J. A. Wise, M. Mouloua & P. A. Hancock (eds), *Human factors in simulation and training*. Boca Raton, FL: Taylor and Francis, pp. 61–73.

Lloyd, B. & Howe, N. (2003) Solitary play and convergent and divergent thinking skills in preschool children. *Early Childhood Research Quarterly*, 18, 22–41.

Magill, R. A. & Hall, K. G. (1990) A review of the contextual interference effect in motor skill acquisition. *Human Movement Science*, 9, 241–289.

Mayer, R. E. & Wittrock, M. C. (1996) Problem-solving transfer. In D. C. Berliner & R. C. Calfee (eds), *Handbook of Educational Psychology*. New York: Simon & Schuster Macmillan, pp. 47–62.

McClelland, J. L., McNaughton, B. L. & O'Reilly, R. C. (1995) Why there are complementary learning systems in the hippocampus and the neocortex: Insights in the successes and failures of connectionist models of learning and memory. *Psychology Review*, 102, 419–457.

Meltzoff, A. N., Kuhl, P. K., Movellan, J. & Sejnovski, T. J. (2009) Foundations for a new science of learning. *Science*, 325, 284–288.

Merrill, M. D. (2002) First principles of instructional design. *Educational Technology, Research and Development*, 50, 43–59.

Meyers, D., (1999) Simulation as play: A semiotic analysis. *Simulation & Gaming*, 30, 147–162.

Michael, D. & Chen, S (2006) *Serious Games: Games That Educate, Train and Inform*.

Nullmeyer, R. T., Spiker, V. A., Golas, K. C., Logan R. C. & Clemons, L. (2006) The effectiveness of a PC based C-130 crew resource management aircrew device. Paper presented at the meeting of the Interservice/Industry training, simulation, and Education Conference, Orlando, FL.

Ortlieb, E. T. (2010) Beyond just books: Sparking children's interest in reading. *International Journal of Education*, 2, E9.

Pellegrini, A. D. (1987) Rought-and-tumble play: Developmental and educational significance. *Educational Psychology*, 22, 23–43.

Pellegrini, A. & Galda, L. (1982) The effects of thematic-fantasy play training on the development of children's story comprehension. *American Educational Research Journal*, 19, 443–452.

Pellegrini A. D. & Smith, P. K. (1998) Physical activity play: The nature and functional of a neglect aspect of play. *Child Development*, 69, 577–598.

Percival, A. (1996) Invited reaction: An adult educator responds. *Human Resource Development Quarterly*, 7, 131–139.

Pepler, J. & Rubin, H. (eds) (1982) *The Play of Children: Current Theory and Research.* Basel: Karger.

Piaget, J. (1950) *The Psychology of Intelligence.* New York: Harcourt, Brace & World.

Piaget, J. (1951) *Play, Dreams and Imitation in Children.* New York: Norton.

Poirier, F. E. (1982) Play – immediate or long-term adaptiveness? *Behavioral and Brain Sciences*, 5, 167–168.

Prensky, M. (2001) *Digital game-based learning.* New York: McGraw-Hill.

Proctor, M. D., Curley, J. & Williams, W. C. (2002) Interoperable training through a simulation game. *2002 European Simulation Interoperability Workshop.*

Proctor, M. D., Panko, M. & Donovan, S. (2004) Considerations for training team situation awareness and task performance through PC-gamer simulated multi-ship helicopter operations. *International Journal of Aviation Psychology*, 14, 191–205.

Ramani, G. B. & Siegler, R. S. (2011) Reducing the gap in numerical knowledge between low- and middle-income preschoolers. *Journal of Applied Developmental Psychology*, 146–159.

Renkl, A. (1997) Learning from worked-out examples: A study on individual differences. *Cognitive Science*, 21, 1–29.

Renkl, A. & Atkinson, R. K. (2007) An example order for cognitive skill acquisition. In F. E. Ritter, J. Nerb, E. Lehtinen & T. O'Shea (eds) *In Order to Learn: How the Sequence of Topics Influences Learning.* New York: Oxford University Press, pp. 95–105.

Roscoe, S. N. & Williges, B. H. (1980) Measurement of transfer of training. In S. N. Roscoe (ed.), *Aviation Psychology.* Ames, IA: The Iowa State University Press.

Rosser, J. C., Lynch, P. J., Cuddihy, L., Gentile, D. A., Klonsky, J. & Merell, R. (2007) The impact of video games on training surgeons in the 21st century. *Archives of Surgery*, 142.

Roza, Z. C. (2005) *Simulation Fidelity Theory and Practice. A Unified Approach to Defining, Specifying and Measuring the Realism of Simulations.* PhD Thesis, Delft University, the Netherlands.

Ryan, E. L. & Deci, R. M. (2001) On happiness and human potentials: A review of research on hedonic and eudaimonic well being, *Annual Review of Psychology*, 52, 141–166.

Salter, G. (2003) Comparing online and traditional teaching – a different approach. Campus wide information systems, *Systems*, 20, 137–145.

Schwartz, S. J. & Waterman, A. S. (2006) Changing interests: A longitudinal study of intrinsic motivation for personally salient activities. *Journal of Research in Personality*, 40, 1119–1136.

Schworm, S. & Renkl, A. (2007) Learning argumentation skills through the use of prompts for self-explaining examples. *Journal of Educational Psychology*, 99, 285–296.

Seligman, M. E. P. & Csikszentmihalyi, M. (2000) Positive psychology: An introduction. *American Psychologist*, 55, 5–14.

Singer, D., Golinkoff, R. M. & Hirsh-Pasek, K. (eds) (2006) *Play-learning: How Play Motivates and Enhances Children's Cognitive and Social-emotional Growth.* New York: Oxford University Press.

Sitzmann, T. (2011) A meta-analytic examination of the instructional effectiveness of computer-based simulation games. *Personnel Psychology*, 64, 489–528.

Smith, P. K. (1982) Does play matter? Functional and evolutionary aspects of animal and human play. *Behavioral and Brain Sciences*, 5, 139–184.

Smith, P. K. (1995) Play, ethology, and education: A personal account, in A. D. Pellegrini (ed.), *The Future of Play Theory*. Albany, NY: SUNY Press, pp. 3–21.

Smith, P. A. C. & O'Neil, J. (2003) A review of action learning literature 1994–2000. Part 1: Bibliography and comments. *Journal of Workplace Learning*, 15, 63–69.

Smith, S. M. & Vela, E. (2001) Environmental context-dependent memory: A review and meta-analysis. *Psychonomical Bulletin & Review*, 8, 203–220.

Stapleton, A. J. & Taylor, P. C. (2003) Why videogames are cool and school sucks. Paper presented at the annual Australian Game Developers Conference (AGDC), Melbourne, Australia, 20–23 November 2003.

Stehouwer, M., Serné, M. & Niekel, C. (2005) A tactical trainer for air defence platoon commanders. *Proceedings of the Interservice/Industry, Training, Simulation, and Education Conference*. Orlando I/ITSEC 2005. Paper No 2066.

Stehouwer, M., Stricker, J. & Gemeren, W. van (2006) Training design for professional development. *Proceedings I/ITSEC 2006*. Paper No. 2513.

Stubbé H. E. & Oprins, A. E. P. B. (2011) *Final report JOT-KM: About the Implementation of Competence-based Learning*. Report TNO-DV 2011 A-143, Soesterberg: TNO Human Factors.

Stubbé, H. M. & Theunissen, N. C. M. (2008) Self-directed learning in a ubiquitous learning environment: a meta-review. *Proceedings of Special Track on Technology Support for Self-Organised Learners (TSSOL08)*. Salzburg, Austria, pp. 5–28.

Sutton-Smith, B. (1998) *The ambiguity of play*. Cambridge, MA: Harvard University Press.

Taylor, K. & Rohrer, D. (2010) The effects of interleaving practice. *Applied Cognitive Psychology*, 24, 837–848.

Udwin, O. (1983) Imaginative play training as an intervention method with institutionalised preschool children. *British Journal of Educational Psychology*, 53, 32–39.

Van Merriënboer, J. J. G. (1997) *Training Complex Cognitive Skills: A Four-component Instructional Design Model for Technical Training*. Englewood Cliffs, NJ: Educational Technology Publications.

Van Merriënboer, J. J. G., De Croock, M. B. M. & Jelsma, O. (1997) The transfer paradox: Effects of contextual interference on retention and transfer performance of a complex cognitive skill. *Perceptual and Motor Skills*, 84, 784–786.

Van Merriënboer, J. J. G., Jelsma, O. & Paas, F. (1992) Training for reflective expertise: A four-component instructional design model for training complex cognitive skills. *Educational Technology, Research and Development*, 40, 23–43.

Van Merriënboer, J. J. G. & Kirschner, P. A. (2007) *Ten steps to complex learning*. Mahwah, NJ: Erlbaum/Taylor and Francis.

Van Merriënboer, J. J. G., van der Klink, M. R. & Hendriks, M. (2002) *Competenties, Van Complicaties Tot Compromis: Over Schuifjes en Begrenzers* (Competencies, from complications to compromise:; about tuning knobs and limiters). The Hague: Onderwijsraad.

Vygotsky, L. S. (1978) *Mind and Society: The Development of Higher Psychological Processes*. Cambridge, MA: Harvard University Press.

Whan Marko, K. & Savickas, M. L. (1998) Effectiveness of a career time perspective intervention. *Journal of Vocational Behavior*, 52, 106–119.

Waterman, A. S. (1990) Personal expressiveness: Philosophical and psychological foundations. *Journal of Mind and Behaviour*, 11, 47–74.

Woodman, M. D. (2006) *Cognitive Transfer Using a Personal Computer-based Game: A Close Quarters Battle Case Study*. Orlando, FL: University of Central Florida.

Yee, N. (2006) The demographics, motivations and derived experiences of users of massively-multiuser online graphical environments. *PRESENCE: Teleoperators and Virtual Environments*, 15, 309–329.

Yee, N. (2007) Motivations of play in online games. *Journal of CyberPsychology and Behavior*, 9, 772–775.

Zimmerman, B. J. (1990) Self-regulated learning and academic achievement: An overview. *Educational Psychologist*, 25, 3–17.

8 Technology-enhanced learning in the workplace

Marcel van der Klink, Hendrik Drachsler and Peter Sloep

In spite of its long history, workplace learning has gained only modest recognition as something valuable for human resource development in organizations. Lately, interest in workplace learning has grown. A number of developments contributed to this, including the emergence of various learning technologies. Through them, workplace learning has also acquired a more prominent position in today's human resource development policies.

This chapter first explores the concept of workplace learning, to be followed by a section that details how the field of workplace learning has evolved over the past few decades. Then, its fundamental features are discussed. What are they, and which factors predict opportunities for learning in the workplace? Subsequently, the focus shifts to how technology enhances workplace learning. Attention is paid to the evolution of technology from media-supported learning, via computer-based training and Web-based training to what now is called technology-enhanced learning. Interestingly, these learning technologies now are deemed prerequisites for creating and organizing learning in the workplace. Technology's power to expand the opportunities for and value of workplace learning is elaborated in a section that presents three examples of contemporary workplace learning. These examples show that modern workplace learning could not flourish or even exist without such technologies as learning networks, microblogging and personalized learning environments. The final section summarizes some main trends and discusses topics that deserve further research attention.

The evolving field of workplace learning

Table 8.1 details how perspectives on workplace learning have shifted over time; it also shows the role technology plays in each period.

Learning in the era of the human relations movement and beyond

From the Second World War onwards until the late 1960s, training sought to prepare employees for entry-level jobs. In many industries new employees received some firm-specific and job-specific training during their entrance period, partly off-the-job but partly also in the actual work setting itself. The latter

Table 8.1 Perspectives on learning in the workplace

	Human relations movement	*Professionalizing organizational training and learning*	*Human resource development*	*Lifetime employability*
Period	Until 1970	1970–1990	1990–	2000–
Aims of training and learning	Apart from preparing for jobs there is attention for employee well-being and commitment	Training is costly but necessary for preparing employees for the increasing pace of change	Training is a necessary investment in the human capital. Emphasis on integrating HRD, HRM and OD	Individual employee becomes increasingly responsible for his/her own learning and career
Dominant types of training and learning	Standardized off-the-job courses	Mainly off-the-job courses	Mix of off-the-job and increasingly on-the-job training and learning	Informal learning at work, use of digital means, learning in networks
Role of technology	Media-supported training. Use of mass media (radio, television, video) in classroom-based training	Computer-based training. Computer as stand-alone, especially for training skills and knowledge in separate computer rooms	Web-based e-learning. Rise of technology, such as Internet, for flexible learning in daily work.	Technology-enhanced learning, strongly embedded in the daily-work setting. Increased use of mobile devices that foster learning in different places and time zones
Content of training and learning	Job-specific but also soft skills and for personal development purposes	Job-specific and emerging attention for career development	Job specific, career development, learning competences	Stronger focus on broad transferable competences. Working and learning increasingly intertwined, thus working becomes learning

Source: based on Van der Klink (2010)

was mainly unstructured in nature and has been called very different names, such as 'sitting with Nellie' or 'follow Joe (or Jane)' (McCord, 1987). There was a growing recognition that organizations are human cooperative systems. In order to assure a better fit between employees and organizations, investments in improving employees' social skills and work motivation were increased (Kaufman, 2001), especially for employees working in supervisory or managerial job positions.

Professionalizing training and learning

The innovations that emerged during the 1970s forced organizations to expand their training investments. It no longer sufficed to train newly-hired employees and managerial staff. The introduction of automated and more complex work processes, followed by the further computerization of work, required more frequent training during employees' careers (Sloep *et al.*, 2011). Now that training had become a means to ensure organizational performance, dedicated training departments were set up. Training expenditure increased accordingly. Most of the training was still classroom-based, in settings removed from the actual workplace. But concern about its actual contribution to employees' on-the-job performance was growing, notably because of the lack of convincing evidence for its effectiveness (Baldwin & Ford, 1988; Latham & Crandall, 1991).

From training to human resource development

During the 1980s, organizations became even more aware of the significance of their human resources for surviving in a globalizing economy. Cost-reduction, permanent attention for quality improvement, elimination of work inefficiencies, flattening and downsizing the workforce are just a few examples of attempts to cope with the rapidly changing circumstances. The nature and division of work fundamentally changed too. Job descriptions became broader, indicating of a wider range of tasks and higher levels of autonomy for individual workers, even for shop-floor jobs (Swanson & Holton, 2008). Improvement and innovation were no longer the exclusive domain of R&D departments but of the workforce as a whole. In turn, this change boosted the integration of work, innovation and learning.

The prominent position training departments now acquired reflected the acknowledgment of their paramount importance for staying ahead of global competition. Training departments were transformed into human resource development (HRD) departments. This was not a mere replacement of labels. It emphasized that training and learning had become a crucial management tool. Organizations attempted to align HRD more effectively with their organizational goals. They redesigned their entire organizational HR policies and practices through integrating HRD with Human Resource Management (HRM) and organizational development (OD) (Ruona & Gibson, 2004).

The lack of evidence for the effectiveness of classroom-based training gave way to a move from off-the-job training to on-the-job training and learning. Evidence became available that suggested learning in the workplace was more effective and more practical, as well as allowing the integration of innovation and everyday learning. Not insignificantly, it was less expensive than conventional classroom-based types of training. Unfortunately, the empirical evidence to support the positive claims of learning in the workplace was, and still is, rather modest (Van der Klink & Streumer, in press).

From lifetime employment to lifetime employability

The first decade of the 21st century was characterized by increasingly unpredictable developments in innovations and global economic circumstances. Once again, this forced organizations to reconsider their HRD and HRM policies. Lifetime employment within the same organization was no longer a prerogative for all employees. The traditional bonds between employer and employee were less self-evident. This was also reflected in the increase in the numbers of self-employed workers, who do not have permanent job contracts anymore but work for a particular employer only during the course of a specific project.

Therefore, today, the notion of lifetime employability seems most appropriate for our understanding of employees' careers. This implies that employees become accountable for investments in their own human capital and hence in their own job security, learning and career development (Van der Heijden *et al.*, 2009). As well as to being competent in a particular occupation, so-called key competences are regarded as crucial for one's employability. They allow one to adapt quickly to occupational changes and guarantee flexibility in moving across the labor market, including transfer to employment different from one's original occupation (European Commission, 2007). An example of such a key competence is 'a sense of initiative and entrepreneurship'; that is, remaining proactive in exploiting opportunities and organizing one's own future work and employment. Today's workforce needs to learn constantly and to be active in different kinds of networks to remain informed about the latest occupational developments. Even more than in the previous decade, the workplace becomes the prime learning environment for today's workforce.

Defining workplace learning

One of the most persistent and discussed problems in the contemporary debate on workplace learning concerns its definition. Such debates are usually rather futile, particularly in growing fields and disciplines such as the present one. Conceptual change reflects the maturing of a field, rather than fundamental disagreement between its practitioners. Any attempt to make permanent a particular definition is counterproductive as it stifles development by focusing on the need for all to agree rather than on the necessity of discussing pending issues. Furthermore, definitions that list characteristics that are each individually necessary and jointly exhaustive – something people in these kinds of discussions often seem to portray as the ideal – are seldom possible. It is much more productive to stick to a list of characteristics that matter but are not individually necessary, and that jointly cover the intended meaning without exhausting it fully.

Such an approach was adopted by Van der Klink and Streumer (in press) and Streumer and Kho (2006). Following them and in accordance with Jacobs and Park (2009), we see workplace learning as the fruitful interaction of two processes, working and learning. Furthermore, we propose to discuss workplace learning in terms of dimensions that allow one to distinguish various kinds of workplace learning. This idea allows nuanced positioning of the various workplace learning practices on each separate dimension. Here two of the main dimensions, formality and location, will be briefly outlined.

What constitutes a workplace?

The terms 'work' and 'workplace' are problematic, 'for their conventional usage tends to ignore important spheres of unpaid work in homes and communities' (Fenwick, 2001, p. 3). Moreover they assume that work is based in unitary, identifiable, geographically organized places and activities.

The expanding opportunities for work that the latest technologies provide only add to these problems. State-of-the art ICT software and tools allow many employees to carry out their work activities in places other than their office, such as their own homes. Also the number of project groups whose members work in different locations and/or in different time zones, is increasing. It is therefore appropriate to define the workplace as any setting in which an employee performs work duties, even if this location is his/her home. In addition, the rise of opportunities for designing high-fidelity simulations of work settings makes the notion of the workplace even more complex. Simulated workplaces are useful as they allow one to learn and experiment safely with situations that cannot be tested in authentic work settings because of potential risks to individuals or work processes. Simulations thus provide an optimal correspondence between potential future work activities and one's competences.

Informal learning in the workplace

Tynjälä (2008) claims that if researchers were asked to mention the most typical feature of workplace learning, most of them would probably refer to the unplanned nature of learning experiences in the workplace, that is its informality. In general, workplace learning experiences occur incidentally, as a spin-off from other (working) activities. Formal learning only represents a minor fraction of the learning that takes place in the workplace (see for example Lave and Wenger (1991) and Resnick (1987)). Marsick (2006) argued that 60% to 80% of the learning in today's workplace occurs informally, whereas Canadian national surveys revealed that even 82% of employees considered themselves to be engaged in job-related informal learning with an average of six hours a week (Livingstone & Eichler, 2005).

The learning potential of the workplace

Onstenk (1997) proposed a well-elaborated theory on the factors that promote workplace learning. His theory is strongly rooted in earlier notions such as the work of the German researchers Baitsch and Frei (1980) and also integrates the findings of quite different streams of inquiry. In this chapter, we mainly rely on descriptions of Onstenk's theory as included in the work of Van Zolingen and

Wortel (2011) and Van der Klink (2004). The likelihood of learning in the work-place is determined by: 1) the repertoire of an employee's competences; 2) the employee's willingness to learn, ranging from resistance to motivation for active and deliberate learning; and 3) the learning opportunities embedded in the work-place (see Figure 8.1).

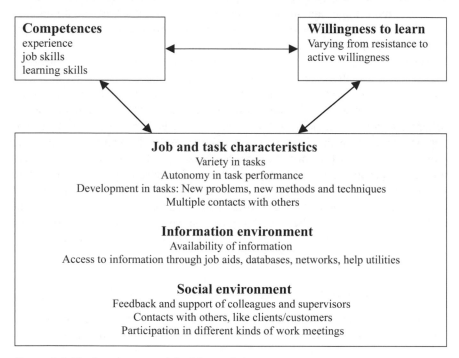

Figure 8.1 The learning potential of the workplace
Source: based on Van Zolingen & Wortel (in press)

Apart from the employee's motivation and his/her competences, opportunities for learning in the workplace depend strongly on: 1) job characteristics, 2) the information environment, and 3) the social environment.

The first factor, the content and complexity of a job, determines to a large extent the learning opportunities within a work setting, especially such character-istics as:

- different types of tasks included in one job: planning and coordination, exec-utive and controlling tasks;
- sufficient autonomy for employees to perform their job tasks;
- opportunities to be regularly engaged in dealing with unexpected problems, so they remain familiar with the latest methods, techniques and products;

- opportunities to build and maintain contacts with significant others (e.g. colleagues, customers) (Onstenk, 1997).

The second factor, the information environment, affects learning opportunities since employees need to have access to different kinds of up-to-date information (availability of computers, access to intranet, the Internet, manuals, and handbooks). Access to publications that present the task execution clearly and simply could be helpful, especially for tasks that are seldom carried out (Van der Klink, 2004).

The third and final factor concerns the social environment. It is relevant since the behavior of others, such as the manager, team members, and other colleagues may provide or inhibit learning opportunities in the workplace. It is vital that employees receive support from their colleagues and manager (through feedback, instructions, and encouragement) for performing their daily tasks and for meaningful and critical reflection on problems and problem solving. In addition, being engaged in different kinds of conversations at work offers employees information and cues supportive for learning purposes (see for example Lave & Wenger, 1991; Solomon, Boud & Rooney, 2006).

During the past decade, several studies have identified factors that are conducive to workplace learning (see for example Ashton, 2004; Lohman, 2005; Skule, 2004; Van der Heijden *et al.*, 2009; Van der Klink & Streumer, 2006). These studies also revealed some unsettling information. The opportunities for workplace learning differ strongly between jobs, companies, and branches of companies (Skule, 2004). Most workplace learning is strongly related to the 'here and now' and is geared to mainly minor changes in tasks, procedures, and methods. It allows one to increase one's competences to perform the current tasks better but, because of its limited scope, it is questionable to what extent it contributes to expanding one's long-term employability (Garrick, 1998; Van der Heijden *et al.*, 2009). In general, current workplaces do not provide sufficient 'space' to reflect thoroughly on work, learning, and career (Boud, 2006; Poell, 2006; Tjepkema, 2003). Additional organizational interventions are necessary to establish more favorable learning conditions at work, especially if workplace learning ought to contribute to the development of new knowledge, or improvements in existing work practices. The recent technological enhancement of learning, we surmise, is the kind of intervention that significantly alters learning at the workplace. In the next sections we will explore technology-enhanced workplace learning further.

From media-supported training to technology-enhanced learning

Technology-supported learning, also known as e-learning, has gone through four phases: media-supported training, computer-based training, Web-based training, and the currently emerging technology-enhanced learning. Each phase is linked to the development of a particular technology. In turn, each phase affords a particular understanding of workplace learning, as displayed in Table 8.2. The technology phases described in this table are not separate developments; most of the technologies still exist and are applied next to each other. The phases described only show the peak-periods of the technologies in question.

Table 8.2 The four phases of technology-supported learning and their relevance for workplace learning

	Media-supported training	Computer-based training (CBT)	Web-based training (WBT)	Technology-enhanced learning (TEL)
Period	Until 1980	1970–1990	1990–	2000–
Applied media	Mass media, broadcasting via radio and television	Not connected PC (stand alone) but interactive training	Connected PCs – Learning management systems (LMS)	Internet as digital habitat, personalised learning environments (PLE)
Dominant types of training and learning	Allows many learners to attend pre-defined fixed learning contents	Designed for individual learners in front of a PC	Designed for online group-based training	Designed for learners with individual learning goals and learning communities
	One size fits all training	First personalized learning approaches by adaptive learning models (learning styles)	Computer supported training systems that are aligned to state-of-the-art education system	Highly personalized delivery of learning content
		Formal learning scenarios, replacing teachers with PCs	Formal learning scenarios, teachers and students remain in traditional roles	Informal learning and social learning scenarios, learning in networks and communities
Content of training and learning	Created by mass media providers	Created by universities and companies	Created by universities and companies	Created by universities and companies
			Learning material standardization (IMS, SCORM)	Partly made publicly available as Open Educational Resources (OER)
				Users generate content
				Mobile learning
				Educational data and learning analytics

Media-supported training

Media-supported training traditionally consisted of paper-based correspondence courses, using the regular mail for communication between teachers and students. This traditional way of training is still applied today in universities that offer distance education and in corporate training. The first electronic media-supported learning approaches were broadcast by radio and later by television. These media stimulated the rise of distance-learning universities that could easily disseminate their courses to schools, companies, and other large organizations (Bates, 2005). Still, many of today's learning scenarios apply a similar approach, although the regular mail, radio or television have been replaced by faster, computer-supported communication techniques.

Computer-based training

Computer-based training (CBT) consists of self-paced learning activities that are accessible via a computer. CBT was initially delivered by CD-ROMS or DVDs and presented the training content most of the time in a linear way, similar to reading a book. The added value of CBT was the extension of text with interactive animation and videos, as well as assessment tests. CBT is often used for teaching facts, procedures, or guidelines. Examples include mastering new software (e.g. word processing), learning safety procedures, or training in product features for marketing staff (Pritchard, 1989). Especially during the early 1990s, CBT was applied on a broad scale in universities, schools, and enterprises, but the rise of Internet significantly diminished its use. However, even today there still is a market for CBT. A huge variety of different learning topics such as languages, mathematics, and games are offered and it is especially valued by parents who want their children to use computers sensibly.

Web-based training

Web-based training (WBT) marked a new decade of media-supported training. The training content is no longer delivered via CDs or DVDs but via the Internet. The Web-based learning technologies stimulated the development of infrastructures for education and training within organizations (Mioduser *et al.*, 2000). At present, various learning management systems (LMS) appear as an open-source (e.g. Moodle) or commercial (e.g. Blackboard) product for the delivery of online courses. The main purpose of LMS is to deliver learning content, offer communication facilities, and keep track of the learners from an administrative point of view. LMSs are still used in larger organizations and by almost every university. The rise of LMS also forced several standardization processes, such as those involving SCORM[1] and IMS-LD,[2] to make course contents exchangeable between different systems. LMS have similar features. They are strongly tailored to ideas such as instructional design and formal training models.

Typical features are:

- Course management;
- Administration of learning content;
- Self-assessment quizzes;
- IMS and SCORM importer and exporter;
- Asynchronous (email, forums) and synchronous communications (chat, whiteboard, teleconferencing).

Technology-enhanced learning

Technology-enhanced learning (TEL) focuses on the technological support of any pedagogical approach that utilizes technology, including informal learning approaches.

TEL deploys technologies from various technology-driven research fields. In that way, it creates new kinds of learning scenarios and enhances the development of novel learning and teaching approaches. Besides the traditional features of LMS systems, the emerging technologies help learners to reflect (e.g. Wopereis, Sloep & Poortman, 2010), connect peer learners (e.g. Van Rosmalen *et al.*, 2008), and offer personalized information support. Examples of these emerging technologies are tools for measurement, collecting data, analysis and reporting data about learners and their contexts, for purposes of understanding and optimizing learning and the environments in which this learning occurs.

The growth of educational data created by CBT, WBT, Open Educational Resources, and the increasing amount of user-created content on the web are a driving force for TEL. This growing amount of data made information retrieval technologies applicable for the educational domain (Johnson *et al.*, 2011; Retalis, 2006). Such technologies are used to analyze data and offer personalized information for the needs and context of individual learners. It is expected that increased opportunities for personalized learning will have a dual effect – reduction of delivery costs accompanied by more effective learning experiences, accelerating competence development, and increasing collaboration between learners. This matters in higher education as well as in workplace learning scenarios (Schoefegger, Seitlinger & Ley, 2010).

Thus, TEL can play a role in documenting the development of employees throughout their learning trajectories. Furthermore, knowledge exchange and social interactions can be made visual. Such visual representations of knowledge exchange can bring new insights and enhance reflection on learning at the workplace.

Emerging practices in workplace learning

Learning technologies have not gone unnoticed to workplace learning. This section presents three examples of technology-supported workplace learning. The examples describe novel practices. Although the authors have anecdotal evidence that they result in more effective workplace learning, no rigorous evaluations have yet been attempted. However, we still present them as they represent interesting and challenging attempts at innovating workplace learning. Before presenting them, we discuss a few fundamental, shared characteristics.

First, the examples demonstrate that people tend to learn and work in different settings (home, office, on-the-road, holiday), which questions the notion of a geographically demarcated workplace. Second, they point to the critical role people themselves have in organizing their own learning. Technology-enhanced workplace learning tends to be informal. It is far less designed by trainers or controlled by employers and it allows, or maybe even demands, that people act as self-directed and independent learners who are able and willing to steer their own learning. Third, all examples show learning opportunities that are enabled because of the use of a specific technology. This does not necessarily imply that the learning opportunities only occur because of the existence of particular technology. However, it does point out that technology truly helps to create learning opportunities that were not obvious to the point of being practically absent.

Learning networks

Contemporary social networks, such as Facebook and LinkedIn, encourage people to contact others, become 'friends,' and stay informed about each other's lives and work experiences. In short, they are about communicating. A learning network is in many ways akin to these social networks, but differs from them in that they are specially designed to foster learning, emphasizing informal and non-formal kinds of learning. Learning networks have two central features.

First, they focus on supporting learning processes in which people learn with and from each other. In them, a participant has access to both other participants and resources that are accessible through the learning network. Instead of adopting primarily a re-active consumer role, the participant becomes a proactive co-creator of his/her own competence development, actively searching for resources, and asking for input and feedback from fellow participants. Moreover, participants can easily and actively contribute to enlarging the existing body of knowledge stored in the learning network, for example through answering questions posed by other members, and by adding information themselves, like documents, blog posts, videos, etc.

Second, as already indicated, learning networks are online environments that have explicitly been designed to support learning processes. They could be built from scratch, make use of a blend of existing social software tools only, or be designed as a mix of both.

An example of such a learning network is the recently launched Handover Toolbox (see Figure 8.2) for medical professionals (note that 'toolbox' is a little confusing). It addresses the issue of the mistakes that are made at the 'handing over' of patients between medical professionals. Usually patients receive hospital treatment from multiple medical professionals. They do not always hand over all the relevant patient information to each other and this then results in errors which can seriously affect a patient's health. A group of well-informed medical professionals worked on collecting a broad range of information, grouped into subtopics in the Handover Toolbox. This learning network offers opportunities for retrieving information, for discussions, and/or for sharing their own ideas (by posting blogs or adding documents).

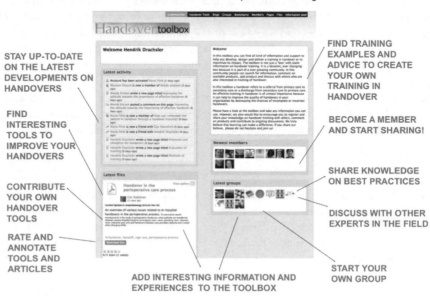

The Handover Toolbox as an example of a learning network

Figure 8.2 The homepage of the Handover Toolbox

To facilitate the process of knowledge sharing, groups are formed that are dedicated to particular subtopics, which support participants in finding others with highly similar interests (see Figure 8.3). Examples are a group working on training methods (effective training methods to increase professionals' skills in performing handovers), and a group dedicated to improving handovers in developing countries. To further encourage knowledge sharing, the learning network offers advanced options, for example RSS feeds for 'subscribing' to the latest ads on particular topics, or search utilities to quickly find persons and materials related to one's search terms.

In practice, learning networks differ strongly with respect to the topics they specialize in, their openness and their purposes. Networks vary, for example, in their membership policies. Some of them are developed by and restricted to a closed, predefined group, such as employees of a particular company; other networks rather attempt to attract a broad range of potential participants.

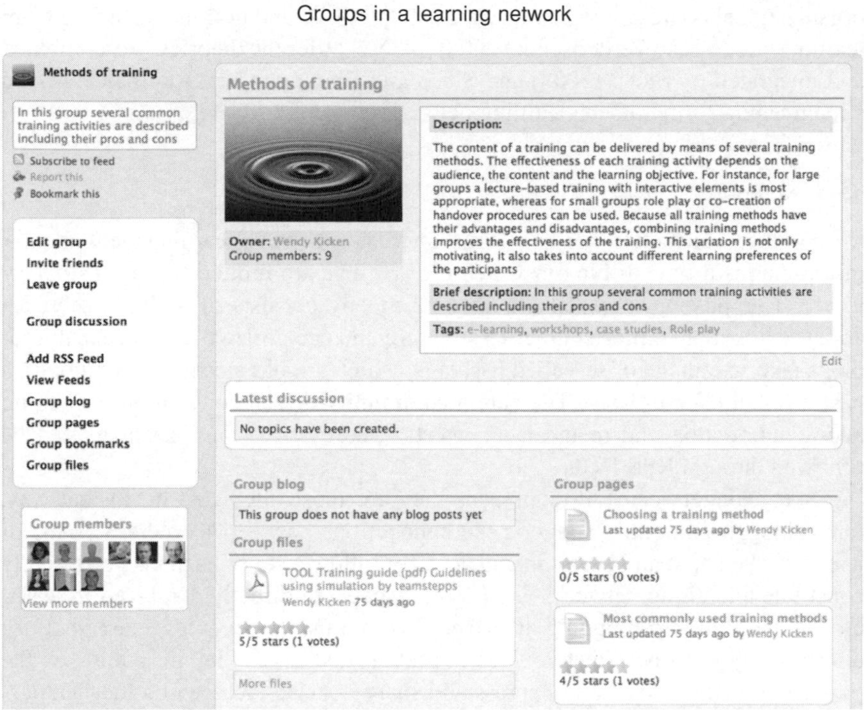

Groups in a learning network

Figure 8.3 An example of a group within the Handover Toolbox

Although from the viewpoint of a company it is quite understandable to remain cautious about open entrance policies, for example, to ensure that vital information is shared with competitors, networks that attract heterogeneous groups of participants appear to be more in demand and successful in the long run (Sloep, 2008). The ultimate success of any learning network lies in its potential to attract large groups of people who are interested in learning through sharing and creating knowledge. A successful learning network usually has a number of communities that concentrate on learning about specific subthemes (e.g. the groups in the Handover Toolbox example).

The purposes of learning networks range from a principal focus on sharing ideas and exchanging information to a focus on the actual development of new knowledge. In the latter example, sharing existing knowledge is then usually considered as a valuable precondition that supports participants in establishing common ground.

The concept of the learning network is strongly grounded in theories on communities of practice (Wenger, White & Smith, 2009), that investigate conditions under which digital groups will flourish in their learning endeavors, theories on social learning phenomena (Bandura, 1977), notions on social capital in organizational contexts (Nahapiet & Ghoshal, 1998), and notions regarding team learning processes (Verdonschot, 2009). These different theories are combined and integrated by Sloep (2008) and Sloep and Berlanga (2011) in their work on strengthening further of the learning network concept.

Micro-blogs

Mirco-blogs can create very dynamic and fast growing learning networks. A micro-blog is a type of blog in which the postings are limited to, say, 140 characters. This posting is called a tweet and mostly consists of a single sentence and/or a link to an online source. To structure and categorize these tweets, micro-blogs take advantage of so-called hashtags, which are like normal tags but with a hash symbol ('#') in front. They are a community-driven convention for adding additional context and metadata to tweets. Like normal tags, hashtags can be followed through RSS feeds.

Micro-bloggers can follow persons they are most interested in. In that way, micro-blogging strongly supports the connections between learners. Groups of learners who share an interest in and actively follow a set of hash tags effectively constitute a learning network. The posted tweets are directly displayed in learners' personal micro-blogging interface. From this, it becomes clear that for micro-blogging to be effective, it is important that all tweets are public, as the purpose of micro-blogs is to express and share concise ideas with other learners within the network. The most prominent micro-blogging services are Twitter, Jaiku and identi.ca. More recently, varieties of services and software have been developed. Squeelr, for example, adds geolocation and pictures to the micro-blog with a time line. In that way, the micro-blogs can become contextualized to physical locations and time stamps.

To deal with sensitive and more confidential information, organizations can take advantage of in-house micro-blogging solutions, such as Yammer, that make the tweets available within the network of the organization only. But also in that example the default is that tweets are openly available to all members of the organization.

Mirco-blogs especially support informal learning in the workplace and are therefore very powerful means for fast knowledge exchange. Using micro-blogging for workplace learning has two main advantages. First, micro-blogs generate ideas in a cost-effective way. By posting ideas in a micro-blog, everybody in the network can reply and further develop them. In that way, the collective knowledge within the entire organization can be utilized for sharing and developing knowledge in a way that requires very little effort because there is no need to arrange formal meetings. Micro-blogs increase the possibilities for informal knowledge sharing which usually takes place during lunch breaks or around the coffee machine. Second, most of the micro-blogging tools are also available on mobile devices such as smartphones and provide access to the latest information anywhere.

Micro-blogging combined with mobile devices could lead to unexpected and interesting micro-blogging networks, such as, for example, the tweeting farmer community in Nebraska that exchanges weather updates and other relevant information regarding farming in that region (CNN Tech, 2009). Not only do farmers follow other farmers in that network, but they are also followed by tourists and market traders who are interested in the latest news about the region and the new crop. The traders receive much more quickly an impression of the quality of the new crop and do not have to rely any more on research studies forecasting the amount and quality of the future crop. The information that is presented in these studies is usually less up-to-date compared to the knowledge shared in the farmers' tweeting network.

Personalized learning environments (PLEs)

People need tools to organize and manage the increasing amount of information available in their social networks, social bookmarks, blogs, and micro-blogging systems. Personalized learning environments (PLEs) help to organize the information in a way comparable to the traditional newspaper that combines different kinds in one view. The main difference between PLEs and a traditional newspaper is that the information supplied in PLEs is provided by many individual contributors. Furthermore, PLEs have certain functionalities that go beyond a traditional newspaper; they are perhaps better understood as some kind of highly interactive cockpit. PLEs aggregate different Internet sources and combine them in a personal view (see Figure 8.4). A web browser to surf through the Web can be seen as standardized cockpit (Figure 8.4, left picture). Such a cockpit can be adapted and enriched with additional Web 2.0 functionalities (Figure 8.4, right picture). An adapted cockpit is a highly personalized environment as it contains a set of tools that an individual user prefers. It is a personal learning environment to navigate through the Web and learning networks.

Figure 8.4 A standardized (left) and adapted cockpit (right)

Examples of personal cockpits (see Figure 8.5) are iGoogle or Netvibes, which allow their users to add and combine different information sources into one website. In their simplest forms, PLEs support informal learning as they require no institutional background, curriculum structure, and are free to use. Their functionalities focus on the needs of the individual learner rather than on institutional needs such as those of, say, a human resource Development department. Although they are most appropriate for informal learning, PLEs could be integrated and aligned with formal learning programs in universities and companies (Behnam, Martin & Sandra, 2009). PLEs possess more functionalities than micro-blogging systems and they can combine different social media sources in one environment. Users of PLEs usually integrate their micro-blogging system into their own PLE.

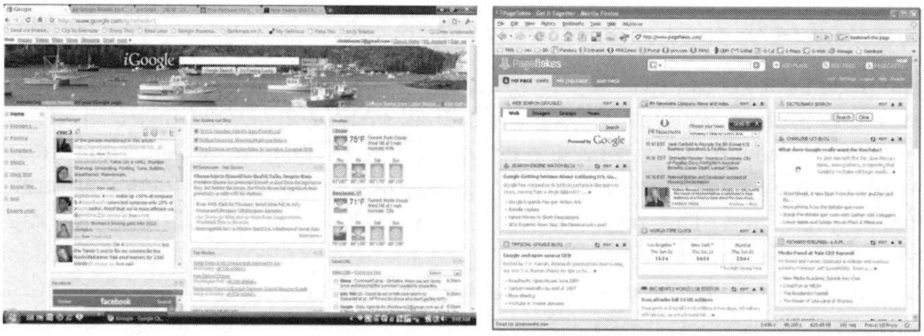

Figure 8.5 Screenshots of personalized learning environments of Google (left) and Pageflakes (right)

Conclusions

In this chapter we argued that technology-enhanced workplace learning is increasingly recognized as a meaningful and promising concept that deserves further exploration. This section presents the main conclusions and highlights the issues that, in our opinion, deserve attention.

First, there is a shift from formalized training to everyday informal learning in the workplace. Traditionally, a highly structured and organized way of training was deemed indispensable to efficiently teach students, using teaching methods, a syllabus, assessments, and certificates. This model of training is nowadays being increasingly replaced by learning practices that are not necessarily structured and organized according the received logic of training. That does not necessarily imply that everyday learning in the workplace is by definition unstructured, organized and devised by a mindset different from the traditional training philosophy.

Neither does the increased attention for informal learning in the workplace necessarily imply a significant devaluation of traditional training. Training certificates are still considered to be important and observable tokens of one's expertise and we do not expect this deeply engrained societal belief to change overnight.

Second, closely related to the move away from formalized training is the changing role of employees. Society no longer sees them as passive consumers of training modules, but they are expected to demonstrate high levels of agency and need to direct their own learning. The growing numbers of self-employed professionals must rely on their own initiatives to learn about the latest developments within their occupation.

Third, it goes without saying that the emerging technologies are essential for many workers to stay in touch with the latest developments. The emerging technologies, as for example applied to learning networks, allow us to find different types of information and to become connected to others who share similar interests. What is very consistent in the evolving field of technologies is that they are under-used for the learning purposes for which they are most appropriate. For example, many workers regard their learning network as a traditional website, and they do not use it as an interactive environment that allows them to connect with their fellow workers. What they miss is its instrumental value in connecting with colleagues. Admittedly, the way in which such sites have been designed and laid out often encourages this kind of thinking. So, the notion that they themselves can generate and add content to the learning network is, especially for novice members, at least one bridge too far. Apart from an interactive design that better highlights the networked character, learners almost invariably need guidance and support in utilizing the new opportunities for learning in a learning network. The availability of technology is no guarantee for its most effective use and people need to be supported in becoming more advanced users of the latest technologies.

Fourth, technology-enhanced workplace learning is an under-researched field. A comprehensive understanding of its potentials and pitfalls requires significant research efforts. The lack of sound research findings follows both from the speed with which new technologies become available, thus leaving researchers always in pursuit of the latest and the newest, but it also follows from the relative novelty of the field. As we sketched in the above, we have just started to witness a re-evaluation of the formal training methods of the past, let alone that we could already have an evidence-based opinion of the opportunities of the present. We will discuss briefly what we see as the current, most prominent research topics that need to be addressed.

It is expected that the next generations entering the labor market will have more experience in the latest technologies and therefore are more willing to utilize them for learning purposes. Many high-school students cannot imagine what life would be like without a mobile phone and permanent access to social media, like Facebook. So, we may surmise that the eagerness to use new technologies is presumably not the issue, but is it? It is gradually becoming clear that while the younger generation is more inclined to use social media, they do not necessarily use them better or more sensibly. And even if they did, other challenges remain that have to do with the best ways, for example, of supporting these next generations in advancing their abilities to find their way efficiently and effectively in an ever expanding and overwhelming load of information. This is about information literacy, if you like. Solutions for this overload can be partly technology-driven, like developing and implementing smart devices, such as recommender systems, that select and structure the information according to the user's requirements. But in addition to these devices, people need to advance their skills in finding and retrieving the most appropriate information (Pirolli, 2007; Gruwel-Brand & Wopereis, 2010).

Next to the required skills and knowledge there is also the need to raise awareness about the possible negative consequences of having a presence on the Internet. So, people need to learn that online friends and offline friends are different entities, with different social rules of 'engagements' attached to them (Boyd, 2006). We are only starting to scratch the surface of the vast and profound consequences this will have on our online social life. More research, resulting in a better understanding and perhaps guidelines, is needed.

Related to this research topic is the need to maintain a coherent, online social identity, which is the online equivalent of our offline presence. As much as learning and work experience at the workplace are automatically associated with the physical persons that we are, this is far from the case in the online world. There, we may have several, fragmented online identities that are spread over the various social networking sites and online learning providers that we happen to visit. And yet, a coherent online social identity matters. It matters, as it allows us to receive recommendations for learning events and opportunities that are better targeted to suit our own individual needs and preferences. It matters for our clients and employers, as they both can get a better impression of someone's suitability for a particular project or job. This requires research at the level of understanding what an online social identity is, what it entails in terms of privacy and regulations, and what it requires in terms of technical infrastructures and interoperability standards (Berlanga & Sloep, 2011).

This set of prominent research topics can be extended, encompassing fields as different as the sciences of learning, social science, and computer science. We predict that technology-enhanced workplace learning has an interesting and bright future!

Notes

1   SCORM – (Sharable Content Object Reference Model) is a collection of standards and specifications for Web-based e-learning. It defines communication between client side content and LMS systems. For instance it allows e-learning courses to be exported from one LMS and imported into another LMS system (http://scorm.com/scorm-explained/technical-scorm/).

2   IMS-LD IMS Learning Design supports the use of a wide range of pedagogies in Web-based e-learning. It provides a generic and flexible metadata structure to show how a resource should be applied in certain pedagogies. It can be used to demonstrate many different pedagogies. The language was originally developed at the Open University of the Netherlands (OUNL) and is now IMS-Global standardized http://www.imsglobal.org/learningdesign/

References

Ashton, D. N. (2004) The impact of organizational structure and practices on learning in the workplace. *International Journal of Training and Development*, 8, 43–53.

Baitsch, C. & Frei, F. (1980) *Qualifizierung in der Arbeitstätigkeit* (Becoming qualified at work). Bern: Verlag Hans Huber.

Baldwin, T. T. & Ford, J. K. (1988) Transfer of training: A review and directions for future research. *Personnel Psychology*, 41, 63–105.

Bandura, A. (1977) *Social Learning Theory*. Oxford: Prentice Hall.

Bates, A. W. T. (2005) *Technology, E-learning and Distance Education*, 2nd edn. London: Routledge.

Behnam, T., Martin, E. & Sandra, S. (2009) Personal learning environnments for higher education: A mashup based widget concept (Electronic Version). Second Workshop Mash-Up Personal Learning Envri, onments (MUPPLE09) in conjunction with 4th European Conference on Technology Enhanced Learning (EC-TEL09), 506. Retrieved September 29, 2009 from http://ftp1.de.freebsd.org/Publications/CEUR-WS/Vol-506/.

Berlanga, A. J. & Sloep, P. B. (2011) Towards a digital learner identity. In F. Abel, V. Dimitrova, E. Herder & G.-J. Houben (eds), Augmenting user models with real world experiences workshop (AUM). In conjunction with UMAP 2011. July, 15, 2011, Girona, Spain. Girona, Spain. Retrieved from http://www.wis.ewi.tudelft.nl/aum2011/aum-proceedings.pdf

Boud, D. (2006) Creating the space for reflection at work, in D. Boud, P. Cressey & P. Docherty (eds), *Productive reflection at work*. London/New York: Routledge, pp. 158–169.

Boyd, D. (2006) Friends, friendsters, and fop 8: Writing community into being on social network. *First Monday*, 11. Retrieved from http://firstmonday.org/issues/issue11_12/boyd/index.html

CNN Tech (2009) Retrieved June 8, 2011 from http://articles.cnn.com/2009-07-02/tech/twitter.farmer_1_smartphones-farm-puresense/2?_s=PM:TECH.

European Commission (2007) *Key Competences for Lifelong Learning. European Reference Framework*. Luxembourg: Office for Official Publications of the European Communities.

Fenwick (2001) Tides of change: New themes and questions in workplace learning. *New Directions for Adult and Continuing Education*, 92, 3–17.

Garrick, J. (1998) *Informal Learning in the Workplace. Unmasking Human Resource Development*. London/New York: Routledge.

Gruwel-Brand, S. & Wopereis, I. (2010) *Word Informatievaardig* (becoming skilled in information). Groningen/Houten: Noordhoff Uitgevers.

Jacobs, R. L. & Park, Y. (2009) A proposed conceptual framework of workplace learning: Implications for theory development and research in Human Resource Development. *Human Resource Development Review*, 8, 33–150.

Johnson, L., Smith, R., Willis, H., Levine, A., Haywood, K. (2011) *The 2011 Horizon Report*. Austin, TX: The New Media Consortium.

Kaufman, B. E. (2001) Human resources and industrial relations. Commonalities and differences. *Human Resource Management Review*, 11, 339–374.

Latham, G. P. & Crandall, S. R. (1991) Organizational and social factors. In J. E. Morrison (ed.), *Training for performance*. Chichester: John Wiley & Sons, pp. 260–285.

Lave, J. & Wenger, E. (1991) *Situated Learning*. Cambridge: Cambridge University Press.

Livingstone, D. W., and Eichler, M. (2005) Mapping the field of lifelong (formal and informal) learning and (paid and unpaid) work. Joint keynote at the Future of lifelong learning and work international conference, Toronto, June 20, 2005.

Lohman, M. C. (2005) A survey of factors influencing the engagement of two professional groups in informal workplace learning activities. *Human Resource Development Quarterly*, 16, 501–527.

Marsick, V. (2006) Informal strategic learning in the workplace. In J. N. Streumer, (ed.), *Work-related learning*. Dordrecht: Springer, pp. 51–69.

McCord, A. (1987) Job training, in R. L. Craig (ed.), *Training and Developing Handbook: A Guide to Human Resource Development*. New York: McGraw-Hill, pp. 363–382.

Mioduser, D., Nachmias, R., Lahav, O. & Oren, A. (2000) Web-based learning environments: Current pedagogical and technological state. *Journal of Research on Computing in Education*, 33, 55.

Nahapiet, J. & Goshal, S. (1998) Social capital, intellectual capital and the organizational advantage. *Academy of Management Review*, 23, 242–266.

Onstenk, J. H. A. M. (1997) *Lerend leren werken: Brede vakbekwaamheid en de integratie van leren, werken en innoveren* (Learning to learn to work: Broad competence and the integration of learning, working and innovating). Nijmegen: Universiteit Nijmegen.

Pirolli, P. (2007) *Information foraging theory: Adaptive interaction with information.* Oxford, New York: Oxford University Press.

Poell, R. F. (2006) *Personeelsontwikkeling in ontwikkeling. Naar een werknemersperspectief op human resource development* (Human resource development in development: Toward an employee perspective on human resource development). Rotterdam: Performa Uitgeverij.

Pritchard W. H. (1989) A review of computer-based training materials: Current state of the art instruction and Interaction. *Educational Technology*, 29, 7.

Resnick, L. B. (1987) Learning in school and out. *Educational Researcher*, 16, 13–20.

Retalis, S., Papasalouros, A., Psaromiligkos, Y., Siscos, S. & Kargidis, T. (2006) Towards networked learning analytics – a concept and a tool. Proceedings of the Networked Learning Conference 2006, Lancaster, UK.

Ruona, W. E. A. & Gibson, S. K. (2004) The making of twenty-first-century HR: An analysis of the convergence of HRM, HRD and OD. *Human Resource Management*, 43, 49–66.

Schoefegger, K., Seitlinger, P. & Ley, T. (2010) Towards a user model for personalized recommendations in work-integrated learning: A report on an experimental study with a collaborative tagging system. In N. Manouselis, H. Drachsler, K. Verbert & O. C. Santos. (eds), *Proceedings of the 1st Workshop on Recommender Systems for Technology Enhanced Learning (RecSysTEL 2010)*. Amsterdam: Elsevier, pp. 213–228.

Skule, S. (2004) Learning conditions at work: A framework to understand and assess informal learning in the workplace. *International Journal of Training & Development*, 8, 8–20.

Sloep, P. B. (2008) *Netwerken voor lerende professionals; hoe leren in netwerken kan bijdragen aan een leven lang leren* (Networking for learning professionals, how networked learning can contribute to lifelong learning). Unpublished inaugural address, Heerlen: Open Universiteit Nederland.

Sloep, P. B. & Berlanga, A .J. (2011) Learning networks, networked learning (Redes de aprendizaje, aprendizaje en red). Retrieved June 22, 2011 fromhttp://www.revista comunicar.com/pdf/preprint/37/05-PRE-10947-Sloep-En.pdf

Sloep, P. B., Boon, J., Cornu, B., Klebl, M., Lefrère, P., Naeve, A., Scott, P., Tinoca, L. (2011) A European Research Agenda for Lifelong Learning. *International Journal of Technology Enhanced Learning*, 3, 204–228.

Solomon, N., Boud, D. & Rooney, D. (2006) The in-between: Exposing everyday learning at work. *International Journal for Lifelong Education*, 25, 3–13.

Streumer, J. N. & Kho, M. (2006) The world of work-related-learning. In J. N. Streumer (ed.), *Work-Related Learning*. Dordrecht/New York: Springer.

Swanson, R. A. & Holton, E. F. III (2008) *Foundations of human resource development*. San Francisco: Berreth-Koehler Publishers.

Tjepkema, S. (2003) *The Learning Infrastructure of Self-managing Work Teams* (dissertation). Enschede: Twente University Press.

Tynjälä, P. (2008) Perspectives into learning at the workplace. *Educational Research Review*, 3, 130–154.

Van der Heijden, B. I. J. M., Boon, J., Van der Klink, M. R. & Meijs, E. (2009) Employability enhancement through formal and informal learning. An empirical study among Dutch non-academic university staff members. *International Journal of Training & Development*, 13, 19–37.

Van der Klink, M. R. (2004) Benaderingen voor het ontwerpen van opleiden en leren op de werkplek. *Handboek Effectief Opleiden*, 5.7-1.01–5.7-1.23. 's-Gravenhage: Reed Business Information.

Van der Klink, M. R. (2010) Human resource development, in F. Kluytmans (ed.), *Leerboek HRM*. Groningen/Houten: Noordhoff Uitgevers-Open Universiteit, pp. 311–338.

Van der Klink, M. R. & Streumer, J. N. (2006) The effectiveness of OJT in the context of HRD, in J. N. Streumer (ed.), *Work-related Learning*. Dordrecht: Springer, pp. 369–392.

Van der Klink, M. & Streumer, J. N. (in press) The boundaries of workplace learning: An introduction. *International Journal of Human Resource Development & Management*.

Van Rosmalen, P., Sloep, P., Kester, L., Brouns, F., De Croock, M., Pannekeet, K. *et al.* (2008) A learner support model based on peer tutor selection. *Journal of Computer Assisted Learning*, 24, 74–86. Retrieved from http://dspace.ou.nl/handle/1820/564.

Van Zolingen, S. J. & Wortel, L. (in press) Workplace learning: A new model applied in a case study in the Netherlands. *International Journal of Human Resource Development & Management*.

Wenger, E., White, N. & Smith, J. D. (2009) *Digital habitats: Stewarding technology for communities*. Portland, OR: CPsquare.

Wopereis, I. G. J. H., Sloep, P. B., Poortman, S. (2010) Weblogs as instruments for reflection-on-action in teacher education. *Interactive Learning Environments*, 18, 245–261. doi:10.1080/10494820.2010.500530

9   Webcam tests in personnel selection

Janneke K. Oostrom, Marise Ph. Born and
Henk T. van der Molen

The advent of graphical user interfaces, large memory capacities, sound and video cards, and the widespread use of the Internet opened the door for the development of various computerized tests that make use of digital media (Drasgow & Mattern, 2006). Current publications have provided a range of examples of this kind of tests, such as computer-based realistic job previews (e.g. Highhouse, Stanton & Reeve, 2004), multimedia situational tests (e.g. Richman-Hirsch, Olson-Buchanan & Drasgow, 2000), computerized in-basket exercises (e.g. Wiechmann & Ryan, 2003), and virtual reality tests (e.g. Aguinis, Henle & Beaty, 2001). All these tests aim to enhance the reliability of the tests; that is the extent to which the format is consistent with how the situation is encountered on the job (Lievens, Peeters & Schollaert, 2008). The present chapter focuses on a test which recently entered personnel selection practices and which makes use of the opportunities provided by digital media, namely a multimedia situational test with a constructed response format. In this test, challenging job-related scenarios are presented to applicants by using video clips. Samples of scenarios appear in Table 9.1. After the scenario is presented, applicants are asked to act out their response, while being filmed by a webcam (Oostrom, Born, Serlie & Van der Molen, 2010). This type of test is usually classified as a webcam test. Figure 9.1 shows an example of a screen from a webcam test.

Many organizations have incorporated webcam tests into their selection practices. However, research regarding this type of test is still scarce. This chapter describes and analyzes webcam tests. First, the main characteristics of webcam tests are described. Second, the benefits and challenges of webcam tests are discussed. After that, a review of webcam test research will be provided. The chapter will be concluded with a discussion of the major issues that need to be addressed in future studies.

Main features of webcam tests

Webcam tests belong to the category of situational tests or simulations, in which contextualized scenarios are presented that mimic key aspects of the future job (Lievens & De Soete, in press). Other examples of situational tests are situational interviews, role-play exercises, situational judgment tests (SJTs), and assessment

Table 9.1 Samples of webcam test scenarios

Introduction:
'A coworker is misbehaving: he doesn't stick to agreements, and his work is below standard or not finished on time. You have talked to him about these problems before. It can no longer go on in this way. You asked the coworker to come to your room (introduction).'

Coworker:
'You wanted to talk to me about something?'

Introduction:
'You have an appointment with an elderly client. The client has been looking for a job for several months now, but has not succeeded in finding a job (oral introduction).'

Job seeker:
'It's obvious why I can't find a job. Who wants to hire someone in his fifties nowadays?'

Note: The first scenario is taken from a webcam test that is intended to measure managerial skills. The second scenario is taken from a webcam test intended to measure effectiveness in consulting job seekers. Both tests are developed by Van der Maesen Koch HRM-Consultancy.

Figure 9.1 Screen display of a webcam test developed by Van der Maesen Koch HRM-Consultancy

center exercises. Situational tests are designed to sample behaviors that are required in actual work behavior (Motowidlo, Dunnette & Carter, 1990). They are based on the basic idea of behavioral consistency (Wernimont & Campbell, 1968). That is, they are based on the assumption that applicants' current behavior elicited by the stimuli of the test will be consistent with their future job behavior (Wernimont & Campbell, 1968). To this end, situational tests aim to maximize correspondence with the future job.

Situational tests can be used to assess different constructs, both cognitive and non-cognitive (Arthur & Villado, 2008; Chan & Schmitt, 2005). They are often multidimensional, as they measure a variety of performance dimensions (Arthur, Day, McNelly & Edens, 2003). Arthur *et al.* (2003), for example, showed that the constructs measured with assessment center exercises can be grouped into six dimensions: communication, consideration and awareness of others, drive, influencing others, organizing and planning, and problem solving. Christian, Edwards, and Bradley (2010) showed in a review of SJT research that a substantial number of SJTs (33%) measure heterogeneous composites, for example clusters of knowledge, skills, and abilities that sample particular job-related characteristics. In some cases, SJTs have been developed to assess specific constructs, most often leadership skills (38%) or interpersonal skills (13%). That most situational tests are designed to measure heterogeneous constructs discriminates them from more traditional selection tests, such as personality questionnaires or cognitive ability tests, which are designed to measure one or more specific constructs (Lievens & De Soete, in press).

Similar to multimedia or video-based SJTs, webcam tests present stimuli via short video clips. Because of this similarity with multimedia SJTs, webcam tests are often labeled as multimedia SJTs with a constructed-response item format (e.g. Lievens *et al.*, 2008; Olson-Buchanan & Drasgow, 2006). However, webcam tests and multimedia SJTs differ in two important features, namely the response format and the scoring method. The response format of a multimedia SJT has relatively low reliability (i.e. realism), because applicants are not asked to show actual behavior. Instead, after the situational stimulus is presented, applicants are presented with a list of plausible courses of action. Applicants are then asked to evaluate each course of action for either the likelihood that they would perform that way or for their effectiveness (Whetzel & McDaniel, 2009). SJTs measure applicants' behavioral intentions or knowledge instead of their actual behavior (Motowidlo, Brownlee & Schmit, 2008). In contrast, the response format of webcam tests has high reliability (Funke & Schuler, 1998). In a webcam test, applicants have to verbalize their own answer immediately after the situational stimulus is presented. The response time is usually limited to one or two minutes. Thus, a webcam test generates actual behavioral samples. The second feature that discriminates webcam tests from multimedia SJTs is the scoring method. Applicants' responses in an SJT are scored by the use of a previously developed scoring key based on theory, the opinion of experts, or on empirical grounds (Bergman, Drasgow, Donovan, Henning & Juraska, 2006). In contrast, applicants' responses in a webcam test are evaluated afterwards by trained assessors, who give their ratings independently of one another and work on the basis of a set of comprehensive scoring instructions.

Regarding their response format and scoring method, webcam tests share clear parallels with situational interviews or role-play exercises. Like webcam tests, situational interviews and role play exercises are evaluated by multiple trained assessors on a number of job-related dimensions (Oostrom *et al.*, 2010). However, whereas webcam tests may be administered to large groups and over the Internet, situational interviews and role play exercises are typically used for smaller samples, at a specific location, with assessors who are physically present (Gaugler & Thornton, 1989). Webcam tests also differ from situational interviews or role-play exercises in terms of their level of interactivity. Situational interviews and role-play exercises are highly interactive, as the applicants have to interact with assessors or role-players and the questions presented might depend on the applicant's answers to preceding questions (Lievens & De Soete, in press). In contrast, webcam tests score lower on interactivity as the stimuli are static and all applicants receive exactly the same set of situational stimuli. The low level of interactivity of webcam tests ensures the standardization of the test (Lievens *et al.*, 2008), whereas in assessment center exercises unintentional variance in situational stimuli may arise (Lievens, 1998).

Benefits and challenges

Webcam tests share several benefits typically associated with other multimedia tests, such as multimedia SJTs (Olson-Buchanan & Drasgow, 2006). The first benefit is the ease of administration. As described above, multimedia tests can be administered over the Internet, which allows to test large groups of applicants at once and on various locations (Lievens *et al.*, 2008), and applicants' responses are automatically recorded. The scoring instructions and applicants' recorded responses become accessible via the Internet immediately after the administration of the test.

Second, using video clips to present situational stimuli and generating actual behavioral samples, makes it possible to simulate detailed and realistic job-related scenarios (Weekley & Jones, 1997). Video clips are representative of workplace stimuli. Voice modulation, facial expressions, and other nonverbal behaviors are similar to what applicants would experience if they were having a real conversation (Drasgow & Mattern, 2006). When it is important for future employees to accurately perceive verbal and nonverbal situational cues, multimedia tests may provide a superior assessment of job-related skills compared to more traditional paper-and-pencil tests. This enhanced realism or reliability indeed has been shown to be related to the criterion-related validity of situational tests. For example, Lievens and Sackett (2006) demonstrated that an interpersonally oriented multimedia SJT has a higher criterion-related validity than its written counterpart in predicting students' performance on interpersonally oriented courses.

Enhanced realism has also been associated with how applicants react to selection tests. Multimedia tests provide a realistic job preview to the applicant and are therefore expected to be more attractive for applicants in terms of interest and motivation than traditional paper-and-pencil tests (Stricker, 1982). Richman-Hirsch, Olson-Buchanan, and Drasgow (2000) demonstrated that compared to a paper-and-pencil test, a multimedia version of the same test indeed yielded more positive reactions. The multimedia test was perceived as more content valid, more enjoyable and also led to more satisfaction with the assessment process. Chan and Schmitt (1997) demonstrated that participants rate the face validity of a multimedia SJT significantly more positively than the face validity of a paper-and-pencil SJT. Previous studies have demonstrated that positive applicant reactions are associated with applicants' intentions to accept the job, the likelihood of litigation against the outcome of the selection procedure, and perceived organizational attractiveness (Anderson, Lievens, Van Dam & Ryan, 2004; Chan & Schmitt, 2005; Gilliland, 1993; Ryan & Ployhart, 2000).

In addition, it is anticipated that the enhanced realism of multimedia tests would not be at the expense of standardization. In other situational tests, such as role-play exercises, the high level of reliability challenges the standardization of the test (Lievens & De Soete, in press). Role-play exercises often revolve unexpectedly, so that no two role-plays are exactly alike. However, in multimedia tests situations are presented in exactly the same way to all applicants, with no unintentional variance due to unexpected behaviors of the applicants or role players' acting performance.

Several researchers have argued that multimedia tests may serve to minimize subgroup differences in test performance (Chan, 1997; Ployhart & Holtz, 2008). Using a multimedia format instead of a paper-and-pencil format has been suggested as one of the strategies to reduce adverse impact. Adverse impact, refers to a substantially different rate of selection in hiring, which in general works to the disadvantage of a minority group (Ironson, Guion & Ostrander, 1982). Although cognitive ability tests have been found to be the best predictor of job performance (e.g. Schmidt & Hunter, 1998), these tests also have been found to produce the highest adverse impact with respect to ethnic minority groups (e.g. Hunter & Hunter, 1984). As many organizations believe it is important not only for business, but also for moral reasons to create a diverse workforce, researchers are searching for valid predictors of job performance that result in less adverse impact than cognitive ability tests. The use of multimedia reduces the reading demands, and subsequently the cognitive load of the test (Ployhart & Holtz, 2008). For example, Chan and Schmitt (1997) examined the effects of ethnicity, reading comprehension, and SJT medium (paper-and-pencil versus multimedia) on SJT performance. A substantial Black-White score difference of almost one standard deviation favoring Whites was found on the paper-and-pencil version of the SJT ($d = -.95$). The Black-White score difference was reduced substantially to about one-fifth of a standard deviation in the multimedia version of the SJT ($d = -.21$). Participants' reading comprehension explained a substantial portion of this effect. Therefore, multimedia tests may be valid predictors which result in less adverse impact than cognitive ability tests.

Thus far, the benefits of multimedia tests in general have been described. Yet, webcam tests also have an important anticipated benefit compared to other multimedia tests, such as multimedia SJTs. Funke and Schuler (1998) argued that the manner of responding affects the criterion-related validity of situational tests, leading to the highest criterion-related validity of situational tests with orally-given responses. As the manner of responding in webcam tests more closely resembles actual work conditions than does the manner of responding in multimedia SJTs, webcam tests are expected to be better predictors of future job performance (Motowidlo *et al.*, 1990).

There are also several challenges when developing and maintaining multimedia tests. The first and perhaps the most important disadvantage of multimedia tests may involve the initial investment required. For multimedia versions of selection tests, the development costs are much larger than for paper-and-pencil versions. Scripts must be written for the scenarios. The scenarios need to be filmed by a professional crew and with professional actors, and the recordings need to be edited. In addition, the administration costs of multimedia tests are higher than for paper-and-pencil tests exercises because technological investments have to be made for administering the test. Furthermore, in a webcam test, applicants' responses have to be rated afterwards by assessors. However, Drasgow, Olson-Buchanan, and Moberg (1999) demonstrated that the per-applicant costs of an interactive video assessment is much lower than the costs of an assessment center using a role-play exercise with actors and trained observers. Besides, the cost effectiveness (the pay-off) of any selection test is not only determined by the development and administration costs involved, but also by its criterion-related validity and an organization's selection ratio (Cronbach & Gleser, 1965). Therefore, a cost-benefit analysis is needed to ascertain whether multimedia tests are cost effective.

Another potential disadvantage of multimedia tests is that there often exists no single correct answer. Similar to role-play exercises, applicants' responses in webcam tests are evaluated by trained assessors (Oostrom *et al.*, 2010). The subjective nature of this judgment process could potentially be considered as a disadvantage of the webcam test. Therefore it is important to carefully select and train assessors preferably with a frame-of-reference training, in which the same evaluative standards are imposed on assessors (Lievens, 1998).

Table 9.2 provides a schematic overview of the characteristics of webcam tests and other situational tests.

A review of webcam test research

Research regarding the psychometric properties of webcam tests until now still is scarce. Webcam tests are a direct successor of tests in which applicants were presented with video clips depicting job-related situations and in which responses were recorded with an audio cassette or with a video camera. Before reviewing the research on webcam tests, we will first discuss research regarding these precursors.

Table 9.2 Schematic overview of the characteristics of webcam tests, multimedia SJTs, and role-play exercises or situational interviews

	Webcam test	Multimedia SJT	Role-play exercise/ situational interview
Ease of administration (e.g. to large group at once)	High	High	Low
Reliability of situational stimuli	High	High	High
Reliability of response	High	Low	High
Adverse impact	Low	Low	Moderate
Criterion-related validity	High	High	High
Standardization	High	High	Low-Moderate
Applicants' favorability reactions	High	High	High
Development costs	High	High	High
Administration costs	Moderate	Moderate	High
Scoring costs	High	Low	High

Stricker (1982) developed the first multimedia test with a constructed response format, called the 'Interpersonal Competence Instrument' (ICI), which was designed to measure effectiveness in dealing with other people. In the ICI, scenarios were presented in which a subordinate talks to a superior in a business setting. The responses of the participants were taped with an audio cassette and assessed for effectiveness and originality. Stricker reports a study in which the ICI was administered to 58 female students. The inter-rater reliability (r varied from .53 to .90) and internal consistency (α varied from .74 to .82) were substantial and the correlations with other tests (vocabulary test, figure test, and auditory measure of accuracy in social perception via spoken language) supported its construct validity.

Based on the findings of Stricker (1982), three multimedia tests with a constructed response format were developed in the Netherlands between 1982 and 1993 to measure the interpersonal competences of managers (Meltzer, 1995). In these multimedia tests, responses were filmed with a video camera. Multiple studies were conducted to shed light on their psychometric properties, with small samples varying between 5 and 59. General findings were in line with the results reported by Stricker in terms of the internal consistency and the inter-rater reliability.

Funke and Schuler (1998) compared the criterion-related validity of six types of situational tests intended to measure social skills. The situational tests systematically differed in the fidelity of the presented situation (either orally or via video) and the fidelity of the responses (multiple-choice responses, written constructed responses, or videotaped constructed responses). In their study among 75 students, Funke and Schuler found that response fidelity but not stimulus fidelity affected the criterion-related validity of situational tests, leading to the highest criterion-related validity for the situational test with videotaped constructed responses. However, an important drawback in the study of Funke and Schuler is their criterion measure, namely role-play behavior. Performance in a role play exercise is inherently different from job performance.

In their review of multimedia tests, Olson-Buchanan and Drasgow (2006) describe a multimedia test with a constructed response format developed by the U.S. Customs and Border Protection to assess future border patrol officers (Walker & Goldenberg, 2004, as described in Olson-Buchanan & Drasgow, 2006). It is unclear whether responses in this multimedia test were recorded with a video camera or with a webcam. Inter-rater reliabilities ranging from .67 to .78 were found. Olson-Buchanan and Drasgow argue that the open-ended response format is an innovative feature of multimedia situational testing, and research regarding the validity of multimedia tests with this response format should be conducted.

Oostrom *et al.* (2010) conducted the first field study on a webcam test, developed by a Dutch HRD-consultancy firm. This test was intended to measure effectiveness in the core task of an employment consultant, namely consulting job seekers, and consisted of 12 scenarios. The scenarios in the webcam test started with an oral description of the situation, followed by a fragment of a conversation between the participant and a job seeker. The responses were filmed with a webcam and assessed afterwards by three subject matter experts (SMEs), with many years of experience as a consultant. This first field study on the webcam test was conducted among 188 consultants working for a public employment agency in the Netherlands. The aim of this study was to shed light on the validity of the webcam test in predicting the employment consultants' job performance. Job performance was measured with job placement success, which is an objective productivity measure, and a manager's appraisal of the consultants' work performance. Furthermore, the unique explained variance of the webcam test was investigated over and above job knowledge. For the webcam test, good inter-rater reliability (ICC = .71) and internal consistency (α = .82) was found. Overall webcam test score manifested a significant and positive correlation with the objective measure of job performance, namely successful job placement of clients ($r = .26$, $p < .05$). The webcam test scores were also found to be related to job knowledge ($r = .22$, $p < .01$). Regression analysis demonstrated that the webcam test had incremental validity over job knowledge in predicting successful job placement ($\Delta R^2 = .04$, $p < .05$). The webcam test and the job knowledge test were not significantly related to the manager's appraisal. Oostrom *et al.* explained these results by several limitations to the manager's appraisal. First, the questionnaire was filled out by 56 different managers. Most managers filled out the questionnaire for only one consultant. Therefore the comparability of the scores on the manager's appraisal may be questionable to a certain degree. Second, the managers had to approve participation in the certification process, leading to a selective sample of motivated participants.

In a second study, Oostrom, Born, Serlie, and Van der Molen (2011) examined the relationship of webcam test scores with personality, cognitive ability, job experience, and academic performance. Data were collected among 153 psychology students at a large Dutch University. The webcam test was designed to measure interpersonally oriented leadership skills. The webcam test consisted of 10 scenarios in which a subordinate talks to a superior in a business setting. In line with the previous study, good inter-rater reliability (ICC = .82) and internal consistency (α = .80) was found. Students' performance on the webcam test, was related to extraversion (r = .26, p < .01), conscientiousness (r = .24, p < .01), emotional stability (r = .21, p < .01), and job experience (r = .26, p < .01), but not to cognitive ability (r = .02, ns). To examine the criterion-related validity of the webcam test two criteria were used, namely grade point average (GPA) and students' observed learning activities during group meetings. Results supported the validity of the webcam test as predictor of academic performance. Scores on the webcam test predicted students' participation during group meetings, how well the students performed their role as a chair during the group meetings (β = .21, p < .05), their preparation for these meetings (β = .20, p < .01), and their learning activities in general, as observed by the students' tutors (β = .22, p < .05). However, no relationship was found between webcam test performance and GPA.

In an unpublished study, Soetiin, Oostrom, and Born (2010) examined the construct validity of a webcam test that was designed to measure sales effectiveness. The webcam test consisted of 12 scenarios in which a client talks to a sales representative. The aim of this study was to investigate the construct validity of the webcam test by examining its relationship with verbal ability, as measured with the Verbal Ability Test (Drenth, 1969), and emotional intelligence, as measured with the Wong and Law Emotional Intelligence Scale (Wong & Law, 2002). Data were collected among 199 students. Results showed that the Regulation of Emotion dimension (β = .19, p < .05) and the Use of Emotion to Facilitate Performance dimension (β = .16, p < .05) of the WLEIS showed a significant relationship with webcam test performance. Verbal ability was not related to performance on the webcam test. However, verbal ability moderated the effects of the Regulation of Emotion dimension (β interaction = $-.16$, p < .05) and the Use of Emotion to Facilitate Performance dimension (β interaction = $-.19$, p < .05) on webcam test performance. The moderation effect is demonstrated in Figure 9.2. The association between the emotional intelligence dimensions and webcam test performance becomes more positive as verbal ability decreases. In other words, emotional intelligence and verbal ability are compensatory with respect to sales effectiveness as measured with the webcam test. Thus, students with low verbal ability are able to show effective behavior in the webcam test if they are emotionally intelligent.

Summary and discussion of webcam test research

Although many organizations have incorporated webcam tests into their selection practices, research regarding this type of test still is scarce. Thus far, research regarding webcam testing has focused on the reliability, the criterion-related validity, and the construct validity of the test (Oostrom *et al.*, 2010; Oostrom *et al.*, 2011, Soetiin *et al.*, 2010). The results are promising.

The subjective nature of the judgment process of webcam tests could

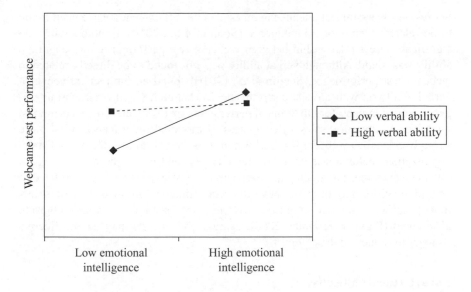

Figure 9.2 Moderating effect of verbal ability on the association between emotional
intelligence and webcam test performance

potentially be seen as a disadvantage. However, by rater training, by using a set
of comprehensive scoring instructions and by the use of multiple raters, it has
been shown that a substantial inter rater agreement can be reached.

Regarding the criterion-related validity, it has been demonstrated that webcam
tests are predictive of both job and academic performance. Moreover, it has been
demonstrated that multimedia tests are able to explain additional variance in
performance over and above traditional tests, such as personality questionnaires,
cognitive ability tests, and job knowledge tests (Oostrom *et al.*, 2010; Oostrom *et
al.*, 2011). These findings confirm that webcam tests can be relevant additional
predictors of job performance. However, to determine the validity of the multimedia tests, thus far only concurrent designs have been used, in which the
predictors and criteria are measured at the same time. It is possible that the results
from such concurrent validation studies might not generalize to applicant
samples. Applicants complete selection tests in high-stakes situations, which are
likely to affect their motivation. Although research has shown that there is little
evidence of differences between predictive and concurrent validation designs
(Barrett, Phillips & Alexander, 1981), we recommend future studies to examine
the validity of multimedia tests in actual applicant samples.

Support was also found for the construct validity of webcam tests. Scores on a
webcam test intended to measure interpersonally oriented leadership skills have
been found to be related to leadership experience, extraversion, conscientiousness, and emotional stability, but not to cognitive ability (Oostrom *et al.*, 2011).

Scores on a webcam test intended to measure sales effectiveness have been found to be related to emotional intelligence (Soetiin *et al.*, 2010). In both studies, no significant direct relationship between webcam test performance and cognitive ability was found. Although verbal ability was not found to be directly related to webcam test performance, Soetiin *et al.* (2010) found an indirect influence of verbal ability on webcam test performance. Verbal ability and emotional intelligence were compensatory in terms of participants' performance on a webcam test intended to measure sales effectiveness. Emotional intelligence was more strongly related to webcam test performance as verbal ability decreased. Many organizations believe it is important for business and moral reasons to create a diverse workforce. The finding that webcam test scores are not directly related to cognitive ability may therefore have important practical implications. As selection tests with smaller cognitive loading will produce smaller subgroup differences (Ployhart & Holtz, 2008), using webcam tests may be an effective strategy to reduce adverse impact.

Future research needs

A number of benefits and challenges of webcam tests mentioned in this chapter have not yet been studied. In this paragraph, we will discuss three anticipated benefits in need of future research, namely applicant reactions, adverse impact, and the effects of response fidelity.

Applicant reactions

In order to realize the benefits of the use of webcam tests in selection contexts, such tests need to be acceptable to applicants. Measuring how applicants react to selection tests has been found to be relevant for applicants themselves and for organizations. Previous studies have demonstrated that applicant reactions are related to intentions to accept the job, the likelihood of litigation against the outcome of the selection procedure, and perceived organizational attractiveness (Anderson *et al.*, 2004; Chan & Schmitt, 2005; Gilliland, 1993; Ryan & Ployhart, 2000). In general, applicants often prefer selection tests that have a clear relationship with the future job (Hausknecht, Day & Thomas, 2004). Therefore, webcam tests are expected to produce more favorable applicant reactions than for example cognitive ability tests or personality questionnaires. Although the simple comparison of applicant reactions to webcam tests to applicant reactions to other selection test is interesting, it is also important to shed light on which distinguishing factors of the webcam test influence these reactions (e.g. the multimedia aspect or the manner of responding). Potosky (2008) recently published a conceptual paper on the role of administration medium in the personnel selection process. In this paper, Potosky posited that administration media can be described in terms of four attributes: transparency (the extent to which the medium facilitates communication), social bandwidth (the number of social cues that can be presented by the medium), interactivity (the pace of exchange between communication partners), and surveillance (the security and anonymity of the medium). Future research should determine the exact standing of the webcam test and other multimedia tests on these attributes and the effects of these attributes on applicant reactions.

Adverse impact

Using multimedia tests instead of paper-and-pencil tests has been suggested as one of the strategies to reduce adverse impact, because the use of multimedia reduces the reading demands, and subsequently may reduce the cognitive load of the test (Ployhart & Holtz, 2008). As described above, two different studies on webcam tests have shown that webcam test scores indeed are unrelated to cognitive ability (Oostrom *et al.*, 2011; Soetiin *et al.*, 2010). Future studies should examine whether this small cognitive load of webcam tests indeed results in less adverse impact compared to other selection tests.

Previous studies have demonstrated that applicant reactions differ across ethnic groups (e.g. Chan, 1997; Chan & Schmitt, 1997; Viswesvaran & Ones, 2004). For example, Viswesvaran and Ones (2004) found ethnic differences in the importance that was placed on different aspects of selection system characteristics that relate to fairness perceptions. Future research should examine whether these ethnicity differences also apply to applicant reactions to webcam tests.

Response fidelity

Thus far, research has supported the construct validity and criterion-related validity of webcam tests (Oostrom *et al.*, 2010; Oostrom *et al.*, 2011; Soetiin *et al.*, 2010). As webcam tests are often seen as multimedia SJTs with a constructed-response item format (e.g. Lievens *et al.*, 2008; Olson-Buchanan & Drasgow, 2006), it would be interesting to compare the construct validity and criterion-related validity of a multimedia SJT and a webcam test, measuring the same construct with the same situational stimuli. By holding the predictor construct constant, conclusions can be drawn about the effects of the response format on the construct and criterion-related validity of both situational tests.

Conclusion

Although organizations have rushed to incorporate webcam tests into their selection systems, research regarding these tests still is scarce. In this chapter, we have aimed to describe the main characteristics, the benefits, and the challenges of webcam tests and to provide a review of webcam test research. Thus far, research has demonstrated that webcam tests can be useful and valuable predictors of academic and job performance beyond traditional measures as cognitive ability tests, personality questionnaires, and job knowledge tests. Furthermore, it has been shown that webcam tests are unrelated to cognitive ability. As selection instruments with smaller cognitive loadings produce smaller subgroup differences, using webcam tests may be an effective strategy to reduce adverse impacts. We hope that future research will be conducted to examine the yet unanswered questions about the use of webcam test in personnel selection.

References

Aguinis, H., Henle, C. A. & Beaty, J. C. (2001) Virtual reality technology: A new tool for personnel selection. *International Journal of Selection and Assessment*, 9, 70–83.

Anderson, N., Lievens, F., Van Dam, K. & Ryan, A. M. (2004) Future perspectives on employee selection: Key directions for future research and practice. *Applied Psychology: An International Review*, 53, 487–501.

Arthur, W., Day, E. A., McNelly, T. L. & Edens, P. S. (2003) A meta-analysis of the criterion-related validity of assessment center dimensions. *Personnel Psychology*, 56, 125–153.

Arthur, W. & Villado, A. (2008) The importance of distinguishing between constructs and methods when comparing predictors in personnel selection research and practice. *Journal of Applied Psychology*, 93, 435–442.

Barrett, G. V., Phillips, J. S. & Alexander, R. A. (1981) Concurrent and predictive validity designs: A critical reanalysis. *Journal of Applied Psychology*, 66, 1–6.

Bergman, M. E., Drasgow, F., Donovan, M. A., Henning, J. B. & Juraska, S. E. (2006) Scoring situational judgment tests: Once you get the data, your troubles begin. *International Journal of Selection and Assessment*, 14, 223–235.

Chan, D. (1997) Racial subgroup difference in predictive validity perceptions on personality and cognitive ability tests. *Journal of Applied Psychology*, 82, 311–320.

Chan, D. & Schmitt, N. (1997) Video-based versus paper-and-pencil method of assessment in situational judgment tests: Subgroup differences in test performance and face validity perceptions. *Journal of Applied Psychology*, 82, 143–159.

Chan, D. & Schmitt, N. (2005) Situational judgment tests, in A. Evers, O. Smit-Voskuil & N. Anderson (eds), *Handbook of Personnel Selection*. Oxford: Blackwell Publishers, pp. 219–246.

Christian, M. S., Edwards, J. C. & Bradley, J. C. (2010) Situational judgment tests: Constructs assessed and a meta-analysis of their criterion-related validities. *Personnel Psychology*, 63, 83–117.

Cronbach, L. J. & Gleser, G. C. (1965) *Psychological tests and personnel decisions*. Urbana, IL: University of Illinois Press.

Drasgow, F. & Mattern, K. (2006) New tests and new items: Opportunities and issues. In D. Bartram & R. K. Hambleton (eds), *Computer-based Testing and the Internet: Issues and Advances*. New York, NY: John Wiley & Sons, pp. 59–75.

Drasgow, F., Olson-Buchanan, J. B. & Moberg, P. J. (1999) Development of an interactive video assessment: Trials and tribulations, in F. Drasgow & J. B. Olson-Buchanan (eds), *Innovations in Computerized Assessment*. Mahwah, NJ: Lawrence Erlbaum.

Drenth, P. J. D. (1969) *Verbale Aanleg Testserie: Handleiding*. Amsterdam: Swets & Zeitlinger.

Funke, U. & Schuler, H. (1998) Validity of stimulus and response components in a video test of social competence. *International Journal of Selection and Assessment*, 6, 115–123.

Gaugler, B. B. & Thornton, G. C. (1989) Number of assessment center dimensions as a determinant of assessor accuracy. *Journal of Applied Psychology*, 74, 611–618.

Gilliland, S. W. (1993) The perceived fairness of selection systems: An organizational justice perspective. *The Academy of Management Review*, 18, 694–734.

Hausknecht, J. P., Day, D. V. & Thomas, S. C. (2004) Application reactions to selection procedures: An updated model and meta-analysis. *Personnel Psychology*, 57, 639–683.

Highhouse, S., Stanton, J. M. & Reeve, C. L. (2004) Examining reactions to employer information using a simulated web-based job fair. *Journal of Career Assessment*, 12, 85–96.

Hunter, J. E. & Hunter, R. F. (1984) Validity and utility of alternative predictors of job performance. *Psychological Bulletin*, 96, 72–98.

Ironson, H. G., Guion, R. M. & Ostrander, M. (1982) Adverse impact from a psychometric perspective. *Journal of Applied Psychology*, 67, 419–432.

Lievens, F. (1998) Factors which improve the construct validity of assessment centers: A review. *International Journal of Selection and Assessment*, 6, 141–152.

Lievens, F. & De Soete, B. (in press) Simulations, in N. Schmitt (ed.), *Handbook of Assessment and Selection*. Oxford: Oxford University Press.

Lievens, F., Peeters, H. & Schollaert, E. (2008) Situational judgment tests: A review of recent research. *Personnel Review*, 37, 426–441.

Lievens, F. & Sackett, P. R. (2006) Video-based versus written situational judgment tests: A comparison in terms of predictive validity. *Journal of Applied Psychology*, 91, 1181–1188.

Meltzer, P. H. (1995) Videotest voor communicatieve vaardigheden, in F. J. R. C. Dochy & T. R. de Rijke (eds), *Assessment centers: Nieuwe toepassingen in opleiding, onderwijs en HRM*. Utrecht: Lemma, pp. 109–122.

Motowidlo, S. J., Brownlee, A. L. & Schmit, M. J. (2008) Effects of personality characteristics on knowledge, skill, and performance in servicing retail customers. *International Journal of Selection and Assessment*, 16, 272–281.

Motowidlo, S. J., Dunnette, M. D. & Carter, G. W. (1990) An alternative selection procedure: The low-fidelity simulation. *Journal of Applied Psychology*, 75, 640–647.

Olson-Buchanan, J. B. & Drasgow, F. (2006) Multimedia situational judgment tests: The medium creates the message, in J. A. Weekley & R. E. Ployhart (eds), *Situational judgment tests: Theory, measurement, and application*. Mahwah, NJ: Lawrence Erlbaum, pp. 253–278.

Oostrom, J. K., Born, M. P., Serlie, A. W. & Van der Molen, H. T. (2010) Webcam testing: Validation of an innovative open-ended multimedia test. *European Journal of Work and Organizational Psychology*, 19, 532–550.

Oostrom, J. K., Born, M. P., Serlie, A. W. & Van der Molen, H. T. (2011) A multimedia situational test with a constructed-response format: Its relationship with personality, cognitive ability, job experience, and academic performance. *Journal of Personnel Psychology*, 10, 78–88.

Ployhart, R. E. & Holtz, B. C. (2008) The diversity-validity dilemma: Strategies for reducing racioethnic and sex subgroup differences and adverse impact in selection. *Personnel Psychology*, 61, 153–172.

Potosky, D. (2008) A conceptual framework for the role of the administration medium in the personnel assessment process. *Academy of Management Review*, 33, 629–648.

Richman-Hirsch, W. L., Olson-Buchanan, J. B. & Drasgow, F. (2000) Examining the impact of administration medium on examinee perceptions and attitudes. *Journal of Applied Psychology*, 85, 880–887.

Ryan, A. M. & Ployhart, R. E. (2000) Applicants' perceptions of selection procedures and decisions: A critical review and agenda for the future. *Journal of Management*, 26, 565–606.

Schmidt, F. L. & Hunter, J. E. (1998) The validity and utility of selection methods in personnel psychology: Practical and theoretical implications of 85 years of research findings. *Psychological Bulletin*, 124, 262–274.

Soetiin, N., Oostrom, J. K. & Born, M. P. (2010) *Het effect van emotionele intelligentie op commerciële vaardigheden*. Unpublished masters thesis. Erasmus University Rotterdam.

Stricker, L. J. (1982) Interpersonal competence instrument: Development and preliminary findings. *Applied Psychological Measurement*, 6, 69–81.

Viswesvaran, C. & Ones, D. S. (2004) Importance of perceived personnel selection system fairness determinants: Relations with demographic, personality, and job characteristics. *International Journal of Selection and Assessment*, 12, 172–186.

Weekley, J. A. & Jones, C. (1997) Video-based situational testing. *Personnel Psychology*, 50, 25–49.

Wernimont, P. F. & Campbell, J. P. (1968) Signs, samples, and criteria. *Journal of Applied Psychology*, 52, 372–376.

Whetzel, D. L. & McDaniel, M. A. (2009) Situational judgment tests: An overview of current research. *Human Resource Management Review*, 19, 188–202.

Wiechmann, D. & Ryan, A. M. (2003) Reactions to computerized testing in selection contexts. *International Journal of Selection and Assessment*, 11, 215–229.

Wong, C. S. & Law, K. S. (2002) The effects of leader and follower emotional intelligence in performance and attitude: An exploratory study. *The Leadership Quarterly*, 13, 243–274.

Index